Heritage under Siege

Heritage and Identity

Issues in Cultural Heritage Protection

The titles published in this series are listed at brill.nl/ichp

Heritage under Siege

Military Implementation of Cultural Property Protection Following the 1954 Hague Convention

By

Joris D. Kila

BRILL

LEIDEN · BOSTON
2012

Cover illustration: Damaged Mural of St. Peter, Matejce Monastery. Photo by Joris Kila.

The research on which this book was based, was co-funded by SNS REAAL Fonds.

SNS REAAL FONDS

Library of Congress Cataloging-in-Publication Data

Kila, Joris.
Heritage under siege : military implementation of cultural property protection following the 1954 Hague convention / by Joris D. Kila.
p. cm. – (Heritage and identity : issues in cultural heritage protection)
Originally issued as dissertation (doctoral) - University of Amsterdam, 2012.
Includes bibliographical references and index.
ISBN 978-90-04-21568-9 (hardback : alk. paper) – ISBN 978-90-04-22853-5 (e-book)
1. Convention for the Protection of Cultural Property in the Event of Armed Conflict (1954) 2. Cultural property–Protection (International law) 3. War (International law) I. Title.

KZ6535.A61954K55 2012
363.6'9–dc23

2012018013

This publication has been typeset in the multilingual "Brill" typeface. With over 5,100 characters covering Latin, IPA, Greek, and Cyrillic, this typeface is especially suitable for use in the humanities. For more information, please see www.brill.nl/brill-typeface.

ISSN 2211-7369
ISBN 978 90 04 21568 9 (hardback)
ISBN 978 90 04 22853 5 (e-book)

A nation that draws too broad a difference between its scholars and its warriors will have its thinking being done by cowards and its fighting done by fools

Thucydides. n.p. n.d. (ca. 430 BC).[1]

[1] Attributed to Thucydides ⟨http://www.quotes.net/quote/38537⟩ [2 September 2011]. Thucydides was the author of The History of the Peloponnesian War, written in 431 BC.

CONTENTS

APPENDIXES

LIST OF ILLUSTRATIONS

ACKNOWLEDGEMENTS

It is a pleasure to thank those who made this book possible. Especially I want to thank my colleagues Prof. Dr. Bram Kempers and Prof. Dr. Rob van der Laarse, both from the University of Amsterdam's Department of Cultural Sciences and Professors Fred Leemhuis and Charles Garraway, for their help and motivating ideas. Special appreciation goes to my old friend Rik Vos. He has made available his support in a number of ways during the entire research. He read many parts of the dissertation version of this book while simultaneously acting as a referee and supplier of inspiration without avoiding risks or being too politically correct. Also I would like to express my gratitude to Paul Koopman from the Institute for Culture and History for his support and to Prof. Dr. Irene Zwiep for making this publication possible by providing matching funds for an appointment so I could do my last year of research and writing. The SNS Reaal fund does a great job in supporting cultural heritage research in the Netherlands and generously donated the initial funding for this project. I want to especially thank Frank Verhagen of that institution for his confidence in my research. A big support was Dr. Roel Amons who kept me going. Much appreciated is the hard work of my U.S. colleagues Dr. Laurie Rush, Jack Rush, and Dr. Jim Zeidler who helped with language problems and provided their perspectives on several issues addressed in this study. The contribution of Charles A. Huff, who did the copy editing, was not only of high quality but inspired me for future publications. Moral support and technical assistance was provided by Karl von Habsburg, Sam Freeke, Dahpne Daponte, Laura Taverne, Winnie Zwetsloot, Rob Schuurman, and Frits Nordsiek. Brigadier General Hans Bosch (ret.), Colonel Chris Herndon and Commander Mike Hallett from IMCuRWG, U.S. supplied military moral support. Lastly, I offer my gratitude to my mother and all who supported me in any respect during the completion of the project.

Joris Kila
The Hague
March 2012

PREFACE

PERSONAL REFLECTIONS OF A DUTCH CULTURAL PROPERTY PROTECTION OFFICER

It was 17 February 2004 when I arrived at Baghdad Military Airport dressed in a Dutch military uniform and armed with a Glock 9mm pistol with the rank of Lieutenant Colonel. My mission was to assess the needs of the Iraqi and Coalition Forces in relation to cultural property protection (CPP). At this time public attention was drawn to Iraq as the Dutch media covered an incident on 27 December 2003 in the Dutch Stabilization Force Iraq (SFIR) Battalion's area of responsibility in South Iraq's Al Muthanna province.

The incident involved a Dutch Marine Sergeant Major who apparently fired two warning shots when Iraqis wanted to loot a container that had fallen off a truck. One of the shots fired killed an Iraqi. The Dutch Military Police arrested the Sergeant Major and he stood trial in the Netherlands. This event caused a public discussion focused on the rules of engagement (ROE) for Dutch Military when on a mission restricted by mandates. It became clear that public opinion did not give much room for the military to use their weapons in cases where they felt threatened. Because of this, I wanted to behave as correctly as possible and comply with all rules of engagement.

At the airport, I was met by a U.S. military convoy that would escort me to the so-called Green Zone. We had to take the dangerous road from the airport leading through the Red Zone. I asked one of the officers in charge of the convoy what the rules of engagement were. He answered while pointing at a suburban car with a driver that had his M16 positioned over the steering wheel, "Colonel, you go sit in the back of this vehicle with your pistol, next to you there will be a sniper, the driver has his own fire power, and next to him there is another guy with a gun. Now for the rules of engagement, if something happens you have to start firing immediately, there is no time to aim so don't bother, there is also no point in opening the window, just shoot right through it as many times as possible. How much ammunition do you have, sir?" I answered that I had five bullets in one clip. In fact, I had to sign for the receipt of these bullets handed over by a Dutch officer in Kuwait where I switched planes; I had to give back the five bullets on my return. The American officer started to laugh and gave me some 500 bullets "that will keep you going for a few days." This personal experience is symptomatic of the practical behavior of the interwoven fabric of interests, cultural backgrounds, and, in this case, rankings that can affect attempts to protect cultural property in the event of and under the threat of armed conflict.

In the anecdote, different perceptions concerning deployment of military experts influenced by geographical and cultural origins play a role. National political strategies, often ambiguous, and corporate cultures as well as military traditions are critical. Overall, communication problems deriving from differences in perception and appreciation linked to cultural backgrounds are a challenge for implementing the military version of cultural property protection. It raises the question whether cultural property experts, while safeguarding cultural heritage according to obligations deriving from international humanitarian law (or their own national law), should carry a status similar to the Red Cross, or, when they are military or militarized, at least like military medical personnel. In other words, within existing legal frameworks, they should be able to operate more independently from direct military command structures. This of course can only happen if commanders and politicians first see the significance of military CPP; I hope that this study will help raise their awareness. Having said this, it seems important to stress that the added value of this investigation is that the subject is, as far as possible, approached and measured from a military perspective. The core topic is an inquiry into the military attitude towards CPP, driven by the initial observation that most military organizations seem not very eager to implement CPP in accordance with International Humanitarian Law (IHL). Nevertheless, during the course of the research it was questioned and debated by civil colleagues whether abstract, contemplative, and reflective dimensions from the civilian cultural heritage debate as conducted by the scientific establishment should have a more prominent position. To put it first bluntly, the answer is no. This needs clarification, of course. The picture generated by this research is to a degree supplemented or influenced by civilian perspectives deriving from the realms of law, politics, sociology, conflict studies, ethics, archaeology and philosophy, to mention a few. Nevertheless, when conceptual ideas or reflections are mentioned, the military point of view is taken into account. If for instance reference is made to asymmetric conflict, the context is more legal and practical than the wider civilian scientific contemplation on post-modern conflict. As a comparison, when conflict is addressed, the issue is more "who is it between" than a reflection on the emergence of another, alternative system of profit and power.[1] Another example is that when safeguarding and protection are mentioned, technical activities within the framework of peacekeeping or other military operations are meant and not the discussion of whether cultural heritage should be physically protected or safeguarded as immaterial heritage.[2] In the current stage of developing and implementing military CPP, the aim should be protecting the actual properties without taking a position in any discussion of what they stand for. Still, within the scope of this study certain asymmetric elements, such as intrastate aspects of conflict, will be taken into consideration since these are directly connected to practical and legal implications that are of importance for safeguarding cultural property.

The military scope does not imply that abstract reflections can not be of value to this inquiry. As an example, when Zygmunt Bauman in *Society under Siege* mentions asymmetric war in the context of global insecurity, he notices that an important feature of this type of war is that "it will not be waged by a grand alliance united to defeat hostile powers but will involve floating coalitions of countries which may change and evolve."[3] Later this aspect is fine-tuned into "Shifting Coalitions." This type of information is extremely relevant for both the military and CPP experts because shifting coalitions contain shifting military cultures as well as changing perceptions and notions of cultural property, especially in cases where such property is connected to identity or has political connotations. My own arrival in Baghdad displays the impact of these shifting coalitions. The reader also will find it apparent when Civil Military Cooperation (CIMIC) is addressed. On the other hand, a lot of ethical considerations and abstract reflections are simply put aside because at this time there is too little field experience and consequently caseload to trigger more profound thoughts like the ones discussed in the international heritage debate. For instance when using the term *urbicide*, the killing of a city, we touch upon matters that have both strategic and tactical connotations in the military and are thus relevant for theoretical, ethical, sociological, and architectural considerations. In the context of this book there is a risk that introducing a concept will create confusion among parties that deal with both civil and military elements. To further clarify, Bevan's *The Destruction of Memory* references urbicide in connection with Carthage's destruction in antiquity, the English

[1] Duffield 1998, p. 66.

[2] Nevertheless, Article 2 of the Convention states that protection comprises the safeguarding of and respect for such property.

[3] Bauman 2002, pp. 90–91.

bombardments of Dresden, and the destruction of Hiroshima.[4] His book makes a connection or at least a comparison between material destruction and genocide and is illustrated in his examination of Carthage, which was demilitarized when destroyed. This is not clearly proven in the other cases, at least not from a military, scientific, or historical perspective. At this point, military scientists and legal experts drop out or get confused since matters are not further argued from legal IHL, especially law of armed conflict (LOAC) perspectives, not to mention arguments in favor of decreasing human casualties via certain military actions that involve damaging or destroying the urban fabric. Nevertheless the topic of urbicide should be (and is) incorporated into the CPP discourse referring to newer situations like Beirut, the Twin Tower destruction, and Libya.[5] As for now, we are first and foremost facing unnecessary and illegal destruction of cultural property in the world's oldest cultural spheres. The current conflicts that raise cultural property issues in Egypt, Libya, Syria, and Cambodia speak for themselves.[6] For now, proactive strategies to tackle protection and cooperation problems should have priority, while reflections should only take place where possible and appropriate. Experiences gained in recent civil-military activities should determine my position in the debate which will hopefully emerge and mature in the reactions, critique, and, with a bit of luck, expanding investigations triggered by this book. Nevertheless I want to mention one example of issues related to the fieldwork of cultural property protectors, namely, possible links between archaeology, conflict, colonialism and selection. Of course selection is a general subject that needs to be studied in depth to be able to answer questions such as who protects, what, where, and why? especially in case of no-strike lists like the ones used in Libya. But while doing so, one can argue that considerations should include historical contexts (e.g. a colonial past could be supported as well as manipulation and certain national identities). Examples can be found in Libya where Roman heritage has multiple identities. It is of general importance and with regards to Libyan archaeology, but it simultaneously represents the Italian fascist identity of the Mussolini period, and therefore was some-

---

[4] Bevan 2006, pp. 18 and 82.

[5] Coward 2009, Verhaert 2006, Sandes 2010.

[6] A report from the Global Heritage Fund states that Palmyra residents say the Syrian army has set up camp in the historic citadel Fakhr-al-Din al-Ma'ani Castle, built probably in the 13th century that overlooks the city of Palmyra and its adjacent Roman ruins. This way the military make the site into a military target which is in breach with The Hague 1954 and protocols, source http://globalheritagefund.org/onthewire/blog/palmyras_ruins, 5 March 2012.

times restored by the Italians selecting especially objects representing and glorifying the Italian past while ignoring or even neglegting heritage from other periods. Having said this, it is still my position that predominantly we are discussing cultural first-aid. To make a comparison when one has a medical emergency and is rushed into a emergency room of a hospital first the damage is repaired or the condition stabilized and later questions of insurance and further treatment are discussed; the same goes for cultural heritage emergency aid.

Let me begin by relating how I became affiliated with the military and what led me to start scientific research on military responsibilities regarding cultural property protection. Trained as an art historian and classical archaeologist, I became involved in an attempt to create a unit of militarized cultural specialists for the Dutch Ministry of Defense (MoD). In 1999, NATO asked the Netherlands to establish a framework for a CIMIC (Civil-Military Cooperation) Group and to invite other nations of the northern region to participate, and I was invited to participate by a CIMIC officer. The idea was to assist in establishing a cultural affairs network within a newly found multinational CIMIC organization called CIMIC Group North (CGN), which is no longer in existence. CGN served as a multinational military organization and, at the time, was based in the Netherlands under Dutch/German command. After accepting the invitation, I was offered the reserve military rank of Lieutenant Colonel and the positions of Network Manager for Cultural Affairs and Advisor to the Commander of CGN for all CIMIC areas. These functional fields are Civil Administration, Humanitarian Aid, Civil Infrastructure, Economy and Commerce and Cultural Affairs. First, the CIMIC concept needs explanation. The NATO defines CIMIC as "the coordination and co-operation, in support of the mission, between the NATO Commander (COM) and civil actors, including national population and local authorities, as well as international, national, and non-governmental organizations and agencies." The exact text can be found in NATO's Civil-Military Co-operation Doctrine AJP-9.[7] Within the context of CPP, it is most likely that the COM mentioned is leading a battalion or battle group in a mission area containing monuments, museums, archives and archaeological sites. It should be noted that the concept of civil-military cooperation is perceived as unclear by many, especially the lack of a unified CIMIC doctrine and international consensus on the CIMIC concept, thus triggering different national approaches to CIMIC in peace support operations.[8] The

---

[7] ⟨http://www.nato.int/ims/docu/ajp-9.pdf⟩ [13 August 2011].

[8] Kristoffersen 2005.

consequence for CPP in a CIMIC setting is that the implementation (if any) differs; for example, the Polish in Iraq had their own quite proactive CPP implementation within their CIMIC capability.[9]

In the beginning, there was much enthusiasm to get the CIMIC organization (including the section on cultural affairs) on the map. To achieve this goal the CGN staff organized courses and seminars in which I participated as both student and lecturer. Initially the focus was to gain an understanding of the CIMIC concept. After a while I tried to specialize on possibilities and challenges connected with implementing CPP. At the same time, I had to study in order to become acquainted with the military culture and fundamental issues that included basic military training. Understanding such matters is essential before beginning work in a military environment. At first glance, CIMIC looked like a perfect structure to house military cultural property protection. This is subject for debate, as will be argued later in this book.

It became clear at an early stage that the only military connection with cultural property in the Netherlands, apart from a set of legal rules, consists of older and historic real estate such as bunkers and fortifications, military terrains and military museums. Apart from this, there was (and still is) widespread confusion about the meaning of the term "culture" as well as a mix-up between CPP and Cultural Awareness and what these terms represent.

These complicated but interesting circumstances provided a stimulus to develop educational materials. In particular, there was and still is a need for CPP training tools containing examples from contemporary conflict situations. Contributing to the shortage is the fact that organizations that normally should provide training materials are not quite able to do so due to insufficient experience in working with the military and lack of expertise regarding civil military cooperation.[10] It should, however, be said that there is no shortage of juridical studies and educational materials suitable for use by military legal advisors as provided for instance by the ICRC and UNESCO.[11] Still, the juridical interpretations, for the most part based on the Hague Convention of 1954 and its protocols, use older case studies. Only a few examples from contemporary asymmetric conflicts were available.

---

[9] Olbrys 2007.

[10] Examples include The International Council on Monuments and Sites, The International Council of Museums, and The International Federation of Library Associations and Institutions, all introduced in the section on taxonomy.

[11] ICRC is the International Committee of the Red Cross based in Geneva. UNESCO is the United Nations Educational, Scientific, and Cultural Organization. See also the Glossary.

Consequently all new materials and studies should as much as possible focus or be adapted to the still-changing types of modern conflict. In this study, issues were first analyzed from a military angle and then as far as possible compared to a wider civil scientific construct.

To summarize matters, there was a need for research to gain the necessary knowledge to serve as a basis for improvement and adaptation of current practices while at the same time creating educational materials. To distinguish and analyze outcomes in a qualitative, sustainable, and credible manner, an appropriate scientific approach was required. Throughout the entire research and especially while exploring suitable methods, choices had to be made concerning theoretical versus practical issues. Consequently, it was determined that a scientifically accepted but still practice-based research method would be the best option, which led me to participant research. Participant research necessitates working from the inside, in this case as a reservist within the Netherlands armed forces. This brought with it the challenge that in the armed forces cultural activities are not considered part of the military core business. What's more, in the Dutch military perception, individuals, normally reserve officers, who do not really belong to the military community, practice CPP.

Reservists share no common past like friendships and networks built while studying at military academies and schools. As a result, the status of a relative outsider makes it difficult to access information, which was a challenge for the research. In other countries, (e.g., the United States), the military community is more receptive to participant research by militarized individuals; the status of a reserve officer is perceived as higher in these other countries than in the Netherlands, making it easier for reservists to function; this was confirmed by my contacts with foreign military in the field. These challenges served as the first indication of difficulties encountered during the entire research process about military involvement in cultural property protection. Overall, many of these nuisances seem triggered by lack of awareness of the subject among parties involved, including different military services and military personnel of dissimilar ranks and various departments. There were cases in which unawareness even led to some degree of antipathy for the topic. Strong opposition comes, for instance, from the (civilian) head of the Dutch MoD section (CAI) responsible for cultural historical backgrounds and information.[12] Resistance against CPP

[12] CAI is an acronym for Cultuurhistorische Achtergronden en Informatie, a section predominantly occupied with cultural awareness and Human Terrain. This department's management is highly risk avoidant, so no research or proactive measures concerning CPP

is apparently not only rooted in cultural differences but correlates with diverse phenomena typically found in corporate cultures. Most apparent are matters of distinction culminating in identity and competence issues combined with bureaucracy-inspired and career-driven risk avoidance.[13] Such issues are often disguised as financial cutback measures. As strange as it may seem, all these challenges inspired me to explore matters from a scientific point of view. My idea was that the research should focus on the handling and protection of cultural heritage in all aspects, that is, heritage as a cultural resource, as cultural property, and seen from both practical as well as theoretical perspectives. Finally, yet importantly, it had to include a description of parties, processes, and mechanisms involved.

Early evaluation included art-historical and archaeological points of view but showed that more dimensions needed exploration to get a complete picture. Obtaining the full picture required a multidisciplinary approach. For instance, sociological and military aspects like identity, security, operational planning, and law of war had to be examined while looking for correlations and interactions. Looked upon from a methodical perspective, the multidisciplinary approach contained participant research evolving into what I would like to call initiating research or the instigation of opportunities to observe and test CPP in practice. In other words, participation in real missions was essential in identifying capabilities, specialists, and players. This resulted in field research using observation and interviews. Sometimes exchange of ideas also took place via correspondence, during conferences, panels, and paper discussions. Apart from these field investigations, the practical functioning of structures and mechanisms that either proved to facilitate or restrain implementation of the Hague Convention of 1954 in contemporary conflicts turned out to be essential.

When my research started in 2003, no cultural property projects were under execution in military mission areas, so the only way to go out in theater was to begin assessments to establish the state of cultural property in respective mission areas. This was not easy to execute because first I had to focus on getting the the topic on the military and political agendas.[14] To achieve this goal, creative solutions were vital along with exploiting oppor-

---

are undertaken. On several occasions the management blocked CPP initiatives coming from other departments. In my case the head of the department made attempts to block foreign presentations made by me on personal title. Sources include but are not limited to internal and external correspondence dated December 7th 2006, February 28th 2008.

13 Another term used is avoidance of uncertainty (Hofstede & Hofstede 2003).

14 Later I found that the Italian Carabinieri and the Polish CIMIC had implemented CPP in Iraq.

tunities. A initial opportunity developed when I managed to do research in theater during a Dutch-led military mission in Macedonia or, as it is officially called, FYROM.[15] An even bigger opportunity was participation in a Dutch CIMIC assessment mission that included identifying cultural needs in Iraq's Al Muthanna province. After the mission a report was written that included recommendations for cultural affairs.[16] A second mission followed in Baghdad in 2004, which enabled me to make international military contacts, in this case with the Americans. From 2005, I more or less pushed CPP education on the curricula of different military courses from the Netherlands Defense Academy's *Instituut Defensie Leergangen* (IDL) and advised the MoD on CPP matters.

In the course of time and despite being repeatedly confronted with opposition that slowed down proper implementation of CPP in the Dutch military organization, I was invited and spoke at international seminars and conferences in New York, Chicago, Baeza (Spain), Jordan, Cairo, Anaheim (California), Tangiers and Tallinn, to mention a few. From 2008, the number of conferences and seminars on cultural property protection and conflict increased at a faster pace, indicating growing international interest in the subject. This brought opportunities to present papers, meet colleagues (including opponents), and initiate interviews with experts. The Pocantico Hills seminar organized by the University of Chicago in August 2006 was crucial.[17] For the first time military and civil officials and specialists met and discussed matters.[18] This event led to an important multidisciplinary publication *Antiquities under Siege*.[19] At this stage, I was no longer part of the Dutch CIMIC because the head of the MoD "embedded cultural awareness" department claimed my position and managed to get me sidelined. Later, through cooperation with the Dutch MoD's operational readiness department, I organized a seminar about CPP and the military. This took place 25 March 2009 in the Peace Palace in The Hague.[20] Part of the activity was the creation of an educational deck of cards about CPP for the military. The

---

[15] The Amber Fox mission that included Task Force Fox (TFF) took place in 2002 in the Former Yugoslav Republic of Macedonia (FYROM). From June until the end of the mission in December, TFF was under Dutch Command.

[16] Kila 2003.

[17] Rothfield 2008.

[18] It was followed by a conference called Protecting Cultural Heritage: International Law after the War in Iraq organized in February 2006 by the University of Chicago Law School focusing on juridical matters.

[19] Kila 2008a.

[20] The Seminar was called Cultural Property Protection in Times of Conflict and included several international speakers.

deck was developed together with the Dutch State Inspectorate for cultural heritage and the Ministry of Culture and was based on the original initiative of the United States Department of Defense (DoD).[21]

As a follow-up to the MoD seminar in The Hague, I wrote a report on its outcomes that included a description of the status of CPP in the Dutch Armed Forces as well as recommendations for the way ahead. Professor Peter Stone from Newcastle University made some valuable contributions to this document, which was intended for the Dutch Chief of Defense. The most significant conclusions were the need for international cooperation and the creation of a small team embedded in the Dutch MoD to assess and implement CPP policies. Regrettably, the document ended up in a drawer. Recent enquiries with the Dutch MoD confirm that CPP still has low priority in the Netherlands and no funds will be made available to support CPP activities; this research will show that this is also a common trend in many other countries.

Recent important gatherings about CPP were the Conference Archaeology in Conflict in Vienna, Austria in April 2010; the course The Protection of Cultural Property in Armed Conflict of International Institute of Humanitarian Law, San Remo Italy that took place 13–15 December 2010; the NATO CPP course in Vienna (November 2011) and a closed conference on Protecting Cultural Property in War Zones held at All Souls College of the University of Oxford on 19 March 2012.

---

21 Made possible by the DoD Legacy Resource Management Program and Laurie Rush (DoD), Jim Zeidler and Tracy Wager (CEMML, Colorado State University).

CHAPTER ONE

INTRODUCTION

Figure 1. Rummy's Magic Vase, courtesy internetweekly. http://www.internetweekly.org/iwr/cartoons/cartoon_rummys_vase.html.

"STUFF HAPPENS" said Secretary of Defense Donald Rumsfeld in a news briefing on 11 April 2003 following the looting and violence that broke out in the aftermath of Baghdad's fall in 2003. Actually, Rumsfeld paraphrased the expression "shit happens" and used a so-called minced oath to diminish the offensive character of the original for the sake of political correctness.[1]

---

[1] Minced oath is a pseudo-profanity.

He added, "Freedom's untidy and free people are free to make mistakes and commit crimes and do bad things, looting is not uncommon during significant social upheaval."[2] Secretary Rumsfeld was not the first to play down the subject of destruction and looting of cultural property; he stands in a long tradition. Two years before, the leader of the Taliban, Mullah Omar, said about the destruction of the Bamiyan Buddhas in Afghanistan "all that we are breaking are stones."[3] Rumsfeld's statement suggests that in certain situations people are justified to loot. On this occasion individuals removed objects they did not rightfully own. Normally national or subsidiary international legislation applies. In this case, at least for Iraq, the Convention for the Protection of Cultural Property in the Event of Armed Conflict, also referred to as the Hague Convention of 1954, applies.[4] However, in the event of a foreign invasion an occupying force (i.e., the United States) is "not completely responsible for every looting in the territory it controls but should exercise due diligence to avoid such looting."[5] Still one can wonder if proper diligence was exercised to prevent or restrain the Baghdad pillaging especially

[2] ⟨http://www.defense.gov/transcripts/transcript.aspx?transcriptid=2367⟩ [1 September 2011]. Kenneth Adelman, a member of Donald Rumsfeld's advisory Defense Policy Board, reports in Vanity Fair about an unsuccessful conversation he had with Rumsfeld in which he criticizes him: "The only thing people will remember about you is 'Stuff happens' and 'This is what free people do.' This is not what free people do. This is what barbarians do." Adelman continues by asking Rumsfeld if he realized what the looting did to the U.S: it legitimized the idea that liberation comes with chaos rather than with freedom and a better life, and it demystified the potency of American forces. Both statements of Adelman are relevant and are supported by cases and situations described in this book, especially since they more or less open the door for identifying the military deliverables that come with effective CPP strategies. http://www.vanityfair.com/politics/features/2009/02/bush-oral-history200902. Vanity Fair, 2 February 2009, by Cullen Murphy and Todd S. Purdum.

[3] Ghaidan, Usam. Damage to Iraq's Wider Heritage. in Stone, P.G. and Farkhach Bajjaly, J. (eds.), *The Destruction of Cultural Heritage in Iraq*. Woodbridge 2008, p. 93.

[4] A legal pact stating that cultural property must be safeguarded and respected in times of conflict. See Article 2 of the Convention. Iraq is a signatory to the Convention and its first protocol since 1967. At the time of Rumsfeld's statement, the United States was not an official signatory; they became a States Party in 2008. Before that, the United States acted in the spirit of the Hague Convention.

[5] Maintenance of law and order is a key aspect of IHL occupation law. Source: International Humanitarian Law and International Organizations in Iraq. Presentation for the Program on Humanitarian Policy and Conflict Research, Harvard University April 2003 ⟨http://www.ihlresearch.org/iraq/pdfs/IHL_IO_Iraq.pdf⟩ [10 October 2010].

The ICRC sees destruction of civilian property and looting as violations of international humanitarian law. Source: Keynote address by Dr. Jakob Kellenberger, President of the in the case of the Iraq National Museum looting on 10 April 2003.[6] In general looting is considered a violation of International Humanitarian Law and is eligible for punishment.[7] However, setting aside legal implications, Rumsfeld's words are, in a strange way, true for my research as will become clear in this publication.

In today's society, many military personnel still see the protection of cultural heritage as a new and unnecessary responsibility that has nothing to do with their core business. Occasionally terms like "mission-creep" are used. However, it seems more likely that "tasks not part of a specific culture are not attended to with the same energy and resources as tasks that are part of such a culture."[8]

In this book, several aspects of military CPP involvement will be investigated. One of these is CPP implementation within the context of the so-called 3D, or comprehensive, approach as practiced by the Dutch Military. The 3 D's (dimensions) stand for Defense, Development, and Diplomacy. Curiously, I found that my research necessarily turned out to be multi-dimensional, too. Actual field implementation of cultural property protection and development of training tools as well as coordination of international cooperation to conduct research had to be initiated. Seen from this perspective the 3 D's in my research stood for Disputed, Dare, and Doing things, as will be argued.

International Committee of the Red Cross. San Remo, 2 September 2004. ⟨http://www.icrc.org/Web/eng/siteengo.nsf/html/64SJR4⟩ [17 July 2011].

Four basic principles of international law underlie an occupation: 1) The occupying power does not gain sovereignty over the occupied territory through occupation. 2) Occupation is considered a transitory phase in which the rights of the population must be respected by the occupying power until formal authority is restored. 3) When exercising authority, the occupying power must take into account the interests of the inhabitants as well as military necessity. 4) The occupying power must not use its authority to exploit the population or local resources for the benefit of its own population and territory. Source: The War in Iraq and International Humanitarian Law, ⟨http://www.hrw.org/campaigns/iraq/ihlfaqoccupation.htm⟩ Last updated May 16, 2003. [17 July 2011].

[6] The Iraq National Museum in Baghdad was looted in April 2003. See Bogdanos; 2006, Rothfield 2008, 2009.

[7] This applies when the courts of the occupied territory shall continue to function. Where this is not possible, the occupying power may set up "properly constituted, non-political military courts" with local or foreign judges to sit in the occupied country; such courts must apply international fair trial standards. Source: the War in Iraq and International Humanitarian Law. ⟨http://www.hrw.org/campaigns/iraq/ihlfaqoccupation.htm⟩ Last updated May 16, 2003. [17 July 2011].

[8] Wilson 1989, p. 101.

Cultural property protection as a relevant topic vanished after World War II, but reappeared on the international agendas triggered by cultural heritage disasters in former Yugoslavia, Iraq, and Afghanistan. This did not automatically mean that CPP returned to military curricula and operational planning schemes as a lack of interest and limited expertise concerning CPP prevented this. In that light, it came as no surprise that start-up issues and implementation problems as experienced in the past by military predecessors (e.g., the U.S. Monuments, Fine Arts, and Archives [MFAA] officers from World War II) reappeared.[9] Examples of such problems include scarcity of (assigned) transportation means for CPP officers, low priority of CPP within military organizations, souvenir hunting or theft of artifacts by one's own troops, and shortage of funding for CPP implementation in the field and for research and education. All of these old challenges recurred during my missions in Iraq: *L'Histoire se répète*. Nevertheless, with the start of my investigations a remarkable exploration began that included encounters with a variety of characters who are nearly caricatures, such as the Indiana Jones-style explorer, warriors of different categories, and anti-military demonstrators at conferences.[10] Within this turmoil, core issues of the investigation became manifest through a number of recurring questions or better, reservations, that are identified and addressed in this book. These more or less continual challenges were of direct influence to both the research process and the practical implementation of CPP. Originating from all parties, they appear to be triggered by the central question of whether the military has to be involved at all in cultural property protection. As will be demonstrated, this is analogous to asking if the fire brigade should be involved when planning capacity and strategies for fire fighting.

The title *Heritage Under Siege* was chosen for this book because it contains key aspects of the subject and the processes and strains surrounding it: heritage, culture, siege, and conflict. These four aspects merit further clarification by taking a closer look at the connotations of the terms

---

[9] Nicholas 1994.

[10] Dr. Zahi Hawass was, at the time, the Egyptian Minister (of state) of Antiquities. He and some of his staff members literally wear Indiana Jones hats that are marketed and sold under the name Zahi Hawass Explorer Hat. They can be bought at: ⟨http://store.exhibitmerchandising.com/emllc/product.asp?s_id=0&pf_id=PAAAIAHILPMLCFEA⟩ [17 July 2011]. The strange thing is that after the Egyptian regime change, the hats are still advertised with a statement that the profits go to the Susan Mubarak Children's Hospital. Demonstrations against military cultural property specialists occurred during 6th World Archaeological Congress (WAC) held at University College Dublin, 29 June–4 July 2008.

"heritage" and "siege." In addition, another overarching key feature must be mentioned, namely the legal aspect that is dominated by the Hague Convention of 1954. The impact of this treaty, whether weak or strong, on all parties involved situates the subject of this study in a polemic perspective that asks to what extent these parties implement the Convention. As will be described, I found myself in a position to pose this question because I worked in the field and could experience and assess whether the directives and tools that IHL gives for CPP actually land on fertile ground.

Heritage

The expressions *heritage*, *cultural heritage*, and *cultural property* contain juridical and material aspects when used in the context of CPP. In the legal sense, cultural heritage is often referred to as cultural property in which case cultural heritage should be seen as a *specialis* under a *generalis*. This is important to consider within the context of rules and legislation such as environmental law. Cases and problems addressed here involve cultural properties such as monuments, archaeological sites, artifacts, archives, and libraries.[11] As will be explained, the terms property and heritage can indicate the presence of matters like ownership, disputes and claims of individuals or certain groups, or, in a wider more reflective perspective, the legacy of humankind. These associations can play a role in a legal sense and—especially in case of conflicts—a political sense.

A different, more conceptual approach emphasizes the idea of heritage.[12] In this context, the idea is constructed as notions of identity, status, social values, philosophical significance, and economic exploitation, and is thus to the same extent subject to change. In a way this can be compared with ideas about history: some perceive history predominantly as a narrative; others see it as a correlation between milieu, procedures, and the construction of a text. Michel de Certeau calls it a heterology, a combination of different knowledges.[13] The latter also applies to cultural property; the perception, appreciation, sometimes even appearance of specific cultural property fluctuates in time or space, and its status can change with the social and political environment.

---

11 Emberling and Hanson 2008; Kila 2008a, 2008b.
12 Gillman 2010.
13 Gunn 2006, pp. 43–53.

Of vital importance is the fact that the types of cultural property described by the Hague Convention in Article 2 can have different or shifting connotations or seem to be of increased importance in the event of conflict or in the period just prior to or immediately following a conflict. This has implications for the planning of military operations. For instance, (working) archives can be of value or danger to military intelligence due to their contents, whereas historical archives can be of importance for the national or ethnic identity of certain involved groups. Often such archives contain contemporary as well as historical and cultural materials. Monuments of architecture can be of strategic importance in the terrain due to height (e.g., sniper nests), and location or strategic use (e.g., weapons can be hidden or stored,); the same applies to prisoners and hostages, who can be used as human shields.

Works of art, books, and manuscripts can have propaganda value, but can be considered icons by certain ethnic, religious, or political groups within a society. Even natural monuments can fulfill such a role (e.g., the tree behind the Anne Frank house in Amsterdam and Uluru [Ayers Rock], the sacred rock of the aboriginals in Australia).[14] Heritage sites can be divided into cultural heritage and natural heritage sites. Different properties recommended by each country are included in the World Heritage List after being screened according to strict criteria defined by the World Heritage Committee.[15]

There is a distinction between material (tangible) and immaterial or intangible heritage. On the latter we can list among others performing arts such as music and theater, national anthems, dialects, languages, oral history, and certain traditional performances like tribal rituals.[16] The List of Intangible Cultural Heritage in Need of Urgent Safeguarding lists elements that are considered endangered and in need of urgent action to be maintained.[17] Intangible heritage can also have links to propaganda, national pride, etc., and can therefore be of relevance for military intelligence and

---

[14] In 2007 there were big protests when the municipality of Amsterdam wanted to cut down a sick tree that is mentioned in Anne Frank's Diary.

[15] The committee was founded 1976 in Nairobi. It was aimed at the identification, protection, and preservation for future generations of the cultural and natural heritage, including buildings, monuments, and landscapes important from a historical, art historical, and scientific point of view and placement of these properties on the World Heritage List by the Committee. The properties vary from cultural to natural to mixed.

[16] See the Convention for the Safeguarding of the Intangible Cultural Heritage, Paris, 17 October 2003.

[17] See: ⟨http://www.unesco.org/culture/ich/index.php?lg=en&pg=00011&inscription=00003&type=00002⟩ [9 September 2011].

give "valuable" information for the planning phase of an operation. Here ethical guidelines and procedures apply in order to maintain impartiality and to prevent undesired assistance to certain parties thus avoiding experts getting compromised.

For the larger part such directives for scientists, subject matter experts, militarized experts, and CPP officers still have to be developed and codified.

A similar approach is utilized in the case of military medical experts and seems to be a logical analogy in this respect.

Culture

There is a tendency to attach different meanings to the term "culture." "The term culture creates immediate difficulties. It is notoriously vague and slippery possessing several different meanings."[18] The various connotations and nuances of the term culture are also in the habit of shifting over time, sometimes triggered for instance by political changes.

Lord Raglan said that culture is roughly anything we do and the monkeys do not.[19] He was right in the sense that culture comes from the Latin *cultura*, meaning to cultivate, for instance a piece of land, something that monkeys leave to humans. In the past it was understood as the tending of crops or animals. From the sixteenth century this became the intellectual and spiritual development of humans that later evolved into matters of taste, while from the nineteenth century the "modern" connotation emerged when culture replaced civilization as the indicator of a particular way of life from a group or a people.[20] Nevertheless, the vagueness of the term culture combined with lack of awareness of the relevance of CPP can sometimes be advantageous. A few years ago, working as a coordinator for the Dutch CIMIC Group North, I received permission to send a reserve officer who was a cultural specialist to Iraq because there was an official request from the Coalition to send an expert for the Iraqi Ministry of Culture. Later it turned out that the request was actually for an engineer to help fix construction damage in the Ministry of Culture (the building). All the same, this "mistake" opened the door to protect cultural property in Iraq. A more than relevant aspect evolving into a connotation is the current perspective that cultural heritage

---

18 Gunn 2006, p. 54.
19 FitzRoy Richard Somerset, fourth Baron Raglan 1885–1964.
20 Gunn 2006, p. 54.

cannot be seen separately from natural heritage. Following this, cultural heritage is an integral part of its environment. The Italians call this *Beni Culturali*. The term stands for archaeological patrimony, archive keeping, and librarianship, as well as historical-artistic, landscape, and environmental heritage.[21] Evidently, this *Beni Culturali* is analogous to cultural property, subject to changing appreciations. The link between cultural-natural heritage and environmental considerations, explained in more detail later, opens new possibilities to embed CPP capabilities in the Armed Forces. Consequently, it will be more likely that CPP is taken into account for military operations.

Siege

Siege in its legal sense is a comparatively small part of warfare and in this case, it refers to armed conflict. Generally speaking this can be either "classical" symmetric warfare or what is called asymmetric warfare within a state even without formal combatants.[22] It is important to consider that armed conflict is not automatically war in the classic sense. Nevertheless, all conflict cases used in this study are a form of warfare, but cannot automatically be classified as siege.[23] Still it is vital to know what conflict is within the context of this study and to take a closer look at different types of conflict to determine if they require different CPP strategies. The Hague Convention uses the term "armed conflict." Nevertheless CPP preparations and training have to take place continuously; therefore, it is better to use the phrase "in the event of conflict" when referring to the total process of preparations in peacetime, military cultural intervention, and post-conflict actvities. International Humanitarian Law (IHL) distinguishes different types of armed conflicts. According to the International Committee of the Red Cross, the prevailing legal opinion on the definition of armed conflict under IHL defines two types: international armed conflict and non-international armed conflict. To be more specific, international conflict refers to two or more opposing states, and non-international armed conflict refers to conflict between governmental forces and non-governmental armed groups,

---

21 Source: Home page of the Faculty of Arts and Philosophy University of Verona.

22 "Formal" has to be understood in the juridical context.

23 In naval terms, a siege is a blockade. It can also refer to surrounding a fortress or city and cutting off supplies, communications, or an attack. It can also be used to indicate juridical implications.

or between such armed groups. IHL treaty law also establishes a distinction between non-international armed conflicts in the meaning of common Article 3 of the Geneva Conventions of 1949[24] and non-international armed conflicts falling within the definition provided in Article 1 of Additional Protocol II. Legally speaking, no other type of armed conflict exists. One type can evolve into another form of armed conflict. Other terms used are intrastate conflicts or inter-communal conflicts often with causes of an ethnic or religious nature, civil war, and transnational conflict.

Conflict

The international community, through treaties such as the Hague Convention of 1954, attempts to balance the interests that cause the friction between parties involved in conflict and the protection of cultural heritage. The two aspects, heritage and conflict, are in a constant tension with each other. To more or less control or in the best cases resolve the strains, the international community turned toward legal solutions. The most relevant one for this study is the Convention for the Protection of Cultural Property in the Event of Armed Conflict, to be referred to as the Hague Convention of 1954 and its two protocols.[25] This book will show that utilizing these legal precedents is the best approach toward the protection of cultural heritage during conflict situations. The primary problem, however, is that few parties and stakeholders utilize IHL methods. This study presents and analyzes a number of reasons and circumstances that exacerbate the current situation. Apart from existing tensions and challenges among stakeholders involved in military implementation of cultural property protection, new issues are generated by the Hague Convention of 1954. In spite of the fact that this convention aims at providing solutions for challenges and tensions, the process of adapting existing courses of action and stimulating efforts to implement the convention creates extra tensions among all stakeholders. Where

---

[24] Article 3 is applicable in case of armed conflict not of an international character occurring in the territory of one of the contracting parties to the 1949 Conventions. It also applies to a situation where the conflict is within the state, between the government and the rebel forces, or between the rebel forces themselves. Art. 1 of Additional Protocol II relates to the Protection of Victims of International Armed Conflicts (Protocol I) which take place in the territory of a High Contracting Party between its armed forces and dissident armed forces or other organized armed groups.

[25] O'Keefe 2006.

possible, these strains will be described from different perspectives. In addition, a number of possible solutions are discussed. As mentioned, the research on cultural property protection generally is of a multi-disciplinary nature and in order to show how this works out in practice, necessarily a number of case studies were initiated as well as executed by the investigator. This, plus the fact that outcomes are not only of a scientific but also of a practical use, can give opponents of combined approaches reason to criticize the, in their eyes, less methodological or unorthodox execution of investigations. I consider this not only a result of the project but also a necessary first step in bringing the subject in a more abstract discourse that has to take place but until now could not be realized due to a variety of reasons that are to an extent discussed in this book. Obviously, CPP cannot be dealt with unless the complexity of all involved interests, regulations, and parties is disentangled, resulting in a coherent account that includes obligations and incentives for all constituents. Such a description must consider the sensitivity of cultural property in relation to identity, authenticity, uniquity, and dispute. These connotations promote strong sentiments among parties expected to deal with the protection of cultural property.[26]

Considering the above, it is possible to compare cultural heritage with explosives as will be substantiated in the case studies. In line with CPP's explosive tendency are certain dilemmas that arise in the process of investigating CPP implementation procedures and strategies. Examples are issues of delegation of authority to handle cultural property in times of conflict and to prepare for this in peacetime while balancing interests of stakeholders to create an effective and sustainable operational model for protection. Any disclaimer to go with cultural property should be the same as warnings that accompany explosives: "If not handled with care by experts, damage and problems leading to conflicts might occur." Likewise, cultural property's fragile and unstable nature can be recognized in its mix of ingredients and conditions of use. Therefore, a good recipe for a balanced mix is difficult to find since cultures are not based on coherent logical patterns. One finds layers of for example different religions and traditions covering or overlapping each other.[27] In all such layers, tensions appear between pragmatic, methodological perspectives and philosophical or contemplative points of view. It seems fair to conclude that both perspectives are

---

[26] Touchiness, for instance related to competence, identity, and distinction issues.
[27] Johnson et al. 2009, p. xii.

needed to present a comprehensive description. In order to create such a complete account, it might be best to give different parties, after analyzing their positions, the opportunity for an equal start. For example, social science contributes to the production of knowledge and buildup of expertise while initiating reflective thinking on the subject; the latter is especially relevant for its military perspective. This way the topic can gradually enter the scientific discourse where heritage issues are debated and analyzed. Consequently, there is an opening for academics and decision makers, as well as experts on military theoretical sciences to join the debate. It does, however, create a risk of producing knowledge suitable for undesired or unethical misuse for military tactical purposes. This threat is real, taking into account that the nature of conflicts changes in the course of time and so do military strategies and weaponry. The established narrative of the classical battle plan is replaced by Foucault's intellectual toolbox approach, according to which units receive the tools they need to deal with several given situations and scenarios but cannot predict the order in which these events would actually occur.[28] Nevertheless, adding expertise and conceptual thinking to CPP and its military dimension can bring the subject into the realm of modern military operational theory.

The development of theoretical approaches specifically for CPP also implies that certain concepts are fit for use in purely military matters. Here too, there is danger of misuse of conceptual and reflective thinking. To give an example, some consider urban warfare to be the postmodern form of conflict. Contributing to this is the fact that in modern conflicts traditional battle plans do not function since there is no clear understanding about the opponent and the environment in which the fighting takes place. Often it is not possible to distinguish fighting groups by, for instance, specific uniforms. Civilians can change into combatants, and vice versa. Identities can change and genders can be feigned. Apparently, this atmosphere inspired certain people to start experiments imposing theoretical reflections on operational strategies.

This use of social science, more specifically theoretical postmodern philosophy (e.g., Deleuze and Guattari) can result in out-of-context contributions to modern military techniques and concepts that are certainly not

---

[28] Source: blog "I cite", Why the Israeli Army Loves Deleuze. ⟨http://jdeanicite.typepad.com/i_cite/2006/09/why_the_israeli.html⟩ [17 July 2011].

aimed at protecting cultural heritage, but more to facilitate state terrorism as is described by Weizman.[29] Potential misuse of scientific concepts and data cannot, however, be a reason to stop examinations thus neglecting obligations to protect cultural property under IHL. Further debate and research might bring about more specific regulations or ethical codes.

This book contains four main parts. First, there is a preface containing personal experiences and opinions followed by an introduction interpreting a number of key expressions found in the book's title and their posssible connotations and an explanation of research methods, sources, and different scientific disciplines used. Finally, a number of characteristics referring to cultural property such as its military relevance and volatility are addressed. Chapter 2 begins with a first part that presents a picture of the CPP playing field and its users in which all parties and stakeholders involved in CPP are introduced. Chapter 3 contains a number of recent case-studies from different conflict areas. Chapter 4 presents conclusions and suggestions for future directions while balancing the respective interests of parties involved as well as a clarification of legal aspects to consider when implementing CPP. Overall, cases of different size are presented to demonstrate a number of suppositions that concern the behaviors of CPP stakeholders.The same method is used to show implications (e.g., legal and sociological consequences) as they happen in practice. In this approach, the cases speak for themselves.

Research Methods, Sources Used, and the Multidisciplinary Nature of the Subject

As mentioned, multiple methods were essential to conduct the research for this book. Overall, qualitative research and field research were used, including participant observation. Furthermore, the use of different sources (e.g., literary sources, interviews and a multi-disciplinary approach) were needed. Important disciplines were, for instance, cultural policy studies, archaeology, and law. All methods used are, as far as possible, clarified using practical examples. Qualitative research on different levels took place to analyze and consequently understand the behaviors of the CPP stakeholders as well as their relations and interactions. Field research, which included

---

[29] Post-Structuralism as "Operational Theory" was used by the Israeli Armed Forces who in Nablus understood urban fighting as a spatial problem. Travelling through walls is a simple mechanical solution that connects theory and practice (Weizman 2006). See also Hollow Land (Weizman 2007).

working inside a military organization, served to bring together original data. Participant observation was especially required to watch situations during exercises, planning, and missions in theater. Part of the empirical research had to be initiated to test solutions and safeguarding strategies. For the whole investigation, observation was a significant technique to study military practices and for that matter the behavior of all stakeholders.

Much empirical, or in fact participant, research inevitably took place in conflict areas where disputes were fought out; these disputes were linked to cultural differences with, as side effects, looting, illicit traffic, and iconoclasm.[30] All these conditions together provided a rich data source. However, it should be noted that the military tendency to keep things secret or at a distance, particularly when referring to new and in their view complicated issues, proved to be a challenge. Participant research in theater did not come naturally; the only possible way to initiate it was through implementation of cultural property protection. Real situations and projects were vital in order to observe the dynamics and courses of action involved. Even though at the time I started my investigations a small network of militarized cultural specialists was already created as will be described in the CIMIC description below, this did not mean that these experts were automatically deployed. Therefore the challenge remained. Initiating access to conflicts required a proactive acquisition strategy.[31] First and foremost, military consciousness on the subject had to be increased since within the Armed Forces appreciation of the relevance of cultural property protection determines the extent and quality of implementation and research. This strategy paid off as described in the cases from the Former Yugoslavian Republic of Macedonia (FYROM), also by some addressed as Macedonia, and Iraq.

There were also other reasons for the described *modus operandi*. First, it is nearly impossible to extract information from military sources or environments without being considered more or less an insider. Second, it is normally not feasible to travel to conflict areas as a civilian. A complicating factor was that military CPP projects in conflict areas were virtually nonexistent at the time the work started, so not only on-site observation but

[30] The most relevant participant research took place when I was in Macedonia in August 2002 as network manager of CIMIC Cultural Affairs and in Iraq in August -September 2003 as acting Chairman of CIMIC Cultural Affairs and in February 2004 as a Cultural Military Specialist and CIMIC Chairman in Baghdad.

[31] Asymmetrical warfare (conflict) is a term that appears to date from the early 1990s. In it, a relatively small and lightly equipped force attacks points of weakness in an otherwise stronger opponent by unorthodox means. All guerrilla activity, especially urban terrorism, falls within this definition. Source: World Wide Words © Michael Quinion, 20 Oct 2001. ⟨http://www.worldwidewords.org/turnsofphrase/tp-asy2.htm⟩ [24 July 2011].

also the processes leading to CPP projects had to be initiated (while also observed). All of this had to happen within an organization that was not interested in the subject. Undoubtedly, field research opportunities could only derive from new military tasks in the context of peacekeeping and reconstruction missions. CPP fits well into these types of missions because it has the potential to generate jobs, a feeling of security, and it also strengthens identity and thus unity within a population. To get permission for cultural assessments that could lead to projects, common denominators, and deliverables for different parties had to be identified. A win-win situation had to be created. This strategy looked to be the right way to convince commanders to send me out to conflict areas. It worked; I managed to carry out participant, in-theater research in Macedonia and Iraq.

Describing and testing military cultural property protection implementation in times of contemporary conflict was not only relevant from a research perspective but also to generate new lessons learned and case studies. New cases obtained in theater led to the discovery of new opportunities to establish CPP capabilities. A good example that surfaced this way is the potential for organizational embedding and implementing of military CPP through obligations deriving from environmental concerns codified by the North Atlantic Treaty Organization (NATO).

The NATO Standardization Agreement or STANAG on this topic includes cultural resources management; see appendix 5. A recent case in which the relevance of following such doctrines is clearly proven is the Forward Operating Base (FOB) Wolverine case that is addressed in Chapter 2 of this book. The good news is that compared to cultural property responsibilities environmental obligations are more appealing to and acceptable for the military. The military engineers, in the Netherlands called the *Genie*, are especially involved in environmental issues. These departments see natural and cultural resources management as a structured, organized, and embedded military activity. Therefore, broader opportunities for military CPP implementation appear to be connected with natural resources protection. To be more specific about NATO's policy, CPP is referred to in environmental doctrines such as the earlier-mentioned STANAG 7141 EP; a policy document regarding environmental protection during NATO-led military activities. The U.S. military uses elements of this STANAG in its CENTCOM Regulation 200-2, (see Appendix 4). Nevertheless, in Europe, the cultural heritage components of this NATO doctrine are not particularly recognized because the content of 7141 EP is not well known. Raising awareness is not encouraged because a number of countries including the Netherlands do not want to allocate financial resources for CPP since it is considered to be of low priority. As the Dutch MoD put it in a letter, "the world is constantly changing and priorities shift."[32] In fact, this statement appears to be the Dutch version of Rumsfeld's credo "Stuff Happens."

Sources included both published and unpublished materials. Military sources were indispensable and required for a special approach or, in fact, preparation. No thorough research on military sources such as training manuals, operation plans, doctrines, and policy notes could be carried out without basic military training in order to obtain a fundamental understanding of military cultures, codes, structures, and abbreviations. This training is only available for military personnel, so I had to enlist in the army. Nevertheless, this proved to be vital, too, for interpreting the information collected through observation. Roughly, the literary sources can be divided into military and scientific materials. Access to military sources was gained through my position within the Dutch Ministry of Defense and via various international contacts. It seems appropriate to split military data like doctrines, orders, documents, and classified or unclassified papers, some not meant to be (openly) published, from scientific publications generated by military academies and research institutes. The latter should be categorized with civil scientific sources. Apart from studying military and other documents, reading the academic and scientific literature was an important part of the research.

At the start of the investigations, suitable empirical studies on the subject were scarce. Contemporary publications on military involvement in protecting civil cultural property were even rarer. However, *Thieves of Baghdad* by U.S. Marine Colonel Matthew Bogdanos was a source for current information from a practical military perspective.[33] His book also gives an insight into the modern American military mindset. Bogdanos personifies the proto-type of the conservative (U.S. republican) warrior but with a significant nuance: the Colonel is very interested in cultural heritage and the arts and has a Master's degree in the Classics. Consequently, his publications and especially his lectures proved to be an important instrument to communicate to the international military community the importance of

[32] This letter was an answer to the Chairman of the Hague Peace Palace Seminar on CPP sent one year after the seminar explaining why the recommendations of this seminar were completely disregarded, source: letter of the Dutch MoD dated 28 April 2010 reference BS 20104157.

[33] Bogdanos 2006, Reserve U.S. Marines Colonel Matthew Bogdanos is in civilian life an Assistant District Attorney in New York City.

cultural heritage and demonstrated to them that it was not just a hobby for sissies. Later in the research process, more literature was found containing information from European military perspectives like a publication from the Austrian Defense Academy titled *Protection of Cultural Property in the event of Armed Conflict—A Challenge in Peace Support Operations*, edited by the now-retired Generals Edwin R. Micewski and Gerhard Sladek. This publication is especially important because it is a rare example of high-ranking military officers writing CPP.[34] An article from Polish archaeologist Miroslav Olbrys, who was embedded with military, gave a European view, as opposed to the American perspective, on what happened in Babylon and other parts of Iraq. It should be noted that perspectives and examples discussed in these publications are not representative for all military organizations, nor can they be adapted to be of general use. Missing in most literature were so-called lessons learned, meaning the incorporation of practical knowledge gained by experience. Normally in the military system, field experiences about topics like cultural protection are processed into case studies and educational tools based on lessons learned. Apparently, this did not happen in the case of cultural heritage experiences. At present, the processing of such military experiences in theater into lessons learned comes mostly from civil scientists, or, in the best case, from military reserve experts and civilians working for the military.[35]

Literature written by these experts tends to deal with cultural heritage in a general context, either from practical or conceptual perspectives. Sometimes such sources contain small sections that give a vision on military implementation or criticize destructive actions. However, normally they are not underpinned by adequate military background knowledge nor analyzed from military perspectives.[36] This is all good reason to initiate production of more comprehensive knowledge on the subject by exploring literature from different perspectives like (art) history, military history, and sociology while considering all of the relevant aspects of military establishment.[37] Art historical sources opened the door for me to a better understanding of intrinsic, often iconographic, characteristics of cultural objects plus their potential relation with, and influence on, military and social codes and

---

34 Micewski and Sladek 2002.

35 See for instance Kila 2008, 2008b, 2010, 2010b, Rothfield 2008, 2009 and Rush 2010.

36 See for an example of an art historical approach by Nelson and Olin 2003.

37 For history see Nicholas 1994, Lowenthal 1996, Akinsja and Koslov 1996, Bevan 2006. For sociology see: Bourdieu 1984, Mac Ginty 2004.

meanings in the context of conflict. A good source referring to these aspects is Robert Bevan's *The Destruction of Memory*, while an excellent historical source dealing with CPP during World War II is Lynn Nicholas' *The Rape of Europa*.[38] Her book gives valuable information on the first, more or less contemporary military involvement in CPP during armed conflict. Also worth mentioning are the proceedings of the symposium *The Spoils of War* that took place in New York in 1995. This was the first major international gathering that drew attention to the subject of looting and theft in times of conflict, though it focused on World War II, and the event did not yet include military experts.[39] Indispensable sociological sources that were critical to explore aspects of distinction, identity, and conflict are Bourdieu's *Distinction* and Roger Mac Ginty's article on the concept of looting, "Looting in the Context of Violent Conflict."[40]

While looking into the characteristics of today's military and studying structural features of military organizations, more links and parallels connected with military sociology and strategy became apparent (e.g., the features of the military way of thinking and its evolution). For the same reason, explorations for possibilities to build a conceptual framework to mark CPP's position in the contentious area of heritage-related activities and studies led to identification of additional sources. They came from the realms of theoretical art history and cultural theory such as *Monuments and Memory, Made and Unmade* by Nelson and Olin and Simon Gunn's theoretical perspectives as described in *History and Cultural Theory*.[41] The domain of cultural policy provided sources that give insight into the current academic cultural heritage debate.[42] The first steps for a dialogue between military and civil CPP parties were initiated in 2006 by the Cultural Policy Center of the University of Chicago through a series of seminars and meetings. Of course, within cultural policy studies also new trends and mechanisms related to art and culture such as the arts market including illicit traffic are studied.[43] Furthermore, possible protection

---

[38] Nicholas 1994 and Bevan 2006.

[39] Simpson 1997.

[40] Bourdieu 1984, Mac Ginty 2004.

[41] Nelson and Olin 2003, Gunn 2006.

[42] Cultural Policy: Rothfield 2008 and 2009. Cultural heritage debate: van der Laarse 2005, Grijzenhout 2007 and Tilmans, van Vree, and Winter 2010, especially van Vree.

[43] A good example is the work of Dr. Neil Brodie, one of the world's foremost experts on the illicit antiquities trade and the impact that looting-for-profit and artifact smuggling has on our knowledge of the past and the future of archaeology.

strategies are researched via, in this case, the Chicago Center that I am affiliated with as a community fellow. Finally, cultural policy is the domain where implementations of national and international obligations that are subject to governmental and private compliance are studied. Put simply, this research examines how respective governments, organizations, and individuals deal with obligations to safeguard and protect cultural property.

Bogdanos, Stone, Farchakh, and Rothfield described recent events and cases focusing on Iraq.[44] It must be noted that during the period of research and thanks to an increasing number of conferences and seminars, new publications started to become available. As mentioned before, in some of them I was able to publish results of my work that form part of the case studies presented in Chapter 3.[45] Rothfield's *Antiquities under Siege* included my first major account on cultural property protection and the military. This publication that focuses on the war in Iraq was the result of a seminar following a juridical conference that took place in February 2006 at the University of Chicago Law School, focused on legal issues involving wartime heritage looting. The related seminar in Pocantico Hills (the former Rockefeller Mansion near New York) was organized by The University of Chicago's Cultural Policy Center and, for the first time, brought together a wide range of stakeholders that included the military. The most significant result was the dialogue between civil and military experts and a set of recommendations that paved the way for more international debates. My contributions to and participation in both the *Antiquities under Siege* publication and its two seminars inspired me to title this book *Heritage under Siege* since "heritage" comprises the many dimensions that are addressed in this study instead of antiquities alone. A source briefly mentioned indicating contemporary misuse of architectural theory by the military is *Hollow Lands* by Eyel Weizman.[46] The book describes the military maneuvers by Israeli Armed Forces that took place in the West Bank City of Nablus. The Commander in Charge, the Israeli Brigadier General Aviv Kochavi, characterized them at the time as "inverse geometry," meaning changing the urban syntax. Soldiers avoided roads, streets, courtyards, doors, and windows that normally define logical movement. In fact, it was destroying people's houses by literally going through walls by first punching holes.

---

44 Bogdanos 2006, Rothfield, 2008, 2009; Stone and Farchakh 2008.

45 E.g., Rush 2010 and Kila 2010b.

46 Weizman 2007, pp. 185–218.

Contemporary technical developments like utilizing Geographic Information Systems (GIS) and archaeological remote sensing technologies are introduced and discussed in a publication by Egyptologist Sarah Parcak.[47] GIS and Remote Sensing are of special interest for the military as this type of data can help avoid targeting and damaging cultural sites. But it can also convince commanders to start implementing CPP since they have access to GIS data as a perk. It goes without saying that misuse of GIS or Satellite data has to be prevented and the military can contribute to CPP by sharing their own GIS information and aerial pictures with CPP experts.

A final format of written sources suitable as research material and at the same time a potential outcome of this study are educational materials. Currently, appropriate education tools not only derive from practical experiences in the field but also from existing CPP training programs for the armed forces. Especially worthy of mention are products of the DoD Legacy Resource Management Program and the Cultural Resources Program at Fort Drum, including U.S. Cultural Heritage Training Websites for Iraq, Afghanistan, and Egypt developed for the military in cooperation with the Center for Environmental Management of Military Lands (CEMML) at Colorado State University.[48] The same source was responsible for the first modern military training *in situ* in Saqqara (Egypt) that included new tools such as special soldier pocket and playing cards, historical timelines, and innovative insights on training methods.[49] More publications on CPP are expected in 2012 while in 2008, 2009, 2010, and 2011 multiple publications were published by the author of this study.[50] A number of articles, papers, and publications used are from conferences and seminars in which the author participated, is quoted, or acted as a referee.[51] Other resources comprise materials such as various CPP training decks of cards from the U.S. and from the Netherlands. There are several military CPP dedicated websites that either began recently or are about to be launched. These include: ⟨http://aiamilitarypanel.org/⟩, a site affiliated with the Archaeological Institute of America, the CEMML site ⟨http://www.cemml.colostate.edu/cultural/⟩ that gives direct information and personal tests for U.S. Defense

---

47 Parcak 2009.

48 See: ⟨http://www.cemml.colostate.edu/cultural/cptraining.html⟩ [17 July 2011].

49 In 1943 the British reserve Lt. Col. and archaeologist Sir Leonard Woolley was involved in training the military *in situ* in Cyrene (Libya). Source: interview with Laurie Rush July 2010. See also the paragraph on Libya.

50 Kila 2008a, Kila 2008b, Kila 2009, Kila 2010a, and Kila 2010b.

51 Rothfield 2008, Olbrys 2007, and Rush 2010.

personnel and a new web portal of the Combat Command Historical Cultural Action Group (CCHAG), see: http://www.cchag.org/.

A third research technique includes interviews, some of them conducted more or less informally using opportunities provided while exchanging information with military peers at work. Furthermore, I interviewed a number of civil experts and key players during conferences and seminars especially in relation to the Iraq conflict. Though these interviews were carried out not within a survey structure but as dialogues, important first-hand information was obtained. Consultations with U.S. Marine Corps Colonel Matthew Bogdanos, who led the investigations following the looting of the Baghdad Museum, and U.S. Army Major Cori Wegener, who at the time was the only serving military cultural property expert of the American forces, were especially valuable. Other important informants were Professor McGuire Gibson who provided the geographical coordinates of Uruk and the late Professor Donny George, former director of the Baghdad museum.[52] An initial supportive exchange of thoughts with Dr. John Curtis, Keeper of the Middle East collections of the British Museum, later evolved into a debate about ethical considerations concerning working with military that involved a number of pro and contra scientists. It was reason for Dr. Curtis to withdraw from the *Antiquities Under Siege* publication. As he put it himself in a recent publication about ethics and working with the military: "I had not been willing to contribute a chapter to Larry Rothfield's book, even though I had participated in the original conference organized by the Cultural Policy Center of the University of Chicago in August 2006. My reluctance was based on the fact that I was unhappy to write about what should be done to protect cultural heritage in the event of an invasion when, to my mind, an invasion could hardly ever be justified."[53] Although I have the deepest respect for Dr. Curtis, who, unlike many others, was never afraid to go "in theater" during the war, I must disagree with him. More to the point, criticizing the ethics of engaging with the military to safeguard cultural property is useless since there currently is no substantial nor sustainable cooperation on this with most military. If the international community succeeds in establishing military CPP capabilities and they start to function for a while, then there can be reason for reflective thinking and for ethical considerations. One should question whether arguing about things that are not happening

[52] See Bogdanos 2006. Major Cori Wegener is now retired from the army and became the president of the American Blue Shield Committee.

[53] Curtis 2009.

is not a waste of time. Of course, any incidental misuse should be dealt with according to IHL as for instance happened in the Pavle Strugar case that is discussed in this book. Actually, Curtis touches upon a basic issue that needs to be stressed and argued: namely, that this book is not about the history of military cultural property protection. It is a study about attempts to develop military CPP within the legal framework of the Hague Convention of 1954. If any ethical issues should be debated, they should be positioned in the perspective of cases, legal obligations or limitations, and historical interpretations that play a role in initiatives to implement military CPP, but not from the standpoint that military CPP is fully in existence. A comparison is possible with, for instance, military health services, military juridical services, or military pastoral care, all scientific disciplines that have functioned within the military for a long time and that are probably evaluated on a regular basis and subject to ethical codes. I hope my discussions on the subject presented here, including ethical issues, will be about the development of military CPP implementation.

Several discussions and exchanges of ideas took place with acknowledged international experts and key players such as W. Hays Parks and Dick Jackson, both from the Pentagon; Professor Charles Garraway formerly United Kingdom Army Legal Services and the Red Cross, Professor Peter Stone, formerly Cultural Adviser to the UK MoD during the Iraq conflict; Professor Patrick Boylan who designed the 2nd Protocol to the 1954 Hague Convention; Professor Jiri Toman, formerly ICRC; Dr. Laurie Rush, archaeologist and cultural resources manager for 10th Mountain Division, Fort Drum, New York; and Jan Hladik from UNESCO. Finally, I want to mention Karl von Habsburg, President of the Association of National Committees of the Blue Shield (ANCBS), who is a great source of expertise concerning intangible cultural heritage. All interviews are listed in this book.

Two issues that are intermingled were vital for both the research process and its outcomes, namely the production of knowledge about CPP and raising awareness on the subject of CPP. The outcomes of this study are produced and presented within the context of a systematic framework that comprises case studies combined with new research results. These results are meant as contributions to the production of knowledge on the subject. The findings that can be used as educational materials but can also help raise awareness among stakeholders are incorporated. Where possible, cases are used; this preference needs further explanation. Considerations are threefold. First, if presented in the right fashion, real-life experiences will be very effective at demonstrating the complexity of military cultural property protection to all parties involved. Second, at the same time the groundwork is laid for a theoretical structure, an in-depth analysis of related dilemmas and challenges is given. Third, by identifying problems, recurring processes and challenges, it is possible to recommend solutions and strategies to protect cultural property in times of conflict.

Case examples presented vary in size. The smaller ones show how aspects like media exposure and ethical considerations become manifest and can be of influence. Big case studies from Iraq, Afghanistan, Egypt and the Former Yugoslavian Republic of Macedonia (FYROM) are in Chapter 3, some of them I published before but are now updated in order to demonstrate in full the complexity, multiple layers, and different implications of military cultural property protection.[54] Nevertheless, it is of vital importance to continuously identify and, if appropriate, incorporate new factors that shape operational planning, strategy, and tactics. Especially the newer case studies, like the Uruk, Egypt, and Matejce accounts, can be of use as educational materials while raising general awareness on CPP.[55] The thought behind this is that when an adequate degree of understanding and appreciation is reached among militaries and policy makers, more field research and teaching programs will be possible. Finally, the creation of military CPP capabilities embedded in the whole military organization is absolutely essential because MoDs can only prove this if the relevance of the subject is acknowledged. To obtain a full picture and grasp the multidisciplinary context, it is necessary to look into the past before addressing the present situation and introducing its actors. The history of the issue is described in the section containing historical trends until 1954. The future is introduced in the section on the current state of affairs regarding the implementation of CPP and by providing insight into new approaches and strategies within U.S., European, and NATO forces. Different methods and tactics are described that are specifically aimed at solving military CPP implementation problems. Finally, yet importantly, a possible way ahead is presented as the valorization of this research in a set of recommendations in Chapter 4 of the book.

[54] It is possible to work with military or temporarily militarized experts.

[55] Kila 2008a, 2008b, 2009, and 2010a.

The Relevance of Military Cultural Property Protection

Cultural aspects of conflicts can give reason for a party to destroy an opponent's cultural heritage, thus damaging their identity and consequently their presence or position in the historical memory of humankind. Side effects like looting, stealing, and illicit traffic of cultural artifacts during or directly after conflict reemerged in Iraq, former Yugoslavia, and Afghanistan. These are all good reasons for cultural property to be considered of strategic importance for belligerents as well as for military peacekeeping, stabilization, and reconstruction operations. This relevance is underlined by the fact that monuments "do not reflect their past so much as they work to create memory in the present."[56] This is without a doubt an interesting aspect for today's military in that they have to deal with memory and identity issues during peacekeeping operations. It is already good reason for more research and debate by military and civil parties dealing with this type of military mission. To create a perspective and starting point, a variety of aspects and challenges as they occur in different contexts need to be addressed. Most relevant is, for instance, the possible intrinsic iconic value or symbolic power of objects. When representing an identity, objects are often inherently charged with the past, or most likely an idealized reconstruction of the past that is found in the present. Clearly, this historical reconstruction does not take place according to set rules, but depends on constantly shifting local, political, and social circumstances.

In lectures for the military, I demonstrate this concept by comparing Duchamp's so-called readymade Mona Lisa (Figure 3) with the damaged mural of Saint Peter in the Matejce Monastery (Figure 4) in FYROM.[57]

---

56 Quote from art historian Professor Michael Ann Holly in a comment about Nelson and Olin (2003). This comment is on the back flap of Nelson and Olin (2003).

57 Kila 2010b.

Figure 2. What is it communicating? Saddam Hussein gathering flowers. Oil on canvas, 100 × 80 cm, 2nd half of the twentieth century. Artist unknown.

Figure 3. Mona Lisa L.H.O.O.Q. Marcel Duchamp, Nouvelles Images SA. Editeurs © ADAGP.

Figure 4. Damaged Mural of St. Peter, Matejce Monastery. Photo by Joris Kila.

Both look like paintings damaged by graffiti, but one is actually a creation of Marcel Duchamp.[58] This example triggers quite fundamental questions raised by military students: How can military personnel recognize cultural objects? What is the difference between cultural property and art? What are the methods for making basic or in fact iconographic descriptions and assessing possible damages? Is the damage in this context the destruction of art or of identity? What is art? What is heritage? Whose heritage is represented in art? When written down, these issues look quite sophisticated and therefore difficult to communicate to soldiers, but they should actually pop up during a lesson following an anecdote or pictures. These questions essentially illustrate the level on which cultural objects are perceived by the common soldier and for that matter the average government official.

[58] L.H.O.O.Q., a cheap postcard-sized reproduction of the Mona Lisa, upon which Duchamp drew a mustache and a goatee. This "readymade" done in 1919, is one of the most well-known acts of degrading a famous work of art. The title, when pronounced in French, puns the phrase *elle a chaud au cul*, translating colloquially as "she has a hot ass."

Government institutions that normally make decisions about whether military operations take place at all should be more aware of and concerned about political and juridical claims than territory and identity. Political claims are often linked to contested memory or notions of the past often created or intensified by the same CPP stakeholders that are described in this study. In such cases, cultural belongings that are infused with memory and identity are not only of scientific value, but are also politically empowered. Consequently, players seeking to appropriate and defend memory for political purposes characterize the playing field. For example, state narratives are increasingly contested or supplemented by a growing number of "counter histories" from "below" (e.g., ethnic minority groups) and "above" (e.g., trans-national memory practices, including UNESCO's cultural heritage program).[59]

After established identity as a crucial ingredient in the mix of cultural property protection, conflicts, and reconstruction, it is essential to examine how identities themselves are distinct. There are several kinds of identities including social, personal, racial, religious, gender, and overlapping or collective identities. Different types are of relevance for CPP.[60] Examples from social identities are actually meanings attributed to others in order to place them in social space like "teacher" or "mother." They also include personal identities or meanings attributed to oneself like names. There are collective identities overlapping with social and personal identities, which are therefore constructed rather than biologically determined.[61] Clearly, this last category is invested with constructed meanings regarding cultural property. Collective identities often have unambiguous connections to cultural objects and to intangible cultural heritage.[62] Collectively claimed objects, including works of art, can be empowered with meaning deriving from an identity or can be still in the process of being attributed to a certain identity. This quality of cultural objects makes them a potential driving force behind history, progress, and economy. The protection of cultural property

59 Thomassen 2010.

60 Snow 2001.

61 Of course there are exceptions. Jewish identity, for example, is a complex amalgram of biological, cultural, and religious factors, with some Jewish communities and individuals giving more weight to their cultural and religious life than others; similar spectrums can be seen in Irish Catholic immigrant communities in the United States. But even in these cases, biology is rarely the *only* factor in constructing identity.

62 E.g., Freemasons, soccer teams, military regiments, social organizations, religions. Intangible heritage can be rituals, music, poetry, languages and music, to mention a few.

for that reason forms an integral part of the entire composite of mechanisms linked to conflict and conflict resolution that is taken into account in planning and implementing peace keeping and stabilization operations. From this perspective, protection of archaeological sites and premises like museums, archives, libraries, and monuments is essential, as well as preparing for such protection in peacetime.

An effective and often sole mechanism to protect cultural heritage in the event of conflict is by utilizing military logistics, tools, and personnel. Military cultural assistance is especially needed when the safety situation does not allow national and international civil experts to be deployed and when local entities like the police are not functioning. Although many of them do not realize this, military personnel have a strategic interest, too, in the careful handling of cultural property. They want to achieve military goals as quickly as possible and complications deriving from damaging cultural properties can harm their mission. To demonstrate military interests to commanders and policy makers, examples are required that will be acknowledged by them as deliverables; in other words, outcomes that help commanders end a mission as soon as possible and strategies for successfully considering circumstances. These incentives can persuade military commanders to pay attention to protection of cultural properties during all phases of a conflict including the planning and post-conflict or reconstruction phases. This reasoning is in accordance with the thought that in today's situation the concept of armed conflict stretches out from the pre-to-post-conflict phases. A basic problem in this context is that military technicalities and force multipliers seem quite abstract to civilian stakeholders while at the same time the military certainly understand the jargon but do not see the connection with cultural property. Here again case examples, later to be processed into lessons learned, are useful to demonstrate the existence of military deliverables linked to CPP in any discussion with military leadership.

An important military deliverable is that CPP contributes to an overall atmosphere of general security.[63] Another crucial matter to consider is that regional or worldwide negative press backlash can be unleashed when cultural property is removed or destroyed. This consequence can be avoided through protective and safeguarding measures. Examples are the bad press the U.S. suffered after the Baghdad museum looting and the mishandling

[63] Feil 2008.

by coalition forces of the important archaeological site of Babylon that was damaged due to its use as a military camp. Typical examples of headlines in news media varied from "US government implicated in planned theft of Iraqi artistic treasures" to "Babylon damaged during US occupation: UNESCO."[64] An understanding of heritage combined with respectful behavior is a "force multiplier" for any global military operation.[65] This leads us into the military vocabulary where force multipliers and force acceptance are important military arguments to engage in cultural protection activities.[66] To give a specific example of a culturally connected force multiplier: cultural property protection can disturb the illicit antiquities market thus reducing a possible source of funding for the opposing forces such as insurgents.[67] It has the potential to mitigate the tactical value exploited by non-state actors.[68] Apart from this, the reduction of negative cultural heritage incidents will improve the operational environment for another type of non-state players, namely contractors in military operational zones. Finally, its protection reduces chances for collateral damage during targeting decisions. This will improve the public relations environment and reduce the vulnerability to litigation.[69] Still, it is clear that caution is required when linking knowledge, in this case cultural property knowledge, to intelligence. Not only is there a communication challenge deriving from the gap between military and civil jargon, but there is also a gap concerning use of military terms between U.S. and European military. This difference in understanding plus connotations causes extra and unnecessary challenges in the communication and interpretations about the subject between international civil stakeholders. A case in point is the use of the sensitive term "counterinsurgency." The U.S. military speak in this context of a force multiplier or more

---

64 ⟨http://www.wsws.org/articles/2003/apr2003/loot-a19.shtml⟩ [1 September 2011]. ⟨http://www.abc.net.au/news/2009-07-10/babylon-damaged-during-us-occupation-unesco/1348442⟩ [1 September 2011].

65 The term *force multiplier* refers to a capability that, when added to and employed by a combat force, significantly increases the combat potential of that force and thus enhances the probability of successful mission accomplishment.

66 Acceptance by the local population of the presence of armed forces from another power.

67 An example were the lootings of antquities (partially) initiated by Muqtada al-Sadr's Army in Iraq approx 2005, source Rothfield 2009, p. 133.

68 Non-state actors exploit the symbolic significance and financial value of cultural property to tactical advantage (Nemeth 2010).

69 Personal correspondence of the author with Colonel Michael Welch of the Inter-American Defense Board. Organization of American States. Dated 24 December 2010.

simply winning hearts and minds, while in the European approach and, for that matter, the language of civilian parties it has connotations of espionage, commando raids, and the ill-conceived Human Terrain System.

The Volatile Characteristics of Cultural Property

The definition of cultural property according to the Hague Convention that is used by the military is found in the convention's Chapter I, General Provisions Regarding Protection, Article 1. For the complete text, see the appendix containing the whole convention and protocols at the end of this book.

We can say that cultural property is potentially available for manipulation simply because it is present. A well-tried method for manipulation was to take property representing cultural identity and then add it (sometimes claimed as a return) to one's own group (e.g., just before World War II the Nazis defined paintings from Rembrandt as being Nordic and/or Germanic and thus part of the German culture).[70] Cultural heritage can be potentially explosive in relation to conflict when poorly handled by the military. The Jewish archive case (see description in the section about the media) illustrates this. Taking this into account, cultural property is a potential source of conflict. Within the military certain parties or individuals who tend to avoid risks (often for career reasons) or want to cut financial spending might use this potential as an excuse not to implement cultural property protection. However, this is not in compliance with international law. Apart from its manipulative and explosive characteristics, the notion that cultural heritage can be a source of dispute is in itself good reason for the military to pay attention since conflict is their core business.[71]

Modern devastations, including the destruction of Bosnia's national library in 1992, the shelling in 1993 of the Mostar's Stari Most Bridge in Bosnia-Herzegovina, and the demolition of the Bamiyan Buddhas in 2001, show that the perception and consequently status of heritage is changing.[72] Generally

---

[70] See Nicholas 1994.

[71] van der Laarse 2005, Grijzenhout 2007 and van Vree 2010, pp. 257–283.

[72] On 25 August 1992, Bosnia's National and University Library, a Moorish-revival building built in the 1890s on the Sarajevo riverfront, was shelled and burned. Some 1.5 million volumes, including over 155,000 rare books and manuscripts; the national archives; deposit copies of newspapers, periodicals and books published in Bosnia; and collections of the University of Sarajevo were lost. Source: Riedlmayer 1995.

speaking, it appears that cultural heritage was in the past not perceived in the same fashion as it is today. Ownership of what we now consider heritage, of course not an objective perspective, was not particularly disputed, and cultural objects were no regular source of conflict. Apparently, there used to be a dissimilar or less strong connection with identity unless religious identity was at stake. This changed perception and appreciation of cultural property has a military parallel, too, as can be seen in the continued adjustment of military ways of thinking. The military mindset is not only influenced by the factor of time, but also by cultural, socio-political, and geographical circumstances as is well-illustrated in the already mentioned phenomenon of looting. Soldiers used to loot objects, including cultural property, as a form of pay, but have today they have been transformed into protectors of cultural property. This change suggests the existence of an interaction between history and the social conditions to which the military approach adapts, in this case looting. If this premise is true, military-civilian interaction will, to a certain extent, also apply to other phenomena like iconoclasm and the military implementation of development aid. Assuming we want to explore looting as a phenomenon that is associated with other aspects of the military relationships with civilian populations, it is essential to understand more about looting of cultural objects from a conceptual point of view.

Looting and Poverty

The terms "looting" and "looters" are generally considered depreciative.[73] The negative label prevails over an objective description of looting as a certain activity. Many looters choose not to interpret their activities in a negative way, but see these activities as justifiable and legitimate. Some point to the fact that they are unemployed and need to provide for themselves and their families. Others justify looting as an act of taking back items that were in possession of a regime by entering its former facilities or as an act to express their anger by just vandalizing objects. A recent example was, for instance, the takeover of Khadaffi's house in Tripoli by rebel forces during which statues and even a golden mask of the Colonel were damaged in anger as a form of revenge. From that perspective, certain looting can be even explained as redistribution or, as the former British Defence Minis-

[73] Mac Ginty 2004, pp. 857–870.

ter Geoff Hoon stated in 2003 referring to plunder in Iraq, "liberating those items that are in the charge of the regime by entering its former facilities and the secret organizations and redistributing that wealth among the Iraqi people."[74] This is an opinion that in a way is shared by the looters in the UK that pillaged stores during the recent sudden mob lootings in London and other cities in the UK.[75] From another perspective, looting is regarded as a byproduct of violent protest and riots especially in the so-called flash or mob lootings happening through sudden outbursts. Looting of cultural objects can take place by being commissioned or at least triggered by collectors and the international antiquities market. Finally, yet importantly, looting can be organized by one's own government to serve as a motive to take tough action against protesters, while withdrawing fighters or armed forces can deliberately destroy objects because they do not want the winning party to take them in possession. It is obvious that looting has several perspectives that have to be considered specifically in relation to military cultural intervention. One of the aspects of looting that can restrain or, just the opposite, promote cultural property protection by military is its interaction with poverty.

New techniques like satellite imagery led to methodical innovative research demonstrating cultural property's connection with poverty. Elizabeth Stone, Professor of Mesopotamian Archaeology at Stony Brook University in New York, started to study the commercially available high-resolution satellite imagery taken by the Digital Globe Corporation of Colorado.[76] Shortly before the 2003 invasion, Digital Globe began taking satellite photographs of southern Iraq for the Pentagon. Stone started buying the images and examined approximately two thousand sites using reference materials dating from before the sites were possibly damaged. Intervals of one month between photos of looted sites were used to develop a perspective on the chronology of looting.[77] In this way it was possible to answer questions like: Are specific type of sites preferred for targeting? Is the size of a site relevant? How selective is the looting? Are certain archaeological periods more favored by looters than others (thus indicating what type of

---

74 Ibid., p. 857.

75 See for instance London riots: Looting and violence spreads ⟨http://www.telegraph.co.uk/news/uknews/crime/8687978/London-riots-Looting-and-violence-spreads.html⟩ [1 September 2011].

76 See homepage ⟨http://www.digitalglobe.com⟩ [17 July 2011].

77 As described in Stone 2008.

finds to expect)? How deep are the holes (to be distinguished by their blackness on the imagery indicating deep trenches that reach down to the earliest stratum of human history in the specific area)?

The link between looting and poverty, in its turn often part of development (aid) issues, brings a potential challenge for the implementation of military cultural property protection. Through the apparent interaction with poverty, looting becomes politicized and ripe for manipulation; consequently, attempts to get military cultural property protection implemented can be hindered.

Nevertheless, we have to distinguish between the act of looting and the perspective of the looters, on the one hand, and the political and social drivers of looting, on the other hand. More simply phrased, is the looting criminal or politically driven? For instance, there is a debate about the above addressed recent mob lootings in the UK (August 2011). Are they of a socio-political nature or just plain criminal acts?

Prevention of looting is an essential task within military cultural property protection. Nevertheless, when certain NGOs that consider poverty fighting their core business notice the link with poverty, they might take the opportunity to oppose to military involvement. It can even go further: several NGOs argue that they can operate cheaper than the military and therefore automatically claim all activities that in their opinion are not part of the military tasks, including cultural property protection. Not unlike commercial companies, NGOs tend to defend their market shares. This is not just theory; there are examples of military cultural activities that had to stop for this reason.[78]

Currently discussions take place about the idea of outsourcing certain military tasks that are normally executed under the threat of violence to contractors, often private companies called PMCs like Blackwater.[79] Fortunately, in the case of CPP any outsourcing seems unlikely since there is a purely military motive legitimizing the military to fight looting and illicit traffic as described in the paragraph on the relevance of military cultural property protection. One can assume that the military will not outsource such tasks. Guarding sites is nevertheless an activity that can be outsourced

---

78 Kila 2008a, pp. 177–178.

79 PMCs are Private Military Companies. Blackwater is a private military company founded as Blackwater U.S.A in 1997. It has a wide range of divisions, subsidiaries, and spinoff corporations. The organization as a whole has stirred much controversy. It is currently named Xe Services LLC.

to private security companies. Another aspect to take into account is the gradual shift in the military mindset culminating in today's dual military role of warrior and peacekeeper. The latter is a contemporary phenomenon that appears to be a *contradictio in terminus*. It is in sheer contrast with the time that looting was not always regarded as being illegal and abject. For example, the Romans allowed their soldiers to plunder as a form of wages.[80] Even today, the traditional tribal militia in Afghanistan and Pakistan, the Lashkar, are not paid salaries but share in loot captured from the enemy.[81] Fortunately, they are an exception since in most countries modern operations and legislation forbid this form of pay.

It seems that the military attitude is not only subject to gradual changes in time, but that more sudden changes can be triggered through social, political and cultural circumstances. In the context of this study and while anticipating future developments in the protection of cultural property, it seems relevant to take a closer look at possible reasons for global changes in the military state of mind. Of influence are (a) the development of international legislation on the subject and (b) the slowly increasing awareness about cultural property protection's value as a military deliverable. In addition, cultural property is often important for the identity of (local) populations involved. Samuel Huntington already predicted in *Clash of Civilizations* that in the twenty-first century and then especially the post-Cold War world, the primary source of conflict would be people's cultural and religious identities.[82] Furthermore, there is the fact that at present the state normally has the monopoly on violence and pays soldiers so the necessity and permission granted to loot as a form of payment is no longer there. Finally, the increase of tourism causing cultural property to gain value as a means to generate jobs and income is a valid motive to refrain from looting.[83] Considering that the military mindset is part of the military identity and assuming that

---

80 Nicolet 1980, p. 118.

81 There was a clear understanding with the Lashkar that when they captured Srinagar, they would be allowed to loot the treasury and the palace in lieu of payment. This was the accepted mode of warfare. Source: Lashkar invasion of Kashmir: the truth by Prof Farakh A. Khan (19. 8. 07) posted on several blogs and forums.

82 Huntington 1993; Huntington 1997.

83 Towards the end of the fifteenth century, group travel already started to take place on a modest scale. As early as 1650 the first known primitive travel agency started operations in Paris, while in the eighteenth century in England excursions to the mainland were offered. The big breakthrough came in 1841 when Thomas Cook (1808–1892) started organized, cheap excursions helped by the development of faster means of transportation. All of this led to today's mass tourism in which CP plays an important role.

identities not only shift in time but are also influenced by socio-political circumstances, it seems fair to conclude there is a causal link with the change in motivation to protect cultural property. Whether this assumption is supported by actual events and intentions will be explored in the section on historical trends in Chapter 2.

CHAPTER TWO

THE PLAYING FIELD OF CULTURAL PROPERTY PROTECTION

Setting the Stage

In descriptions of business concepts and market models that include competitors and suppliers, the term *playing field* or *level playing field* is often used. Those that have a position or stake in an organization or project are usually referred to as stakeholders while those that want to enter a market become a player or party. In a business context, the playing field is leveled in the sense that all participants play according to the same rules.[1] The use of the playing field metaphor seems appropriate in this study because CPP parties or players (e.g., NGOs, museums, and universities) are in constant competition with each other while stakeholders (e.g., IOs and Ministries) tend to defend their positions. Still, all compete not for victory but for control of the CPP market and to substantiate their identities. In fact, it is somewhat analogous to behaviors of parties using and abusing cultural property in the event of conflict. One could say there is a CPP market/playing field and a CPP battlefield where the first arena has to solve the problems created on the latter. This comparison is used here in an attempt to clarify matters and does not pretend to be appropriate in another context. Using the two identified fields together can make matters more complicated since some players described in this research as being part of the CPP playing field can be placed in the CPP battlefield as opposite forces (e.g., illicit traffickers, opposing military forces, and certain antique dealers). Finally, there are (potential) stakeholders such as the military of some countries that want to get out of the playing/battle field or do not want to enter it because they consider CPP not part of their core business or competence. These stakeholders can also have financial motives for not entering or staying in the market (e.g., financial cutbacks at MoDs). From a pure technical point of view, a playing field gives indications of parties, their respective positions, and the way they are interrelated, so in fact networks are described. The parties addressed here are the military, the media, governmental organizations,

---

[1] http://www.businessdictionary.com/definition/level-playing-field.html [17 July 2011].

non-governmental organizations, international organizations, workgroups and advisory groups, and stakeholders related to commerce, crime, law, religion, and science.

Before giving an account of these parties and their networks, some issues have to be addressed that directly relate to the setting of the stage. This is necessary to put CPP as a relatively new subject in perspective. If needed, contextual explanations and practical cases will be given of the respective stakeholders and players. This includes giving cases of good and bad practice while mentioning opposing, sometimes conflicting, interests or implications. The playing field cannot only be described in terms of international and multinational dimensions since it contains interagency and interdisciplinary elements, too. Apart from this, the playing field comprises more than conflict areas. Art and antique auction rooms as well as high-class antique dealers in major western cities, museums, universities, and criminal courts and international tribunals set the scenery, too. The information in this section does not pretend to be complete, but merely aims at giving an impression in which the main players, beneficiaries, and legal obligations are identified, described, and explained. In addition, experiences in theater and peacetime preparations, as well as procedures and events taking place after conflicts if they concern cultural property protection by civilian and military parties are taken into account.[2]

One important party that will not be addressed extensively is local and national populations sometimes referred to as local communities. These have a variety of interests ranging from economic to identity and safety issues and are, just like the military always *in situ* in times of conflict.

It is a basic assumption that in peacetime the military focus on training and the creation of networks. These should provide for so-called reach-back capabilities to be used in times of conflict, military exercises, and natural disaster. Examples of reach-back resources are curators, restorers, universities, cultural NGOs, and international organizations.

Civil parties in countries that ratified the Hague Convention of 1954 are legally expected to work on risk preparedness in the event of conflict as well as in the event of natural disasters. The latter demonstrates that the number and type of parties involved in preparations can differ from those taking part during military operations. Consequently, the actors mentioned do not participate at the same time or to the same extent in all possible situations. This depends on whether the activities happen before or during

---

2 Not to be confused with national risk-preparedness for natural and manmade disasters.

an operation but also on the types of action. A peace-support operation, for instance, can differ from a counterinsurgency or combat operation. Apart from this, it is questionable if, for example, scientific reach-back capabilities, needed by the military for expert advice, can engage with secret military operations. The military apparatus as a whole consists of a collection of acronyms; it is a matter of culture or at least corporate culture. The use of military acronyms in this book is therefore inescapable, not only to make the text more readable but also to open up the information for military officers used to reading and using acronyms. At the end of this publication is a glossary explaining the abbreviations used.

As touched upon earlier, the identity aspect of cultural heritage is vital. Identity is not only one of the three key elements (identity, authenticity, and uniqueness, referred to as uniquity) in the civil heritage debate, but is also a driver for many contemporary conflicts and disputes. In Bevan's *The Destruction of Memory*, the connections of cultural property with identity and conflict and potential openings for strategic use by military or opposing forces are analyzed.[3] As an example of denying a people its past as well as its future, he discusses the so-called Kristallnacht of 1938 that caused the destruction of German synagogues. Bevan labels the activity of destroying identity markers such as certain buildings as "forced forgetting." This sounds logical, but it has to be noted that historians will argue against Bevan's claim that the Kristallnacht was a preconceived goal of the Nazis to delete Jewish identity from the memory of humankind.[4] A historically correct example would be the 1993 destruction of the Mostar Bridge in former Yugoslavia. Seen from Bevan's perspective, and when applied to conflict, there is a military interest; to be exact, the defeat of the enemy that can lead to "exterminate this enemy by obliterating its culture." The scope is relatively wide since the threat to common objects, especially buildings, is considered a threat to identity as well as to the collective memory maintaining a group's consciousness. Here we are at a no man's land between cultural "scapes" that are in Bevan's context probably typical neighborhoods, and autonomous cultural objects that include monuments that are freestanding buildings.[5] If such typical neighborhoods are considered part of cultural

---

3 Bevan 2006.

4 The attack came as a reaction to the killing of a member of the German Embassy staff in Paris by a young Jew in retaliation for the poor treatment his family suffered at the hands of the Nazis in Germany. Source: ⟨http://www.historyplace.com/worldwar2/timeline/knacht.htm⟩ [17 July 2011].

5 The term scapes is currently used as an indicator for different environments e.g. landscapes, cityscapes, sound-scapes, nature scapes, trauma scapes etc.

identity, CPP will be even more complex than it is now and additional expertise to assess the presence of sensitive areas in case of military operations will be needed.

The current scientific discourse is expanded with a debate about the link between heritage sites and cultural/natural landscapes, or to be more precise, the cultural and natural aspects of heritage.[6] When one takes a closer look at cultural and natural characteristics, a specific military link becomes apparent, namely the connection of cultural resources with natural resources within the environmental approach towards operations. The environmental connection that aims at protecting and safeguarding the environmental milieu including implications and opportunities, will be described and analyzed in other sections of this book.

Established groups of people tend to identify themselves with certain (cultural) objects. Additionally, they want to appropriate these objects for themselves or their group as heritage. Through this process, the objects reflect and represent certain identities and receive (added) intrinsic values.[7] This quality is not evident at first glance but gives the property significance for opposing parties in a conflict. For instance, a mosque is not simply a mosque, but it can represent to an opponent the presence of a community marked for erasure. By the same token, a library or even an art gallery can be a cache of historical memory. A memory legitimizes a community in the present and in the future, but it also gives an opponent room for selecting objects and places carrying meaning such as cultural landscapes, battlefields, and memory/memorial sites, for intentional destruction aiming at oblivion, or in other words, erasure from memory. These mechanisms are interesting from a military point of view, but have to be controlled from a CPP perspective. National and international legislation applies to prevent misuse both from military and civilian stakeholders such as politicians. Practical cases, to be presented later, will show that identity can also influence the position and actions of CPP stakeholders on a micro level. Identity on this level can be hidden in different phenomena such as traditions, corporate cultures, and bureaucratic behavior.

The contemporary scholarly debate on cultural heritage is of vital importance, but occurs at a more profound level compared to the military-driven discussion and related issues that are addressed in this study. The main reason for this difference is that issues on military CPP form a new debate about

---

[6] See Luengo 2009 and the Convention concerning the Protection of World Cultural and Natural Heritage, ⟨http://whc.unesco.org/archive/convention-en.pdf⟩ [17 July 2011].

[7] Bevan 2006.

a new discipline that in its current phase is still underdeveloped. In addition, it should be noted that there is a civil scientific trend that tends to value methodology over content or to have function follow form instead of vice versa, resulting in highly abstract approaches that appear not in concurrence with today's issues concerning heritage in conflict and disaster. Of course, everything is open for debate and the perspectives need to be in balance with each other. Nevertheless, transferring knowledge and raising awareness among the military concerning CPP should start on a functional level where it can gradually grow to a more sophisticated level. That said, we cannot ignore the strong need for scientific research that informs efforts to raise awareness and stimulate participation of the military.

There are multiple angles for a categorization of CPP stakeholders, so choices were made that best fit the current situation. An interesting approach comes from U.S. Civil Affairs Colonel and archaeologist Mark Yanaway.[8] He distills the CPP stakeholders from what he calls the Paradoxical Trinity: the Government, the Army, and the People, or in fact Clausewitz's Trinity.[9] He uses the site of Babylon as an example.[10] First, to clarify, in the 1980s, Saddam attempted to create a major tourist attraction there aimed at glorifying himself. This led to inferior reconstructions on the site while restaurants and other facilities were erected on site. Saddam identified himself with the ancient ruler, Nebuchadnezzar. He even believed he looked like him and had been "given" the vision to restore the once great empire and serve as its ruler. What survives today of the original Babylon is generally only the lower courses of the walls or simply their foundations. As it was put in the press, "the site has the aura of a theme park touched by the ambition of dictator Saddam Hussein and the opportunism of looters: Modern walkways run beside crumbling old walls, a reconstructed Greek theater and a palace built for Saddam atop an artificial hill."[11] Even so, Babylon is still perceived as an important cultural property and demonstrates through an examination of the situation during and after its occupation until December 2004 that many stakeholders can be classified under

---

[8] A presentation at the AIA conference military panel January 2011 in San Antonio TX see: ⟨http://aiamilitarypanel.org/events/aia-2011-workshop/⟩ [17 July 2011].

[9] Clausewitz 1968 (1832).

[10] Babylon (Iraq) was the capital of a city state in Mesopotamia, located on the eastern bank of the Euphrates River. Babylon was founded at the end of the third millennium BC, and lasted through the 2nd century AD.

[11] ⟨http://www.msnbc.msn.com/id/27669499/ns/technology and_science-science/t/iraq-can-ancient-babylon-be-rescued/⟩ [20 August 2011].

government. In this case, the U.S. Government and its institutions were in charge during the U.S. occupation. These institutions included ORHA, OCPA and CPA, the Federal Government of Iraq, and the Provincial Government of Babil Province. The example shows how different governmental segments can have conflicting and complementary interests. Implicitly this is an acknowledgement from a military expert of paradoxes and contradictions within the CPP field, and as such a military recognition of the importance of cultural property. Yanaway compares his trinity with Clausewitz's original trinity: emotion, chance, and reason. Opinions will differ on this sort of classification or comparison of parties based on emotion, chance, or reason. Besides, a government is not always present in today's asymmetric non-state conflicts, and ruling parties can substitute governments. Still, the point is valid that mutual discussions between civil and military experts that may lead to combined research can be fruitful and constructive.

A first and basic classification of stakeholders must include military and civil parties, which are sometimes also opponents in the protection of cultural property; certain entities can also belong to both groups (e.g., juridical experts, trainers and military and civilian archaeologists). A second categorization concerns parties according to their interests. These can, for example, be classified as groups, factions, nations, tribes, etc., that foster their identity while protecting and preserving objects representing these identities. Examples include the Copts, the Roma, Free Masons, and the like. When referring directly to CPP stakeholders, distinctive entities like archaeologists, government officials, architects, and antique dealers enter the picture. When economic and financial interests are at stake, entities such as the tourism industry, restorers, auctioneers, antique dealers, and of course, artists can be distinguished. A third possible classification is mentioning and describing all relevant stakeholders by their professional or group's name. To obtain a detailed insight, this appears to be the most functional method. In the following pages a selection of seven key players will be discussed while explaining how they relate to each other within the field of heritage protection. Practical examples show that some parties look upon CPP as a subject that is presented to the world as invented by them. Consequently, it is a challenge that parties not only need to cooperate in raising their awareness on the relevance of the subject, but also have to acknowledge that CPP should only and necessarily be implemented in a multidisciplinary fashion. Parties addressed are the military, the media, political organizations, including governmental institutions, non-governmental organizations (NGOs), international organizations (IOs), scientific disciplines and universities, and working or advisory groups; see also figure 7. Finally, a number of parties are addressed under their own name since they are not classified within the groups mentioned.

The Military

The military is sometimes addressed as the armed forces, MoD, or DoD. Within the framework of this study, they comprise paramilitary police like the Italian Carabinieri and the Spanish Guardia Civil. Therefore when referring to the military as the armed forces it is more effective to speak about ministries of defense (MoD) or the U.S. Department of Defense (DoD). Nevertheless, the official definition of armed forces is important to consider when planning to embed cultural property protection officers since they fall under the same legal regime as the military of such forces. The armed forces of a party to a conflict consist of all organized armed forces, groups, and units which are under a command responsible to that party for the conduct of its subordinates, even if that party is represented by a government or an authority not recognized by an adverse party. Such armed forces will be subject to an internal disciplinary system which, inter alia, will enforce compliance with the rules of international law applicable in armed conflict.[12] The official entity containing the armed forces is normally a country's ministry or department of defense. Cultural property protection resources can be embedded in defense ministries in different ways, for example, in CIMIC or civil affairs units, or environmental departments.[13] It can even occur that they exist as separate capabilities within one or more services like the air force, navy, or army. To make the legal distinction between official combatants and unofficial fighters clear and in an attempt to make it possible for CPP experts to get some idea about the legal conditions in which cultural properties are damaged or attacked during conflicts, let us first take

[12] Source: Protocol Additional to the Geneva Conventions of 12 August 1949, and relating to the Protection of Victims of International Armed Conflicts (Protocol I), 8 June 1977.

[13] Civil affairs (CA) is the long-standing name used by the U.S. military to describe its relations with the civilian sphere. The term is often confused with the term "civil affairs activities." Civil affairs are designated for active and reserve component forces and units trained to conduct CA activities that support civil-military operations. Civil affairs activities are actions performed by CA personnel that enhance the relationship between military forces and civilian authorities in areas where military forces are present. The activities include, for example, the application of civil-affairs functional specialty skills in areas normally the responsibility of the civil government (source: Celik 2005).

a closer look into the international legal definition used to describe and specify the military as a party to a conflict. Apparent and important to distinguish officially recognized armed forces is that they consist of "organized" forces under a "command" that is responsible for the behavior of its lower ranked. In addition it is conditional that there is an internal system of sanctions to enforce violations of IHL or more specific that part of IHL applicable to armed conflict.[14]

Soldiers operate during all phases of a conflict including those in which civil experts are not allowed or unable to function. In fact, they form both part of the problem and part of the solution. That is why armed forces are mentioned in legal documents about heritage protection like the Hague Convention of 1954. In a democratic system, the military only act when ordered by their governments. Therefore, it can be assumed that in most cases they are not ordered to implement CPP as described in the Hague Convention of 1954. For that reason, impediments have to be considered while examining mechanisms and situations regarding implementing and embedding CPP capacity in armed forces. This discussion provides an insight into the norms, ideals, and expertise within military organizations to facilitate further analysis.

It is a simplification to look upon "the military" as one solid entity since "the military" is in fact a collection of parts, (e.g. military academies, alliances such as NATO, military juridical experts, military archaeologists, Ministries, and Departments of Defense and Civil Military Cooperation units). Within the components different cultures connected with ranks, blood groups, regiments, and services can be distinguished, all with distinct characteristics. Yet seen from the outside, the military have their own rather isolated milieu. At the risk of being blunt, it can be said that traditionally they form an almost tribal society predominantly interested in themselves and loyal to their traditions and values. The military hierarchy, envisaged career path, possible qualification for staff positions, and cultural aspects stimulate risk or uncertainty-avoidance; this means military society is generally more risk-avoiding than civil society and subsequently has more problems with changes and influx of new tasks.[15] These special conditions also create a feeling of superiority, which for outsiders makes it difficult to raise awareness of topics like cultural heritage. Soldiers look upon these

---

[14] See footnote 12 above.

[15] Hofstede & Hofstede 2003.

Military Strategic Culture and Subcultures that Interact with Civilian Strategic Culture and Subcultures and Influence Implementation of a Military Cultural Property Protextion Strategy.

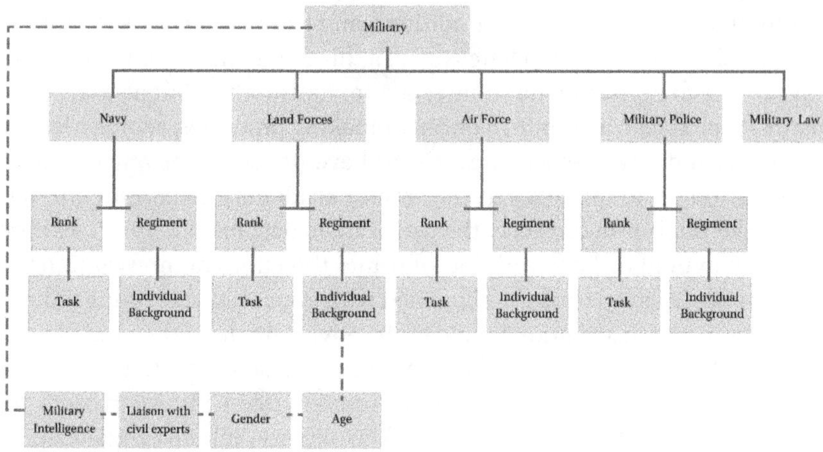

Figure 5. An example of the military social fabric. © Joris Kila.

matters as representations of civil and not military society. Nonetheless, it can be said that today's military appears less afraid of change and more open to tasks concerning development and environmental issues than they were previously. Still, it will take a while until all genetic characteristics that used to be typical for the military have transformed into new attitudes and finally become part of the military collective identity. Cultural and geographical backgrounds of the various armed forces, as well as education and lessons learned, house an influence on this process.

The diagram above (Figure 5) shows an example of military strategic cultures influencing the degree of receptiveness to be educated about, and work with new expertise and subjects like CPP.[16]

Potential incentives for paying attention to cultural property and related civil-military aspects do exist as common denominators. Like most civilians, military personnel are also interested in cultural property, especially when

[16] Strategic culture is that set of shared beliefs, assumptions, and modes of behavior, derived from common experiences and accepted narratives (both oral and written), that shape collective identity and relationships to other groups, and which determine appropriate ends and means for achieving security objectives. Source: Johnson and Larsen 2006. Comparative Strategic Culture Syllabus, Jeannie L. Johnson and Jeffrey A. Larsen, Fort Belvoir, Virginia, 2006.

there is a relation to their business. In this context, we can think of war monuments and museums containing warplanes, weapons, uniforms and the like, and also, for some, famous battlefields. Historical sources describing military history and the art of war are appreciated too, combined with a potential receptivity for codes, traditions, and iconography as is stimulated during military education. There is such a thing as a military mindset or the ways in which personnel not only relate to one another, but also the manner in which they contribute to decision-making processes, exercise leadership roles, and interpret significant world events. Concerns range from an examination of honor codes at the service academies to consideration of topics like nuclear deterrence, the use of biological and chemical warfare, the development of "just war" doctrine, and the ethics of intervention.[17] In recent times, this repertoire is expanded with issues like sustaining military readiness in which attention is paid to the environment in the form of natural and cultural and combined natural/cultural resources.[18] Organizational aspects can hinder implementation of matters like CPP. Apart from the already identified trend of personal risk avoidance, military organizations as a whole tend to avoid change and risks, too. Ministries or Departments of Defense are in most cases large complex organizations. Their staff members have a tendency to value means over ends; they worry more about following the right rule than about achieving the ultimate goal.[19] In the Dutch Defense organization, this is especially apparent in the behavior of those that are destined for higher positions, the so-called staff-qualified, recognized by a special emblem on their uniform shaped as the sun. De facto, this qualifying system is a recipe to create unnecessary risk avoidance, thus suppressing creative and visionary ideas.

Having acknowledged this, one has to take into account that in a military organization, more than in civil organizations, it is customary for people to follow orders from their superiors. This is extremely relevant in wartime, but in peacetime, it contributes to restraining development and implementation of new ideas and strategies. Moreover, the military encompasses many cultures and all of these see various tasks as most relevant. As a result, different individuals are active in the same field, often working against, or in the best case, supplementing each other. In this respect, they do not differ from actors in the civil playing field. In both arenas multiple interests,

---

[17] Source: Ethics and the Armed Forces. Naval War College Library Notes, May 1997 (revised August 1997), Vol. 25, no. 4.

[18] ⟨http://smrconference.com/Agenda/index.cfm⟩ [17 July 2011].

[19] Wilson 1989.

groups, competencies, and political power structures compete. There is one unwritten rule: "tasks that are not part of the culture will not be attended to with the same energy and resources as tasks that are part of a certain culture."[20] This became apparent in many cases examined for this study. A good pars pro toto was the organization of the Dutch military seminar entitled The Protection of Cultural Property in Times of Conflict: The Relevance and Practical Implementation of CPP and its Connection with the Comprehensive Approach during Military Operations, that took place in The Hague in 2009. For instance, the allocated funding for the event was quite limited. In fact, it was too limited to offer the right quality. Fortunately, external funding was offered from the city council, but financial support from non-military partners was not accepted by the Dutch MoD. Other challenges concerned freedom of information about military CPP issues. At the last minute, the press was not allowed to attend the seminar, by the order of the MoD head of communication. No reason was given. After the seminar, attempts were made to get clarification from the responsible official without result. In addition, there was an issue concerning the use, in a Power Point presentation, of apparently classified materials. These experiences seem to support the already presented suppositions that the military have, and want to keep, their own isolated milieu and that protection of cultural heritage is a topic connected to competence struggles and angst for the media, often combined with the urge for distinction. The effects that contradictory rules and competence struggles within the military organization can have on CPP becomes apparent in the two following examples. The first one concerns Civil-Military Cooperation as an example of conflicting strategic cultures while the second involves the issue of ranking functional specialists.

1. NATO defines Civil-Military Cooperation (CIMIC), as "the co-ordination and co-operation, in support of the mission, between the NATO commander and civil actors, including national populations and local authorities, as well as international, national, and non-governmental organizations and agencies."[21]

---

[20] Wilson 1989, p. 101.

[21] There is a difference with Civil Affairs (UK and U.S.) and British CIMIC. Whereas NATO, as an organization, considers civil-military cooperation as "observation, interposition, and transition assistance," the British perceive CIMIC as "direct assistance by conventional troops," and Americans recognize it as force protection, liaison, and limited direct support (Celik 2005). Force protection is a term used by the U.S. military to describe preventive measures taken to mitigate hostile actions against Department of Defense personnel (including family members), resources, facilities, and critical information. Force protection does not

The basic format of CIMIC comprises five branches, as follows: Civil Administration, Humanitarian Aid, Civil Infrastructure, Economy and Commerce, and Cultural Affairs.[22] The latter designation, however, creates confusion. Some countries attempt to implement cultural issues through Civil Military Cooperation; others address cultural matters through Civil Affairs (CA) units. The use of the adjacent word cultural gives room for multiple interpretations. If a country is well aware of its legal obligations concerning CPP, of course depending on the treaties it ratified or signed, there is a greater chance for an interpretation towards "concerning cultural heritage protection." However if there is no special familiarity with this topic, confusion can occur where cultural affairs is equated with cultural awareness. The latter means information on cultural backgrounds; it uses the wide anthropological connotation of the term culture, or better said, all cultural issues are thrown together.

Since the early 1990s, CIMIC appeared on the political and military agendas. In fact, CIMIC is related to the much older concept of civil affairs that is still in use in the United Kingdom and the United States of America. In line with NATO directives, a number of countries started creating CIMIC capabilities within their Armed Forces. Yet most countries did not have the necessary resources such as cultural specialists within their armed forces. Experts had to be found in civil society, painted green (the military expression for militarizing civilians), and deployed as reserve officers, known in CIMIC as functional specialists. While this was a positive development, it became clear that in practice cultural experts were never sent on missions to conflict areas. The only initiated Dutch CPP project in the Former Yugoslav Republic of Macedonia (FYROM) was even stopped because the Dutch Ministry of Development Aid opposed the fact that military experts would do work that NGOs could do.[23] In fact, Dutch CIMIC projects executed in conflict areas were and still are primarily concerned with water sanitation, bridge construction, and commerce. It is probably not a coincidence that these represent typical Dutch export specialties that mainly involved the CIMIC Civil Infrastructure and Economy and Commerce departments and were seldom supported by funding from other ministries than just the

include actions to defeat the enemy or protect against accidents, weather, or disease. Source: Department of Defense Dictionary of Military and Associated Terms 8 November 2010 (As amended through 15 May 2011). ⟨http://www.dtic.mil/doctrine/new_pubs/jp1_02.pdf⟩ [17 July 2011].

[22] Cultural affairs is the name according to NATO's CIMIC Doctrine.

[23] Kila 2008 a and b.

MoD. In this study, however, only CIMIC matters linked with CIMIC cultural affairs will be discussed. With respect to cultural property protection, in CIMIC known as cultural affairs, the AJP-9 or CIMIC doctrine has led to poor results in practice because it was written with more common public policy issues in mind, such as providing humanitarian aid, repairing electricity and sewage systems, and supplying drinking water.[24] Also, there is a certain reluctance since the military does not want to be accused of spending tax money where it is not necessary. They also do not want to be labeled as being in competition with civilian players like NGOs, or accused of devoting resources to objectives beyond the scope of their mission.

Still there is more to consider, such as all kinds of rules and directives that appear to be contradicting each other and that are set out and described in the annexes of operation plans (Oplans) to achieve the end state of a mission. All of these aspects primarily serve military goals. Seen from this perspective by a commander, CIMIC is, in the first place, a tool to reach the end state of a mission faster and easier by creating and keeping good relations with the civil environment of the local population. A real show stopper for CPP projects is the directive deriving from the AJP-9 doctrine stating that all CIMIC activities in a certain area have to meet a basic military criterion, namely to be in support of the commander's mission.[25] Military commanders are rarely spontaneously interested in cultural property, and cultural property advisers who could point out the relevance to them are hardly ever deployed nor employed for that matter. Therefore, the subject is almost never chosen or implemented as a CIMIC activity. Even if it was, a legal contradiction may still arise between a military decision assigning low priority to cultural affairs in the context of the military goals and an action, for instance, to protect an object as mandatory under the Hague Convention of 1954 and its protocols. This contradiction arises because the CIMIC (cultural) activity is judged and started through an order of a military commander and is not (only) subjected to the directives of the 1954 Hague Convention. From this perspective CIMIC does not appear to be the right platform or institution to house cultural property protection officers who by nature feel compelled to follow the Hague Convention of 1954 and other relevant legal instruments. This does not mean that CIMIC cannot

---

24 Kila 2008a.

25 NATO CIMIC Doctrine AJP-9 states: "The co-ordination and co-operation, in support of the mission, between the NATO Commander and civil actors, including national population and local authorities, as well as international, national and non-governmental organizations and agencies."

employ cultural property specialists; they can always be lent out to MoD as embedded cultural property capabilities. In this way cultural property protection as a MoD-dedicated capability will not only solve the problems described, but expertise will at the same time be available for all military services (army, navy, air force and military police). This means that preparation and training can be initiated in peacetime as well as during conflict operations, and the same goes for research on the subject and the building of networks. Such a solution demands making a choice and allocating funding. In practice, this is more complicated than one would expect. When no provisions are made in advance following the legal obligations for instance, the military tend to leave such matters to be initiated by civil policy and decision-makers. This brings an extra complication since the latter often confuse cultural aid with the highly politicized humanitarian aid that, in general, is implemented by NGOs to avoid false competition accusations. Adding to this is the fact that CIMIC commanders and planners are likely to give priority to so-called high-visibility, quick-impact projects, like refurbishing schools and digging water wells in order to win the hearts and minds of a local population.[26] This supports the thesis that the urge for, in this case, individual distinction (to be precise, the upgrading of a personal status) and in second instance, a military objective, stand in the way of protecting cultural property that represent the identity of a larger entity in a conflict situation. Considering this, CIMIC and cultural property protection appear to have no easy mix. The fact remains that when a Commander wants to get a complete inventory of civilian needs, professional advice from experts representing all civil-military functional areas including cultural property protection is necessary. The best way to get this information is through assessments that have to take place before an actual operation. Concerning the cultural heritage situation in a mission area, assessments are not only desired but also mandatory.[27] When cultural property protection capabilities are embedded in a Ministry of Defense, such assessments can be scheduled, prepared, and executed as a regular activity within the military planning process. In most current situations in which the military are not convinced of the importance of CPP, this will remain a challenge.

2. The military organization houses more potential constraints for the implementation of CPP by (CIMIC) Functional Specialists and for that matter

---

[26] This problem is less obvious with U.S. Civil Affairs (CA) commanders who on the average stay longer in theater.

[27] See for instance Chapter 2 of the Second Protocol to the Hague Convention of 1954.

by reservists in general. A tough issue is ranking, in the sense of employing individuals of a certain military rank. It is a subject of discussion within the military, because of (as perceived by professional military) the relatively high rankings that reserve functional specialists, such as cultural property experts, receive. Since there are not enough qualified experts within the armed forces that can be deployed in the CIMIC functional areas, they have to be recruited from civil society. In general, these experts want to earn at least the income they are accustomed to receiving. This is a human resources challenge for most MoDs. In the Dutch Ministry of Defense, for example, two major criteria are used to determine the ranking level. First, within the military, pay is directly connected with rank. As established, in order to be able to recruit highly qualified civilian experts, they must be paid a reasonable salary. Average incomes that MoDs have to offer are considerably less than civilian salaries that are paid to highly qualified expert personnel. Because of the connection between rank and salary, ranks offered to specialist personnel recruited from civil society are relatively high. Second, to be able to properly negotiate in the field with governmental officials, higher foreign military officers, and international organizations, the specialist officer should have a representative (high) rank in order to be taken seriously.

Opposition against the level of ranking occasionally comes from professional military. They frequently argue that foreign military cannot see that a certain high-ranking officer is a functional specialist who is not equally equipped and trained to act in military emergencies, while the (foreign) military of lower rank, which cannot recognize the fact that the concerned reserve officer is a specialist, expect the same officer to act and take command. This can be avoided by having high ranking specialists, when they are sent out in the field, accompanied by at least one professional colleague, probably of lower rank, acting (by mutual agreement) as a so-called functional superior during such a field assignment, as was tested during deployment in Iraq.[28]

From 29 November to 2 December 2011 an event took place in Vienna. It was a course on CPP organized by the Austrian MoD, IMCuRWG and NATO or to be more specific its Allied Command Transformation (ACT) department in Virginia. The course included an exercise on integrating CPP in the military planning process. The supposition was that there were CPP staff officers in the planning process. This exercise made very clear that for

---

[28] For instance during my deployment in al Muthanna; see the Uruk case.

cultural experts it is extremely difficult to understand and apply all military procedures. The participants more or less concluded that it will be easier to train military candidates to become cultural property specialists than the other way around. This implies that CPP officers should be found preferably from within the military.

Even so, it is curious that the troubles described do not seem to exist for military medical, religious, and legal staff, perhaps because these militarized experts have long proven to be necessary in the armed forces, whereas cultural officers and their expertise are seen as something new and, in the eyes of some, unnecessary. Finally, the arguments above, as well as field experiences show, and confirm, that ranking is connected with status and therefore identity. Once again this supports the argument that proper implementation of CPP is restrained because entities that have to solve cultural property problems in practice are facing strategic cultural, often identity-related problems within their own circles. Having said this, it is time to look at external factors that can be of influence to the whole CPP picture. Today's most critical factor to consider is the media.

The Media

Within the context of this research, and taking into account that due to technical advancements their (potential) relevance is rapidly increasing, it has become clear that the media can play a significant role in CPP. When discussing the media, it is important to consider that there is currently a significant variety of vehicles to spread and exchange information. In the past, newspapers, magazines, radio, and television were the ruling media, but times have changed. New media that often cover the whole world will be addressed in this section and it goes without saying that they all have a potential influence on the behaviors of political and military CPP stakeholders. To give an example, the media input regarding the Baghdad Museum looting made the already low international support from within society for the Iraq War almost disappear.[29] In spite of the fact that the United States tried to limit the damage, they got saddled with the image of a "destroyer of culture" that remains intact until today, as is confirmed in the discussion on training in the Egypt/Bright Star case (see below). Today even the public, through social networks, can affect a military mission and a country's reputation. More than ever, information and communication play key

[29] Especially the CNN images of looters and museum staff in the shambles of the museum.

roles since they are capable of provoking negative international reactions or triggering positive media coverage, whereas the latter can generate military force multipliers. One should not underestimate the influence of bloggers and websites that can be driven either by individuals or by specific interest groups and have a great potential to influence opinions. The same goes, to certain extent for social media like LinkedIn, Facebook, and YouTube. A derivative of this is addressed as viral marketing, also named "going viral," referring to marketing techniques that use preexisting social networks to produce increases in awareness concerning brands or certain topics. Viral in this context is used to point at the self-replicating spreading process of viruses. CCHCAG's Paul Kunkel gives an impression of possibilities to use these techniques and media for CPP in a presentation under the title: "Going Viral: A Web Portal Concept for CCHCAG and beyond."[30] Effectively the media can help in getting CPP obligations fulfilled. From this perspective, the "uncertainty avoiding attitudes" of military and governmental decision makers can work positively because they fear "a bad press," in fact meaning negative reports from old and new media alike. This gives them enough reason to exclude unnecessary (personal) risks, and to especially aim at fulfilling legally imposed obligations. Then again, this can also lead to exclusion of the press, as happened in the earlier-addressed Dutch MoD seminar in The Hague that took place in 2009. The head of the Press and Information Department of the Dutch MoD personally banned all press and interviews.[31]

Publications can have an impact too, as can be seen in a number of book titles used in reference to the damaging of cultural property. Some publications dealing with the subject make use of the term rape in their titles (e.g., *The Rape of Europa, The Rape of Mesopotamia,* and *The Rape of the Nile*).[32] Apart from the section with case studies that constitute a separate part in this book, two cultural heritage cases will be addressed here showing the media's influence and weight for bringing these issues out

---

30 Paul Kunkel, SAFE/Saving Antiquities for Everyone, Inc., New York, NY. Paper for presentation at the 112th Annual Meeting of the Archaeological Institute of America, Workshop 4A: Collaboration Between Cultural Heritage by AIA-Military Panel (CHAMP) and CENTCOM Historical/Cultural Action Group (CCHCAG). San Antonio, TX, 6–9 December 2011. ⟨http://aiamilitarypanel.org/events/aia-2011-workshop/⟩ [17 July 2011].

31 An explanation was not given but risk avoidance and lack of knowledge on the subject were most certainly driving his behavior. At the time the author, who was also the seminar organizer, tried repeatedly to get an explanation but no answer was given and all contacts with the head of the department were refused.

32 Nicholas 1994, Fagan 2004, and Rothfield 2009.

in the open. The first is a discussion initiated by both the press as well as internet bloggers about the Human Terrain Systems (HTS), and the second is the case of the Jewish Archives from Iraq.[33]

The Human Terrain Systems (HTS) discussion contains ethical concerns connected with military cultural property protection and as such represents a challenge for implementing CPP. The issue is the current, international, media-driven discussion about ethical issues concerning social scientists who work with the military. Opponents of scholarly engagement with the military use this anthropological involvement in the HTS as a justification to react against all cooperation from social scientists including the realm of military cultural property protection. Their actions restrain the process of making the military aware of the obligations in the 1954 Hague Convention and its Protocols. The core of the problem is that social scientists, working for the American HTS teams, are mistaken for cultural property experts working with the military within the framework of the 1954 Hague Convention and its two protocols or other international legal instruments. Due to this confusion, a relatively small number of archaeologists and anthropologists have spread confusion. During the sixth World Archaeological Congress (WAC 2008) in Dublin, this led to a confrontation.[34] CPP experts working with the military gave papers, participated in panels, and had to face fierce opposition. Intense ethical objections drove remarks and arguments from opponents. During discussions, archaeologists who had chosen to partner with the military were labeled as "part of the problem" and accused of having lost their impartiality. This reminded me of the 1960s when similar allegations were made to individuals collaborating in various capacities with the military. These accusations were often true, but the political global situation and the type of conflicts were completely different at the time. Several articles discuss the ethical problem.[35] A statement

---

[33] HTS is a new proof-of-concept program, run by the U.S. Army Training and Doctrine Command (TRADOC), and serving the joint community. The near-term focus of the HTS program is to improve the military's ability to understand the highly complex local sociocultural environment in the areas where they are deployed; however, in the long-term, HTS hopes to assist the U.S. government in understanding foreign countries and regions prior to an engagement within that region, source: ⟨http://humanterrainsystem.army.mil/⟩ [17 July 2011]. HTS embeds anthropologists and other social scientists with combat brigades (currently in Iraq and Afghanistan) to help tacticians in the field understand local cultures using Human Terrain Mapping.

[34] 6th World Archaeological Congress (WAC) held at University College Dublin, 29 June–4 July 2008.

[35] See for instance David Price 2008 and Dahr Jamail, "How Some Anthropologists Have Learned to Stop Worrying and Start Loving the Army," www.truthout.org/051609Z 16 May

that illustrates the ruling opinion as well as the degree of confusion comes from the American journalist Dahr Jamail who spent eight months in Iraq, from 2003 to 2005, and at the time was one of the few reporters not embedded with the military. He writes that "Social scientists in the Human Terrain System teams embed with the military, ostensibly to improve cultural awareness of the populations in Afghanistan and Iraq. However, this cultural awareness is used to formulate strategies for killing and destruction."[36] The fact that in the U.S. the hearts and minds strategy of counterinsurgency was stressed did not make things better, but triggered even more opposition from experts. The link between counterinsurgency and hearts and minds and subsequently CPP is explained in detail in the section below on the sociology of CPP and the military. Nevertheless, to quote American anthropologist David Price: "The problem with anthropology used in counterinsurgency isn't just anthropologists helping the military to wear different cultural skins; the problem is that it finds anthropologists using bio power and basic infrastructure as bargaining chips to force occupied cultures to surrender."[37] The above clearly describes the problem: confusion about the phrase "cultural awareness," a term often mistakenly seen as part of CPP.

Already introduced to explain the concrete relevance of CPP are the following: (1) common denominators to illustrate the significance of cultural property for civil and military players; and (2) deliverables that can be of tactical and strategic relevance for the military.[38] Military planners and senior leadership, currently largely uninformed, have to be made aware of their existence. If they realize the significance of the deliverables, this will be taken into account when missions are planned. There is, however, no guarantee that things will automatically run smoothly. How matters can develop in practice, especially when cultural objects are handled inconsiderately, is illustrated through the case of the "Jewish archive." The story

---

2009. ⟨http://www.google.nl/search?hl=nl&q=www.truthout.org%2F051609Z&rlz=1I7ADFA_nl⟩ [17 July 2011].

[36] Quote: Dahr Jamail, May 17, 2009 | T r u t h o u t. ⟨http://declarationofpeace.org/published/may-17-2009-engineering-trust-of-the-indigenous-popula⟩ [July 17 2011].

[37] Ibid.

[38] Tactical level is the level at which activities, battles, and engagements are planned and executed to accomplish military objectives assigned to tactical formations and units. The operational level is the level at which campaigns and major operations are planned, conducted, and sustained to accomplish strategic objectives within theaters or areas of operations. The strategic level is the level at which a nation or group of nations determines national or multinational security objectives and deploys national, including military resources to achieve them.

includes several parties that behave as contestants disputing cultural property, which is illustrated by the way they react in the media (used as the battlefield).

On 17 January 2010, an article was published in the Washington Post, "Iraq reclaims a Jewish history it once shunned."[39] During the last war in Iraq in May 2003 U.S. military personnel found in the flooded basement of a deserted building once belonging to the Mukhabarat (Saddam's secret police) a collection of old Jewish books, photographs, and manuscripts. The former Iraqi secret police are believed to have confiscated the items from the small Iraqi Jewish community. These objects, referred to as the "Jewish archive" looked heavily damaged. At the time the U.S. had only one Arts, Monuments and Archives Officer working in Iraq. She examined the objects from the basement and found that they were damp and moldy. The only way to stabilize them for the time being was by freezing, so a refrigerator truck was parked in a warehouse in the back of Saddam's former palace located in the so-called Green Zone. The truck's motor was kept running to sustain the electricity until September 2003. In the meantime, an agreement was reached, and later approved by the Iraqi Ministry of Culture, to move the objects to the United States for preservation.[40] The archive was flown to Fort Worth, Texas, with a military cargo plane and finally ended up in the National Archives and Records Administration (NARA) in Maryland. It was supposed to be returned to Iraq after two years, but the Iraqis have never pushed for its return since they were more focused on surviving the violence in their country. Yet, now (2010) they wanted it back. The problem is that apparently more parties feel entitled to control the collection. This triggers a lot of different, sometimes opposing, statements and perspectives that influence public opinions. Media quotes show how the cultural property at stake is claimed and which arguments are used.

Saad Eskander, the director of the Iraq National Library and Archives, said Iraqis must know that we are a diverse people, with different traditions, different religions, and we need to accept this diversity "to show ... our people that Baghdad was always multi-ethnic."

Abdullah Hamid, the head of Iraq's National Center for Manuscripts and Documents added: "I am afraid that there is pressure from some groups,

[39] Sources: "Iraq reclaims a Jewish history it once shunned," by Rebecca Santana, The Associated Press, Sunday, January 17, 2010; Email correspondence dated January 22, 2010 from the author of this book with Major (ret.) Corine Wegener, the CPP officer involved at the time.

[40] Effectively Iraq was, during this period, governed by the United States-led Coalition Provisional Authority (CPA.)

both inside and outside the United States, in order to prevent the return of these Iraqi manuscripts to their original country."

Doris Hamburg, who directs preservation projects at NARA, denied any pressures and stressed: "Iraq can have the archive back whenever it wants." Iraqi officials at the National Library said they have no indication the Americans are trying to hold onto the archive.

Dov S. Zakheim, an Orthodox Jew who was a senior Department of Defense official under President George W. Bush, warned that if the Iraqis were to claim the archive as their own, it would anger the Jewish community. "It's not theirs. It's just not theirs," he said. "Jews feel very strongly about their heritage."

Mordechai Ben-Porat, who helped Jews leaving Iraq after Israel's establishment in 1948, says the archive should be in the museum dedicated to Iraqi Jews that he runs in Israel. "The books belong to the majority of the Iraqi Jews, and they are not in Iraq. The books should be given to us, as the representatives of the Jews of Iraq."

According to Saad Eskander, the archive's long absence from Iraq has made it politically sensitive. It annoyed Iraqis that the Americans who failed to protect Iraqi cultural treasures were devoting such care to the Jewish archive. "The American national archive did a great job, and we are grateful for their help ... now we will do it here in Baghdad. It is our Cultural Heritage."

Iraqi officials will go to the United States shortly to assess the materials found by U.S. troops and plan for their return. Obviously, publicity concerning this case will not stop for the present. It shows how unpredictable cultural property protection can work out when not treated with the utmost care.

In this one incident, different interests, distinctive identities, legal dilemmas, and media exposure, all triggered by military implementation of CPP, become visible. It should be clarified for the legal context that, at the time the archive was shipped to Texas, the United States was not a state party to the 1954 Hague Convention, but Iraq was. Therefore Chapter III, article 18 of the Hague Convention of 1954 applies, and it seems mandatory to return the objects to the country of origin after the hostilities ended. Nevertheless, this example can illustrate to military leadership that inconsiderate actions regarding handling of cultural property can harm both a military operation as well as the reputation of a country involved.

Another case that, although not directly connected with conflict, demonstrates media influence on handling cultural property is the event involving the chestnut tree of Anne Frank. In 2007, there were large protests when it was announced in the press that the municipality of Amsterdam wanted to cut down a sick tree that was mentioned by Anne Frank in her diary. After many national and international protests and a court case, the tree was allowed to remain standing. The tree was braced and was expected to stand for up to fifteen years. The neighbor of the Anne Frank House put a chestnut from the famed tree up for auction on eBay where it fetched 2,500 Euros. The end of the tree came unexpectedly on 23 August 2010 when it fell down due to excessive wind. Again, many people tried to make a profit by offering pieces of the tree for sale on the internet. The latest news dates from end of February 2012; different Dutch media report that the cuttings taken from the original tree's branches produced roots and were already blossoming. A number of cuttings were donated to the United States.[41]

To conclude, these cases demonstrate that media exposure can draw attention to ethical concerns, thus forcing parties to reconsider certain cultural activities. The second example of the Jewish archive confirms the mechanism described earlier that media coverage can trigger groups or individuals from different geographical descent to identify themselves with certain objects and consequently claim them as heritage, or in this case objects are claimed that are considered part of their (existing) heritage in order to strengthen their present identity. It can also happen that claims are made for financial reasons, or to get a new value, but this seems not to be case here.

A final example of media influence involving new social media, particularly Twitter and Facebook, is the revolt in Egypt (end of January 2011) to be discussed in more detail in a case study in Chapter 3. Social media not only played a substantial role in mobilizing demonstrators and informing the international news media, but also spread news to the world about the looting of cultural property. Some quotes from an email to me by a U.S. archaeologist with direct contacts in the field illustrate this. "I just received this information directly (on Facebook) from Egyptologists and members of the Supreme Council for Antiquities (SCA) who are witnessing the situation ... Verified by Mohammad Megahed: Immense damages to Abusir and Saqqara, all magazines and tombs which were sealed were entered last night. Only Imhotep Museum and adjacent central magazines protected by the military. In Abusir all tombs opened. Large gangs digging day and night everywhere."[42]

---

[41] ⟨http://www.rtvnh.nl/nieuws/74565/Jonge+takken+Anne+Frankboom+staan+in+knop⟩ [27 February 2012].

[42] Email to the author from Dr. Sarah Parcak, University of Alabama at Birmingham, Jan 30, 2011.

These reports, which were all quite timely, when compared to the situations years earlier in Baghdad demonstrate that the social media is not only faster than the older media, but the reporters, who are often the cultural property experts themselves, are less vulnerable to potential censors within governmental and political entities.

Governmental Institutions and Political Organizations

Governmental parties involved in CPP are antiquities services, ministries of culture, foreign affairs, and development aid.[43] Ministries of defense are discussed separately in the section about the Military. "Foreign Affairs has good ideas and a feel for the political landscape, but they are bad at implementing anything. Defense, on the other hand is excellent at logistical stuff, but has blinders on when it comes to policy."[44] This quote shows one of the core problems that affect cooperation, in this case concerning CPP within governmental institutions and political entities: all governmental institutions have different interests and areas of expertise. Nevertheless, a multi-agency approach is always needed because of the variety of CPP stakeholders. In order for assets to be used in support of CPP, the institutions involved need to be aware of incentives that can be generated and of common interests they have as part of the government as a whole. To give an example, many governmental institutions own and use monuments like historical buildings, so that a common interest is conservation and preservation of these cultural properties in Norway, for instance, many historical buildings are owned by the Norwegian Ministry of Defense. Again, practice shows that in order to stimulate institutional attention, CPP's value as an incentive or as a subject that can trigger synergy has to be demonstrated and explained thoroughly. Potential synergy can, for instance, be found in the domain of foreign affairs, especially in the actual ministries, departments, and embassies. Seen from a wider perspective, foreign affairs has a relation with CPP via cultural diplomacy that in its turn plays a role in national politics as well as in reconstruction processes during foreign missions. Diplomacy has always been linked to culture and cultural diplomacy as such has existed since ancient times.[45] The Pharaonic Egyptians, for example, already practiced diplomacy with the inclusion of cultural ceremonies in which objects and

---

43 Such ministries can have different names, e.g., Foreign Affairs, State Department, etc. This differs by country.

44 Wilkie 2008.

45 See also Asgard 2010.

artists often served as gifts. Throughout time, explorers, musicians, and travelers like Marco Polo played a role as informal cultural ambassadors. Cultural diplomacy is defined as "the exchange of ideas, information, art, and other aspects of culture among nations and their peoples in order to foster mutual understanding."[46] Today's military operations abroad can involve diplomatic experts from either state departments or embassies that cooperate with the military and cultural experts. Important contacts with opposing governments or foreign dissidents often start with attempts to connect with intellectuals, artists, and foreign cultural institutions in times of conflict. De facto, any cultural diplomacy policy will not be taken seriously if the implementing country has a reputation to destroy cultural property during military operations or has a reputation for not implementing the directives of the Hague Convention of 1954. Unfortunately, cultural diplomacy as such is declining, since it suffers to a certain extent from the same lack of funding as CPP. Nonetheless, as former cultural diplomat Richard Arndt says "The loss could be repaired. A decent Cultural Diplomacy [of which CPP takes part] costs amazingly little, a shadow of the cost of one wing of fighter aircraft."[47] As with CPP, there are also incentives for defense, whereby troops could be supported by cultural diplomats during missions, including peacekeeping operations. The exact role of cultural diplomacy in CPP or vice versa has not yet been examined, but further research should be undertaken soon. CPP and cultural diplomacy encourage other peoples to give the implementing country the benefit of the doubt on specific policy issues or requests for collaboration, since there is a presumption of shared interests.[48]

Governmental institutions are naturally affiliated with politics. Of all parties involved in CPP, the government (or in reality politics) is potentially decisive when it comes to the implementation of CPP. When the government allocates funding, orders the military to implement CPP in their organization, and provides for coordination and cooperation with civil entities preferably also on the international level, more energy and intellectual input can be spent on the contents of CPP instead of on how to receive permission and funding for implementation. Of course, governmental institutions comprise governments. The governments that are party to the Hague

---

[46] Source: Milton C. Cummings, Jr. *Cultural Diplomacy and the United States Government: A Survey*, Washington, D.C: Center for Arts and Culture, 2003. p. 1.

[47] Arndt 2005 p. xxi.

[48] Source: *Cultural Diplomacy The Linchpin of Public Diplomacy*. Report of the Advisory Committee on Cultural Diplomacy. U.S. Department of State. September 2005. ⟨http://www.state.gov/documents/organization/54374.pdf⟩ [20 July 2011].

Convention of 1954 and other relevant legislation are particularly important for the purpose of this study. To garner an overview of their current behaviors and practices regarding CPP implementation by military organizations, a section at the end of Chapter 4 will present some concrete examples.

Non-Governmental Organizations (NGOs)

The average non-governmental organization is legally constituted and works independently from any government. One can distinguish international and community or national NGOs.

Some NGOs have a consultative status with UN's Economic and Social Council (ECOSOC), while others are affiliated to another UN organization or institutions like the World Bank. Currently, UNESCO has official relations with 348 international NGOs and 20 foundations and similar institutions, which are working in the fields of competence of the organization.[49] Of course, one can also find numerous small NGOs with a formal or even informal legal status. Three categories can be distinguished for the purpose of this study. First, NGOs that, according to their statutes, deal with cultural property such as the World Monuments Fund, Getty Foundation, WATCH, and SAFE.[50] Second, there are NGOs not involved with cultural heritage related matters, such as Doctors without Borders, Oxfam, and Greenpeace. There is good reason to make this distinction, because there is a lack of knowledge within NGO circles about cultural heritage issues since most Non-Governmental Organizations concentrate predominantly on humanitarian aid. The NGO market is also highly competitive and therefore organizations tend to protect their market shares while sometimes not relying on accurate information. This can lead to the situation where organizations without cultural heritage expertise do not want to miss chances concerning a CPP topic often driven by the argument that they do not consider to be a military issue. The motto is everything that is not military core business has to be done by NGOs. This slogan, when combined with the dictum "as civilian as possible, as military as necessary" that some NATO partners and CIMIC departments use is a recipe for trouble and miscommunication. Third, there are NGOs that deal with cultural issues but these

49 ⟨http://portal.unesco.org/en/ev.php-URL_ID=32906&URL_DO=DO_TOPIC&URL_SECTION=201.html⟩ [17 July 2011].

50 WATCH: World Association for the Protection of Tangible and Intangible Cultural Heritage in times of armed conflicts. SAFE: Saving Antiquities for Everyone. ⟨http://safecorner.savingantiquities.org/⟩ [17 July 2011].

activities concern intangible art forms like dance and music or the modern visual arts such as painting and sculpture. These NGOs regularly aim at organizing exhibitions and supporting artists. Good reason for the distinction made between cultural (in the sense of CPP) and non-cultural NGOs is the fact that, in the Netherlands, at least some NGOs confuse cultural activities undertaken by military experts with humanitarian aid. They tend to react strongly against utilizing military experts for everything not directly related to what is their perception of the military core-business. From the NGO perspective, there often seems to be little room for cooperation with organizations not part of the NGO culture, including the military. Motives seem ethically and politically inspired, although an important reason could also be that NGOs are judged and subsequently subsidized and funded according to their market positions. Therefore, they will fiercely defend these positions. Additionally, there is an international debate, often fed by NGOs and civil policy makers, about the argument that Non-Governmental Organizations can work cheaper than the military. It is difficult to determine what costs less, because one has to study comparable projects, and gain access to all financial data including matters like overhead, depreciation, etc. Contributing to the situation is that not many NGOs deal with cultural property protection (nor is information on their field experiences easily accessible). Consequently, it is hard to compare the value and sustainability of projects either undertaken by military or civil parties. The discussion is even more complicated because some claim that funds that could be used for Military CPP were originally meant to be spent on NGO activities.

Nevertheless, there are cases of civil organizations undertaking cultural emergency rescue missions. Examples are the recent ANCBS/IMCuRWG missions to Egypt and Libya that were solely funded by ANCBS and IMCuRWG, Blue Shield (ANCBS)-initiated salvage projects that were undertaken after severe flooding in Poland, in Haiti that suffered from a severe earthquake and quite recently in Cologne, Germany, in support of rescue work regarding the collection of the collapsed City Archives. These type of NGO activities are usually (co-)funded by governmental institutions. Some projects in Iraq, however, were also partly funded by NGOs like the Dutch-based Prince Claus Fund and Italian organizations.[51] Only Italian NGOs were actually on the ground with cultural property projects in Iraq during violent phases of the conflict.[52] In 1980 Austria founded the Österreichische

[51] The fund provided emergency aid for the Central Library of the University of Baghdad; unfortunately, Baghdad's national library that suffered more damage was not helped.

[52] For example, Un Ponte Per Baghdad. This is a volunteer based association established

Gesellschaft für Kulturgüterschutz (ÖGKGS). The aim of this organization is to disseminate the principles and directives for CPP and while doing so to increase the awareness of the relevance of CPP among a wide audience. Instruments used are manifestations such as seminars, exhibitions, publications, and helping individual initiatives.

There is related debate as to whether military logistics and CPP experts could be deployed for natural disasters. This is, of course, the domain of NGOs. However, it would be useful to exchange lessons learned from the military context with civil organizations and vice versa so they can be of benefit for cultural emergencies in times of manmade and natural disasters.[53] Military engagement in natural disasters can be very useful when conditions create a demand for special types of transportation and logistics. A recent example in which (U.S.) military helped in the aftermath of a natural disaster is the earthquake in Haiti. Of course, military cooperation should always be by special request, and there might be juridical implications and other aspects that have to be considered. There are organizations that left and are still leaving their CPP footprints in war-stricken countries such as Iraq. Worth mentioning is an initiative created in 2004 when the Getty Conservation Institute (CGI) and the World Monuments Fund (WMF) joined forces to help Iraq rebuild its capacity to manage monuments and sites. Another organization that is running a program in Erbil is International Relief and Development (IRD). They are establishing a Conservation and Historic Preservation Institute in Erbil focusing on technical and professional training while aiming at improving the professional environment in the Iraq National Museum in Baghdad.[54] Then there is Saving Antiquities for Everyone (SAFE), a U.S. based non-profit organization dedicated to preserving cultural heritage worldwide. SAFE concentrates on raising public awareness about damages that result from looting, smuggling, and trading illicit antiquities. They focus on media campaigns in partnership with academia and the communications, legal, and law enforcement communities.[55] Finally there is ARCA the Italian based association for research into crimes against art. ARCA studies issues in art crime, and art protection and

---

in 1991 working in humanitarian aid mainly in Iraq, and recently in Jordan, Lebanon, Turkish Kurdistan, and the Balkans. In September 2004, a number of their workers, including Italians Simona Pari and Simona Torretta, were kidnapped. UPP was for instance active in trying to save and help Iraqi libraries.

53 See also Euromed Heritage Cultural Heritage Management in times of Conflict, recommendations of the Workgroups, p. 8. Amman April 2005.

54 ⟨http://www.ird.org/index.php⟩ [17 July 2011].

55 ⟨http://www.savingantiquities.org/index.php⟩ [17 July 2011].

recovery while maintaining a network including international police, governments, museums, places of worship, and other public institutions.

International Organizations (IOs)

A variety of international organizations are active in the field of cultural heritage. The most prominent one is the United Nations Educational, Scientific, and Cultural Organization (UNESCO) based in Paris. Other examples are the International Centre for the Study of the Conservation and Restoration of Cultural Heritage (ICCROM), the International Council of Museums (ICOM) that has a disaster relief task force, the International Council on Archives (ICA), the International Federation of Library Associations and Institutions (IFLA), the International Council on Monuments and Sites (ICOMOS), the International Committee of the Red Cross (ICRC), and the International Committee of the Blue Shield (ICBS). In this book, only the cultural heritage protection and safe guarding activities of UNESCO are addressed. The organization has other activities such as education matters, but these UNESCO activities are not at stake here.

To provide an idea of processes and mechanisms that influence the way international organizations operate, it is useful to take a closer look at the cultural heritage activities of UNESCO. In the years 1959–1960, UNESCO made a good impression by mobilizing the international community for an international rescue plan concerning the safeguarding of Nubia's (Egypt) cultural treasures. The cultural heritage of Nubia was threatened with total destruction because of the construction of the Aswan High Dam in the Nile River. The story is well known: many monuments were rescued, and some rebuilt on higher grounds in an international effort. The most famous example was the Abu Simbel Temples. Nevertheless, today the organization is perceived as being not very proactive, especially in times of conflict. For the duration of my missions in Iraq during the last conflict, I never met or heard about any UNESCO representative being in the country. When the looting started in Egypt in February 2011, UNESCO again did not act timely by sending an assessment mission. A direct request was made to the Assistant-Director General for Culture and Director of the World Heritage Centre of UNESCO and no reaction was given nor any action undertaken.[56]

[56] A request was made by IMCuRWG and the ANCBS in a message of which receipt was confirmed dated 4 February 2011. After this appeal without result IMCuRWG and ANCBS set out a mission themselves that took place in Egypt from February 12–16 2011.

When the name UNESCO is mentioned in conversations and meetings about CPP, there are often questions raised about the organization's reputation for not meeting demands and challenges. Issues include, for instance, that UNESCO has no permanent liaison with the military[57] and is often absent in conflict areas, and in general, too passive when cultural property is looted or damaged (e.g., Iraq, Egypt). There are a number of possible reasons for this alleged behavior. We know that cultural property is by nature disputed, thus potentially able to cause political and identity-related power struggles. The same phenomenon, but on a micro level, makes entities that have to do with safeguarding cultural property disagree and compete with each other. Given these mechanisms, it can be dangerous for the career orientated in UNESCO's organization to handle CPP in a proactive manner. Besides, UNESCO is as an organization framed in a highly bureaucratic structure that is controlled by diplomats and officials. This type of leadership tends towards risk avoidance, which in its turn leads to a non-proactive attitude. Also, from a more practical or technical perspective the organization has limitations. For instance, UNESCO is unable to take action in cases of illicit traffic of looted goods. UNESCO has no mandate to either act in case a crime is detected or to take custody of cultural materials. "Its mandate is assisting its Member States in the conservation of cultural heritage. It is without sufficient specialists, (e.g., security, collections, and conservation experts), to undertake detection or custody function."[58] Finally, UNESCO is not a rich organization, as it depends on outside funding by member states, which fosters a cautious attitude. On the positive side, it should be said that UNESCO provided for the Hague Convention of 1954 and other treaties like the 1970 Convention on the Means of Prohibiting and Preventing the Illicit Import, Export and Transfer of Ownership of Cultural Property, and the UNIDROIT Convention on Stolen or Illegally Exported Cultural Objects (Rome, 1995) that was, as a study, requested by UNESCO from UNIDROIT in 1986. But there is little in their power to implement or enforce implementation of these legal instruments. To underpin the suppositions presented here, two examples that concern, respectively, UNESCO and ICOMOS will be addressed.

1. UNESCO: the Commissioner General for the Protection of Cultural Property and the Committee for the Protection of Cultural Property in the Event of Armed Conflict.

---

[57] Recently a representative of the (Para-military) Carabinieri started to advice UNESCO on a temporarily basis.

[58] Prott 2006.

The 1999 Second Protocol to the 1954 Hague Convention and the Constitution of UNESCO give possibilities for practical cultural heritage safeguarding actions. The constitution provides UNESCO's Director General with a general mandate for the protection of cultural heritage.[59] The control system under the convention is composed of three elements: representatives of parties to the conflict, commissioners general for cultural property, and protecting powers. A protecting power is a neutral or other state not a party to the conflict which has been designated by a party to the conflict and accepted by the adverse party.[60] Reference is made to the possibility of nominating one or more commissioners general for cultural property. This option, interlinked with the system of the protecting powers, has only worked once following the Middle East conflict. When the mandates of the two commissioners general accredited in 1967, one to Israel and the other to Egypt, Jordan, Lebanon, and the Syrian Arab Republic, were terminated in 1977, no new commissioner general for the Arab governments concerned was appointed. Because of this, an end was in fact put to further implementation of this institution. Nonetheless, the system is still intact for Parties to the 1954 Hague Convention, but is no longer used. Consequently, the international list of experts mentioned in Chapter I, Article 1 from the Regulations for the Execution of the Convention from which commissioner generals could be appointed has most probably not been updated since 1977. This implies that UNESCO has no official oversight on (current) international cultural property experts.

A fund for the protection of cultural property in the event of armed conflict is established for parties to the Second Protocol of the 1954 Hague Convention. This fund aims to provide financial or other assistance in support of preparatory or other measures to be taken in peacetime. It is managed by the newly founded Committee for the Protection of Cultural Property in the Event of Armed Conflict, in which member countries, not individuals, are represented as well as the UNESCO Secretariat. The resources of the fund shall consist, inter alia, of voluntary contributions made by state parties to the Second Protocol. According to a source within the Commit-

---

59 Article I(2)(c) of the UNESCO Constitution stating that the organization will maintain, increase and diffuse knowledge "by assuring the conservation and protection of the world's inheritance of books, works of art and monuments of history and science, and recommending to the nations concerned the necessary international conventions ..." is illustrative in this respect. *United Nations Educational, Scientific and Cultural Organization, Basic Texts*, 2006 edition, (Paris: UNESCO, 2006) 6.

60 Source: Protocol Additional to the Geneva Conventions of 12 August 1949, and relating to the Protection of Victims of International Armed Conflicts (Protocol I). Art. 2 (c).

tee, the situation in February 2010 was as follows: the fund has 100,000 Euro from a voluntary contribution from the Netherlands.[61] Currently there are no projects undertaken. An appeal has been made to State Parties to nominate cultural property for enhanced protection. Nothing has happened so far. Contributing to this is the fact that the section of the UNESCO Secretariat dealing with the Hague 1954 is understaffed and has not enough financial resources to manage matters in a proactive manner.[62]

2. The ICOMOS Venice Charter from 1964 is also known as the International Charter for the Conservation and Restoration of Monuments and Sites. It is a document that defines the common responsibility of nations to safeguard cultural heritage and cultural landscapes.

Its preamble states that the historic monuments of generations of people remain to the present day as living witnesses of their age-old traditions. In this perspective, people regard ancient monuments as a common heritage. The common responsibility to safeguard cultural property for future generations is recognized and it is regarded as a duty to maintain their authenticity. The latter is, of course, still the subject of an international debate among scholars that includes questions of uniqueness and identity. Nevertheless, it is essential that principles guiding preservation and restoration of ancient buildings should be agreed upon and established on an international basis, with each country being responsible for applying the plan within the framework of its own culture and traditions. Therefore, Article 1 of the charter states "the concept of an historic monument embraces not only the single architectural work but also the urban or rural setting in which is found. This can be the evidence of a particular civilization, a significant development or an historic event." It is specified that this does not only apply to great works of art but also to more modest works of the past that have acquired cultural significance over time.

All of this is not only in complete accordance with the new recognition of cultural heritage as part of the *Beni Culturali* that was explained in the introduction of this book, but it also makes more scenarios and objects vulnerable for military activities. On the other hand, any military effort to avoid destruction or stop pillaging of heritage is in fact a form of preventive conservation. Not only can this feed the scholarly debate by demonstrating a

---

[61] The vice-chairman (at that time) acting on behalf of the Netherlands.

[62] During the meeting of the Parties on 24 November 2009. The situation in December 2010 was that only the Netherlands and Finland (the chair of the committee was Finish now Dutch) paid their contributions.

new perspective for military involvement, but it also fits the principles of the so-called holistic approach often applied in (integrated) conservation strategies. In its turn, this integral concept also plays a role in the debate on development and peacekeeping missions and their military components. The name used in that context is the comprehensive approach. The idea behind this is the creation of strategic partnerships, in the case of cultural property protection between military and civil parties. Consequently, the system as a whole determines for a major part how its components behave. This can create new forms of synergy and help solve the problem of the lack of cooperation and communication on cultural property protection between potential strategic partners such as NATO, EU, and UNESCO. Both examples show that, in spite of positive elements such as the Venice Charter, the UNESCO department dealing with the 1954 Hague Convention restrains proper handling of cultural disasters in the event of armed conflict due to the system and the bureaucratic approach combined with, for instance, understaffing.[63] Furthermore, the lack of voluntary contributions for the UNESCO Committee for the Protection of Cultural Property causes available financial means to be predominantly used for the overhead costs of this committee and not for practical activities. A last development making matters even worse started 31st October 2011. The United States will not pay $ 60 million to UNESCO after it voted to accept the Palestinian mission as a full member, triggering a U.S. requirement to cut off funds. The United States pays $ 80 million a year to UNESCO, which is 22 percent of the organization's overall budget. If this situation is not solved and taken into account the lack of the $ 60 million already not paid UNESCO will become increasingly less active due to financial problems.

Work(ing) and Advisory Groups

Sometimes subjects are difficult to get on the agendas of (potential) stakeholders, as is surely the case with CPP especially when it involves the military. A solution not suitable for the fainthearted and bureaucratically orientated is the creation of initial, not formal-institutionalized, entities like working groups or advisory groups.[64] In order to start a more proactive approach, a number of these informal networks and groups were created to promote military cooperation with civil CPP stakeholders. Some of these

[63] According to a undisclosed source, only one staff member and a part-time secretary.

[64] A term also used is workgroups.

Figure 6. Logo CCHAG. http://www.cchag.org/.

began activities without formal consent of military and political institutions.[65] Their value for starting a dialogue between dissimilar parties and stimulating international cooperation as well as exchange and dissemination of information is huge. Some have created or are in the process of creating web sites that give access to new information. It is fair to say that they fill a gap that many NGOs and international organizations have left open.

A new initiative in which military and civil experts join forces in order to share expertise and resources is the U.S. Central Command or CENTCOM Historical/Cultural Advisory Group (CHCAG). Quite recently, in August 2010, the group's name changed to the Combatant Command Historical/Cultural Action Group (CCHAG) to reflect its applicability to all six U.S. Combatant Commands, see www.cchag.org.

Founded in the beginning of 2008, its mission is to enhance military capacity by promoting historical/cultural property protection during U.S. Combatant Commands a full spectrum operations.[66] Objectives are to develop and implement education and training materials for all combatant commands and its personnel in the field for history, cultural property protection, and preservation. Further aims include the development of policies for protection and preservation, providing CPP planning information, maps, and tools, coordinating with stakeholders to share information and protect historical and cultural heritage, and supporting coalition partners through information exchange, seminars, and training exercises.

---

[65] One potential military member of the International Military Cultural Resources Working Group (IMCuRWG) was even threatened with losing his job.

[66] CENTCOM's Area of Responsibility is 27 nations that stretch from the Horn of Africa through the Arabian Gulf region, into Central Asia.

Finally, a network of subject matter experts and reach-back capabilities is under development; originally the Command of CENTCOM would be advised on relevant obligations under federal laws, international laws, treaties and agreements as well as Department of Defense and service regulations. The founders of CCHAG hope that the initiative serves as a model to the other American Combatant Commands.[67] Unfortunately, due to a change of staff and policy at CENTCOM the yearly workgroup meeting of 2011 had to focus on strengthening DoD-wide cultural property protection training and awareness and the establishment of a DoD-embedded CPP office. As a result, less attention was paid to the indispensable subject of international cooperation that is even more relevant given the current international developments in the Middle East. For now, the officials within CENTCOM that serve as contacts for the CCHAG seem less interested; this development demonstrates that CPP activities though legally mandatory are still too much personality-driven. The group has one international member, the chair of the international working group, to be addressed in the next section below.[68]

The International Military Cultural Resources Working Group (IMCu RWG) that was founded in Phoenix, Arizona, in August 2009 during the Sustaining Military Readiness Conference, involves cultural heritage professionals working in the military context in order to enhance military capacity to implement protection across the full range of operations. At the same time, the aim is to provide a forum for international cooperation and networking, raising awareness, identifying areas of common interest, sharing best practices and lessons learned, and initiating research on CPP and military involvement. Membership is restricted to cultural heritage experts working within the military context. Recognizing that the effectiveness of this group will be its ability to work in a liaison capacity, the group may invite advisors, for example from NGOs and universities.

IMCuRWG works within the context of the 1954 Hague Convention addressing archaeological sites, historic buildings, museums, libraries, galleries, and archives. In the first instance, its focus was on immovable cultural heritage: archaeological sites, cultural and memorial landscapes, historic buildings, and sacred sites, but currently the whole spectrum of cultural property is addressed. Envisaged outcomes of this initiative are: first, a web-

---

[67] CENTCOM is just one of the (Unified) Combatant Commands U.S. there are also (U.S.) EUCOM for Europe, (U.S.) AFRICOM for Africa, PACOM for the Pacific, SOUTHCOM for South America and NORTHCOM for North America.

[68] Currently the chair of IMCuRWG is the author of this study.

site that will explain the role of the working group and provide a vehicle for hosting training materials and other information; second, the development and testing of international on-site training modules and programs for senior leadership; and, third, the collection and sharing of data for Geographic Information System (GIS) databases of immovable cultural heritage for the purpose of supporting military environmental planning.[69] To achieve this, sub-committees on matters like GIS, illicit traffic, training, operational planning, and environmental aspects will be created. Finally, the group will support efforts to establish international military and civilian "rapid reaction teams" for the protection of cultural property during and immediately following armed conflict. In addition, it will be determined if and to what extent such teams can be deployed for natural disasters. At this time, initial members and advisors come from Austria, UK, the Netherlands, the United States, and Libya. A first emergency assessment mission to Egypt took place in February, 2011, followed by missions to Libya also in 2011. All mission were carried out in cooperation with the Association of the National Committees of the Blue Shield (ANCBS). A major achievement in cooperation with the Austrian MoD and NATO's ACT was a CPP pilot course held in Vienna in November–December 2011.

A recently created group is Cultural Heritage by AIA-Military Panel (CHAMP). AIA is the Archaeological Institute of America. Some of the aims of CHAMP are: to build collaborative groups between military personnel and professional archaeologists, to promote understanding of military needs, cultural site preservation, and sensitivities of local populations, and to offer chances for AIA professionals and members to participate in Department of Defense initiatives to enhance global heritage stewardship. CHAMP's webpage went online in January 2011.[70]

Commerce, Crime, Law and Order, and Religion

All parties discussed in this section are in different ways, and to certain extents, connected to each other. Another common denominator is that they attach or add different values to cultural objects. Since this study is devoted to balancing different interests in favor of CPP, it will come as no

---

69 Military defense uses GIS for intelligence, terrain analysis, mission planning, and facilities management. Geographic analysis is critical in military operations, tactical or logistical planning, and infrastructure management. Source: ⟨www.gis.com/content/government⟩ [17 July 2011].

70 See: ⟨http://aiamilitarypanel.org⟩ [25 July 2011].

surprise that this also is a challenge when economic interests are involved. Naturally, there are tensions between the commercial market values of cultural property and the values cultural objects have for identity, science, and art. Various mechanisms, often serving dissimilar interests, apply here; these include power mechanisms in case of conflict where the strongest party wins, the urge for profit in the world's trade and business arena, or the aim for social progress and the desire to preserve and protect historical properties. All these mechanisms have to be brought in line with each other and synchronized to an extent that also makes effective implementation of CPP feasible in times of conflict. Within the context of this study, the contradiction of military interests versus scientific and commercial value is a key issue. This brings us back to the basic dilemma between military necessity that is used as a reason to solve (or end) a conflict as soon as possible and civil interests that look ahead and consider post-conflict conditions. The commercial stakeholders in CPP play a vital role in conflict and peacetime; they are responsible for many of the movements and dynamics that define CPP in both contexts including the relation with crime. The role of collectors, and consequently dealers, is especially criticized since it is believed that they feed the demand for cultural objects of which there is only a finite supply.[71] This results in attempts to increase the worldwide supply through theft and looting while especially seizing opportunities in conflict areas. Sometimes matters are exacerbated by thieves who intentionally break up objects in pieces to be sold separately as so-called orphans.[72] The conclusion seems justified that collectors, art dealers, antique dealers, and auction houses are in the chain of buying and selling cultural objects whereas travel agents, tour guides, and antiquities services are exploiting cultural sites and have an interest in keeping them in good condition. Museums, to a certain extent, are commercial parties too, since many sell tickets for admission or make profits via museum shops, mail orders, and by managing author rights on certain cultural objects.

Bourdieu refers to the reservoir of cultural assets as cultural capital, to be compared to cultural resources as in natural resources.[73] However, the definition or concept of Bourdieu aims at cultural capital in what he calls its "transformed form or scholastic capital" and insofar as he acknowledges a historical opposition between cultural and economical capital in which the latter dominates the first, his concept lends itself for a wider interpreta-

---

[71] O'Keefe, Patrick J. 1997.

[72] See for instance Watson, Peter. The Medici Conspiracy, New York 2006.

[73] Bourdieu and Passeron 1990.

tion.[74] To put it simply, cultural capital shares many of the properties characteristic of economic capital in that it can be invested and exploited and thus generate added value that can, for a certain timeframe and situation, be expressed in monetary figures. Some stakeholders from the commercial segment see this as an extra reason to protect and safeguard heritage. Protection creates more commercial stakeholders like guards, security companies, and manufacturers of surveillance equipment. Interrelated to the interests of collectors and dealers are stakeholders such as auction houses, lawyers, insurance companies and affiliated organizations such as the Art Loss Register.[75] Antique dealers can play dubious roles when it comes to matters of provenance (illicit traffic) and authenticity. It is even said that some try to restrain the implementation of international legislation (e.g., the UNIDROIT Convention on Stolen or Illegally Exported Cultural Objects [Rome, 1995]) using lobbyists.[76] Recent examples of demand-driven theft and traffic are the looted and stolen objects from Afghanistan, often commissioned by the Taliban, smuggled out through the Kandahar military airport and ending up in expensive antique shops in Brussels, Belgium. In this example, parties that are addressed in this publication such as the military, opposing forces, commerce, and law are all involved.[77]

The tourism industry as a CPP stakeholder is potentially capable of creating strong economic incentives. Certainly after a period of conflict or turmoil, earnings, often hard currencies, generated through tourism (e.g., souvenir factories, tour guides, hotels, etc.) can make a difference in restoring economy and thus society. In this context, there are direct interests for restoration architects, restorers, security personnel, contractors and certainly the military that see restoration of a safe society as the end state of their mission. By the same token, it is true that tourism decreases or even stops when a country is suffering from conflict, turmoil, or natural disaster (e.g., Egypt). Criminal parties can be found within the whole spectrum of CPP stakeholders. However, in the context of this study the most interesting are looters, insurgents, and, in some circumstances, even dealers and curators (when they sell or buy objects without provenance) and scholars that authenticate objects that lack provenance. If crime is at stake, there are also parties that are involved in imposing sanctions and the returning of stolen

[74] Bourdieu and Passeron 1990. pp. vii, xi, xvi, 93, 157. Swartz 1997. p. 79.
[75] ⟨http://www.artloss.com/⟩ [17 July 2011].
[76] See ⟨http://www.unidroit.org/english/conventions/1995culturalproperty/main.htm⟩ [17 July 2011].
[77] See ⟨http://www.deredactie.be/cm/vrtnieuws.english/news/1.592370⟩ [22 July 2011].

objects like the police, customs, lawyers, prosecutors, insurance companies, and even the military. Parties in the juridical sphere comprise lawyers, police, and forensic accountants. This study deals with parties involved in conflict situations, so, for the sake of argument, opposing forces in the military sense and insurgents will be included among them. As described earlier, such opposing forces can intentionally damage cultural objects as part of actions against their opponents, and they can also exploit cultural property to gain revenues by selling products of illegal excavations or lootings to obtain financial resources to fund their operations. Looters and smugglers fit into this picture as intermediaries that perform certain activities commissioned by the opposing forces or by civil criminal players. It goes without saying that law and order parties such as customs and police and including organizations as EUROPOL and INTERPOL as well as national and international courts of justice, play a decisive role. The latter will make use of independent or institutionalized specialists for advice and to serve as expert witnesses at trials. Legal and other art crime experts can be organized as well. Some random examples are the Lawyers' Committee for Cultural Heritage Preservation, a non-profit association based in Washington DC, and the earlier mentioned Association for Research into Crimes against Art (ARCA). ARCA is an international interdisciplinary research group on contemporary issues in art crime and cultural property protection based in Amelia, Italy.

The last large stakeholder to be discussed here is religion, a party that traditionally used to commission the production of cultural objects and that still owns many cultural properties. To be more precise, and in concurrence with defining the military, when speaking about religion, this refers to church leaders, Islamic religious leaders, religious or civil personnel in charge of managing churches, mosques, temples and other religious institutions. Their relationship or lack thereof with the military depends on the degree of religiousness of a country. In Austria, for example, there are strong connections between armed forces and the Catholic church while religion has a strong connection with art and thus to an extent to cultural objects. This is demonstrated by the Austrian expression *Kunst als Ausdruck des Glaubens*, or "art as an expression of faith." In most North European countries like the Netherlands, official connections between the church and the armed forces are almost absent. Having mentioned this, it has to be taken into account that in this publication, religious property will be considered part of cultural heritage. However, there is a debate among scholars as to whether objects of a religious nature should not be regarded as a separate category based on the argument that religion is not culture but something intermingled with culture.[78] Regardless of this discussion, there are valid arguments to involve religious property within this research. One is the fact that it is mentioned as such in the Hague Convention of 1954, for instance in Article 53 of Protocol I, (applicable to international armed conflict) which prohibits use in support of the military effort of all places of worship which constitute the cultural or spiritual heritage of a population. Seen from the art-historical perspective, it is obvious that, certainly in history, the larger parts of cultural property are religious objects and monuments. Finally, religious objects play an important role in many contemporary conflicts such as in the Middle East (e.g., the Al Aqsa Mosque in Jerusalem) and Asia (e.g., the Preah Vihear temples in Cambodia and Thailand). It would be rather unwise to separate them from other categories while raising awareness and facilitating training and education about CPP amongst the military. There is, however, a problem with some religious cultural property. The reason is that certain objects have significance for more than one religion. At the same time, those beliefs can be in conflict with each other. For instance, Iraqi cultural property in Babylon and Ur is biblical heritage for Christians while simultaneously the national heritage of (Islamic) Iraqis. Another clear example is the Temple Mount in Jerusalem that is a constant source of political unrest and violence.[79] Religious connotations are not always making things worse for CPP. A remarkable but positive development involving religion and CPP is an attempt to utilize fatwas as a means to prevent looting of cultural property.[80] This case is described in my chapter *Can White Men Sing the Blues?* in the volume *Archaeology, Cultural Property and the Military*.[81] The case shows

---

78 See for instance: Shireen Hilmi, Culture and Religion: A Mixed Race Relationship. 6 December 2011. ⟨http://www.the-platform.org.uk/2011/12/06/culture-and-religion-a-mixed-race-relationship/⟩ [27 February 2012]. Amin Abdullah, Analytical Perspective In The Study Of Religious Diversity: Searching For A New Model Of Philosophy Of The Study Of Religions. 6 May 2010. ⟨http://aminabd.wordpress.com/2010/05/06/analytical-perspective-in-the-study-of-religious-diversity-searching-for-a-new-model-of-philosophy-of-the-study-of-religions/⟩ [27 February 2012].

79 The Waqf, the religious Muslim endowment that rules the Temple Mount, decided to banish archaeological supervision after the "Tunnel Riots" in September 1996, during the government of Benjamin Netanyahu. These riots were about the opening of a tunnel along the Temple Complex's Western Wall, to the Muslim Quarter. During the fierce fight, around 70 Palestinians and 17 Israeli soldiers were killed.

80 A fatwa is issued by a recognized religious authority in Islam. Since there is no hierarchical priesthood or anything similar in Islam, a fatwa is not necessarily "binding" on the faithful. Source: ⟨http://islam.about.com/sitesearch.htm?q=Fatwa&SUName=islam⟩ [17 July 2011].

81 Kila 2010b. pp. 41–59.

how a fatwa normally associated with negative matters such as spells (e.g., the Salman Rushdie Fatwa), can be used as a tool to save cultural property.[82]

Science

The scientific arena consists of various players that can have or do already have interests in CPP. These include think tanks and university-based research institutes as well as faculties that provide teaching curricula. They can be either civilian institutes or military academies. A crucial element needed for implementing, developing, and sustaining CPP expertise is empirical scientific research, although reflections and explorations are also essential to integrate CPP's military aspects into the scientific discourse. As established, there is in the existing civil academic cultural heritage debate enough reason for military scientific institutions and civil academia to examine military aspects in CPP to be able to participate in and compare to the civil discourse. However, experience shows that for military-based scientists this will probably only happen if the subject is first added to the curricula of military schools, academies and universities. Because of its multi-disciplinary character, choices have to be considered and made for approaching the subject. Research can be initiated from cultural heritage related disciplines like archaeology and art history, or from a wider construct of social sciences. The latter will make it easier to introduce CPP as a topic for further research at military educational institutions. In the Netherlands some attempts were made although they proved not to be sustainable.

Lectures were for instance given by the author of this book at the so-called *Instituut Defensie Leergangen*, but they were discontinued due to financial reasons and opposition from Dutch MoD cultural awareness experts. In addition, the NATO School in Oberammergau, Germany started to incorporate lectures in their environmental course but stopped for financial reasons.[83]

Currently there are plans and discussions within NATO's Allied Command Transformation (ACT) to pay attention to the subject from within their organization, thus creating an institutionalized opportunity to get the subject on NATO educational curricula, including *in situ* training on archaeological sites. The last result was the previously mentioned first course

[82] Source: Hugh Eakin, The Devastation of Iraq's Past. *The New York Review of Books*, Volume 55, Number 13. August 14, 2008.

[83] See the section on Opportunities for Effective Implementation of Military Cultural Property Protection.

on CPP co-hosted by NATO. The invitation stated that NATO Allied Command Transformation (ACT), the International Military Cultural Resources Working Group (IMCuRWG) and the Austrian National Defense Academy (NDA) conducted a Pilot Course on cultural property protection in order to train NATO and NATO partner personnel on cultural property protection in accordance with The Hague Convention on the Protection of Cultural Property in the Event of Armed Conflict (1954) and NATO Standardization agreement (STANAG) 7141 EP JOINT NATO DOCTRINE For Environmental Protection During NATO Military Led Activities from 29 November to 2 December 2011. This event was a big success and at the moment plans and proposals are prepared for more pilot courses in Vienna, Copenhagen and Turkey (Izmir). It is encouraging that NATO begins to see the relevance and value of CPP as a force multiplier and a primary strategic communication tool. Already NATO's press departments emphasized the success of the heritage no-strike list used during the Libyan campaign. On the so-called NATO TV Channel several short films can be found about Libyan Cultural Heritage and the no strike list see: ⟨http://www.natochannel.tv/⟩.

Most probably the fastest way into NATO institutions will be CPP's connection to environmental issues. Another positive development can be found in the Austrian MoD. A large contribution has been made through their *Institut für Human-und Sozialwissenschaften* that is part of the Landesverteidigungsakademie in Vienna. Currently they have one officer, a colonel, occupied with research on CPP and seminars and publications on the subject are initiated on a regular basis.

At present, apart from the Austrian example, no special research is undertaken by military academic institutions, but there is some outsourcing done by the military. The Center for Environmental Management of Military Lands (CEMML) is a research and service unit within the Warner College of Natural Resources at Colorado State University (CSU).[84] Professional services and technical support are provided to the U.S. DoD in conservation, environmental planning, and natural and cultural resources management. CEMML assists military planners, trainers, and land managers in the maintenance of diverse ecosystems to support sustained, realistic training, and testing exercises. Part of this assistance involves management planning and technical support for the full range of installation cultural resources to ensure that diverse non-renewable resources are adequately protected and managed in compliance with applicable federal and state legislation

[84] ⟨www.cemml.colostate.edu⟩ [17 July 2011].

without impeding the military training mission. CEMML also supports and produces web pages, military cultural property playing cards, and publications on cultural property protection.

The American Academy in Rome granted a fellowship to one of the Army archaeologists of the U.S. DoD to spend a year's research to develop a cultural heritage curriculum that can be used to educate military personnel. The research includes interviewing members of the Italian Carabinieri about setting up effective police forces for archaeological site protection and the use of management models from archaeological sites in Italy to develop military site management handbooks for fragile Middle Eastern and South Asian cultural properties.[85] Also other, university-based research institutions like the Illicit Antiquities Research Centre (IARC) at the University of Cambridge, UK, (the Centre is no longer in existence) and the Cultural Policy Center at the University of Chicago played a role in research and quite recent the All Souls College of the University of Oxford organized an expert seminar. In 2006, the Chicago center first organized a juridical seminar about the protection of cultural heritage during the war in Iraq, followed later by the previously mentioned conference of August 2006 that for the first time brought together scientists and the military. A number of archaeological faculties, juridical faculties, and cultural sciences faculties work on the subject, most of them restrained by lack of funding. In the Netherlands Leiden University's Archaeological Faculty gave some attention to the subject through a number of guest lectures and a seminar called "Legacy and Legislation" that took place in April 2010. The author of this publication gave several lectures and presentations.[86] The University of Amsterdam, supported by the SNS Reaal Fund, appointed the author of this book to carry out research on CPP at least for one year. Doctoral research on the subject, in one case from a juridical perspective, is taking place at the University of Antwerp (Belgium)[87] and the University College Dublin. Apart from their important role in research and the scientific discourse, academic institutions can (and some already) serve as reach-back capabilities for military experts in theater and can also participate in training and development of education materials.

Academic institutions are potentially vital for CPP research in general and for research concerning heritage, culture, siege, and conflict in partic-

---

85 Source: correspondence with Dr. Laurie Rush.

86 See for a list: ⟨http://home.medewerker.uva.nl/j.d.kila/⟩ [22 July 2011].

87 PhD Thesis by Sigrid van der Auwera titled: de bescherming van culturele goederen tijdens en na gewapende conflicten: naar een integrale preventiestrategie. 29 May 2012.

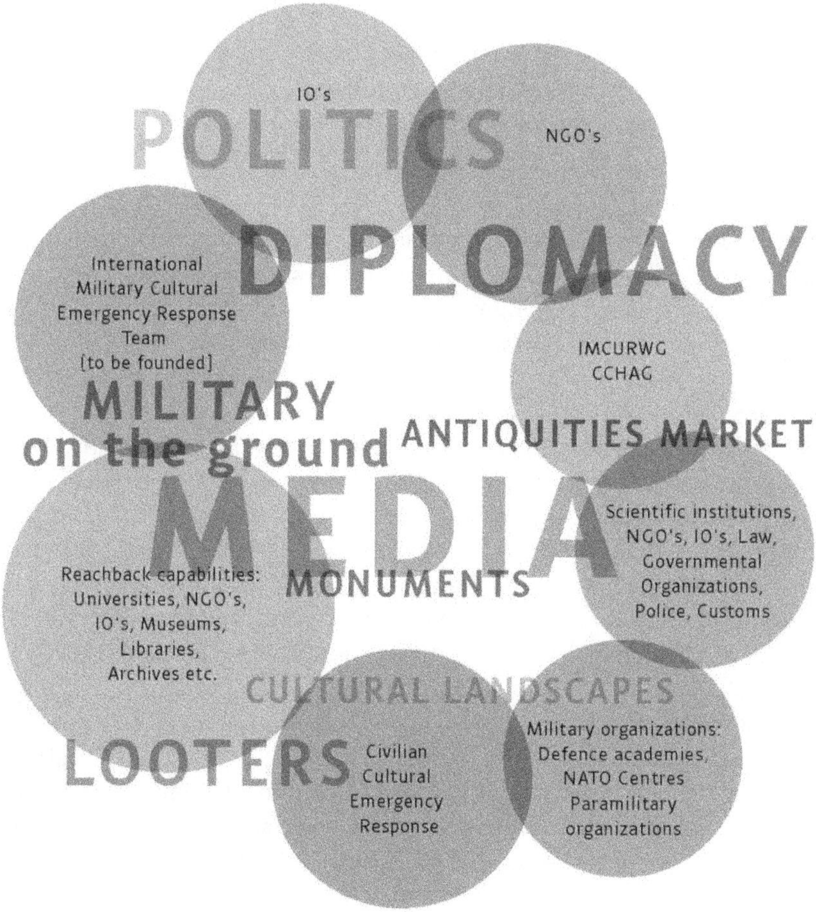

Figure 7. Network of CPP Stakeholders © Joris Kila.

ular. As we have seen, there are tensions between the players and stakeholders involved in CPP and the situation and awareness of CPP by external parties leaves much to be desired. Science houses all disciplines that are involved in CPP reflections and the sociology of CPP and the military. Since the subject is multidisciplinary, synergy can be created and, as a result of the first reflections presented in this book, more research from other disciplines can be triggered. There are, for instance, legal and environmental aspects that need research, but also the current situations in Asian countries such as China and the South American countries concerning military CPP are never assessed or researched. The subject of CPP and its relation to conflict and identity deserves a place within the field of heritage studies and should be on the curricula and research programs of universities, including military academic institutions.

Trends in Cultural Property Protection until 1954

History shows that CPP, or for that matter cultural property destruction, is not a new phenomenon. This section provides past examples and trends. It will become clear that many of the CPP parties and stakeholders presented in this book were also involved with the subject in the past. Nevertheless, as Bourdieu has stated, the past is produced in the present, which is clearly demonstrated by the varying status and perception of cultural heritage throughout time.[88] Still for every here-and-now history provides examples. An ancient reference of the wish to protect cultural properties comes from the Greek historian Polybius and dates from before 146 BC. Polybius acknowledges that there may be reason to appropriate gold and silver from other peoples because of the limited supply and as a means to weaken a group after a conflict, but every other form of wealth should be left where it is since this is more glorious or, in today's terms, more honorable. Polybius does not want his nation's glory to be based on abundance of (appropriated) paintings and statues, but on its sober customs and noble sentiments. He hopes that his thoughts will inspire future conquerors not to plunder the cities subjugated by them, and not to make the "misfortunes of other peoples the adornments of their own country."[89] In fact there is a relationship between this statement and Grotius, who was inspired by Polybius, Marcellus, and Cicero, and who made a plea in 1625 to spare things that when destroyed do not weaken the enemy. His contribution will be discussed in greater detail later.

As mentioned, the military used to capture loot during conflicts since this was the right of the victor and common practice in antiquity.[90] Apart from this, damage to cultural objects was sometimes part of erasing the identity of opposing parties or other cultures. Early examples are found in Pharaonic Egypt. Numerous bas-reliefs and statues still *in situ* bear witness as can be seen in cartouches in which names have been removed (e.g., the names from Queen Hatshepsut and King Akhenaten who both fell from grace).

---

[88] Bourdieu 2000.

[89] Merryman 2005, Polybius 1960.

[90] Source: H.D. Szemethy, Patterns of Art Theft, Looting and Plundering of Cultural Property, *Forum Archaeologiae* 55/VI/2010 ⟨http://farch.net⟩ [17 July 2011].

The Romans knew this phenomenon under the name *damnatio memoriae*, a posthumous dishonor.[91] Although it is not possible to compare historical motives one on one with today's political and military reasons, this is in fact early evidence of governmental involvement in a cultural property issue. The pattern of conquest established by the Romans allowed victors to appropriate cultural treasures from conquered peoples as trophies of war, to be put on display in triumphal marches and later installed in the Roman Forum.[92] More incidents took place throughout history since there were always conquering powers that aimed at exterminating a defeated enemy's identity through eradicating objects associated with their culture. Simple examples are the destruction of Carthage by the Romans in 146 BC that ended the Third Punic War (149–146 BC), and what has become known as the first Byzantine iconoclastic outbreak. Sometime between 726–730 AD, the Byzantine Emperor Leo III, who was against the worship of images, began this iconoclastic campaign ordering the removal of an image of Jesus prominently placed over the main ceremonial entrance to the Great Palace of Constantinople, also known as the Chalke gate. This is a good example of the involvement of religion as a stakeholder in cultural property issues. Another case from the Netherlands is the big iconoclastic outbreak of 1566, the so-called *Beeldenstorm* caused by a religious conflict between Calvinists and Catholics resulting in large scale damage to church interiors and monasteries. Because of this historical trend, from time to time initiatives were taken to promote protection of cultural objects. The Dutch scholar Grotius addressed the protection of heritage in 1625. In *On the Law of War and Peace* he states "reason compelled the sparing of those things which, if destroyed do not weaken the enemy nor bring gain to the one who destroys them, such as colonnades, statues and the like."[93] This is an early example of science as a CPP stakeholder. Even so, many years earlier in 1598 Alberico Gentili condemmed the wartime pillaging of art in his book *De Jure Belli Libri Tres*.[94] In 1697 the defeat of Mesoamerica was completed when the last Maya capital,

[91] "Condemnation of the memory" was an ancient Roman process dealing with individuals judged unfit to be members of a community. This posthumous dishonor was the worst thing that could be done to a former senator. In Tacitus Annals 3.17, Tacitus describes what was done to condemn the memory of Piso. Acts included scratching names and titles from inscriptions, defacing likenesses, confiscation, and destruction of the condemned man or woman's writing, annulling of wills, mutilation of corpses, and more. The senate, the emperor, or the army could start the condemnations. Source: ⟨http://ancienthistory.about.com/b/2010/01/14/thursdays-term-to-learn-damnatio-memoriae.htm⟩ [14 January 2010].

[92] Merryman 2005 p. 13.

[93] Grotius—Hugo de Groot 1573–1654, De iuri belle ac pacis Paris 1625.

[94] O'Keefe 2006, p. 6.

Tayasal, was burned and wiped out by the Spanish Conquistadors, thus ending the entire Mesoamerican culture. Another important advocate for the sparing of cultural property in the event of conflict was Emer de Vattel (1714–1767), who argued that cultural property was in the interests of humankind and human society, and added the importance of beauty.[95] It seems fair to say that Polybius, Gentili, Grotius, and de Vattel, though recognizing the primacy of military necessity, think in the same direction as General Eisenhower, who did not want military necessity to be confused with military convenience.

A phenomenon that turned out to be vital for the transformation of certain cultural objects into bearers of (national) identities was the so-called Grand Tour, which began in the late sixteenth century and lasted for approximately 300 years. The idea was to introduce Englishmen, Germans, Scandinavians, and Americans to the art and culture of France and Italy by visiting Paris, Venice, Florence, and especially Rome. Travel, at the time and throughout the period, was difficult and expensive, so the Grand Tourists were a privileged class consisting of mostly aristocrats. The Grand Tour shaped Northern Europeans ideas about the Greco-Roman world and helped foster neoclassical ideals. Ambitious tourists visited excavations at such sites as Pompeii, Herculaneum, and Tivoli, and purchased antiquities to decorate their homes.[96] Van der Laarse in *Bezeten van Vroeger* brings an interesting perspective to this, what he calls "multiplier experience."[97] He notes that the touristic transfer of people that, as described, started in the sixteenth century was accompanied by a displacement or relocation of cultural objects (art and souvenirs) and perceptions of landscape settings. These were appropriated by the travellers in such a successful way that in their respective native countries these objects and perspectives became part of national identities. Here one can see a parallel with the military throughout the ages whereby soldiers took objects from mission areas to strengthen their status (or their regiment's honor) and as a memento.

In France, decrees and rules on the protection of certain "condemned treasures and monuments" were made as early as in 1791.[98] This did not prevent Napoleon from taking antiquities from Egypt after concluding his Egypt expedition in 1801. The British confiscated antiquities collected by the

---

[95] Merryman 2005.
[96] Sorabella 2000.
[97] Van der Laarse 2005 p. 59.
[98] O'Keefe 2006.

French as trophies of war after the final defeat of Napoleon's troops. Among these was the famous Rosetta Stone, still at the British Museum, an object often at issue when the subject of looting is discussed since Egypt wants it back from the British Museum.

Looting or Elginism, a term created by the actions of Lord Elgin, who between 1801 and 1805 "illegally" transported the Parthenon Marbles from Greece to London is often considered an act of (cultural) vandalism. It should be said that there is a debate about whether the activities of Lord Elgin were illegal. Some (especially the Greeks) strongly disapprove of Elgin's actions while others give arguments that justify his deeds. Currently the appropriation of artifacts taken from poorer nations to richer ones is especially referred to as Elginism.[99]

Safeguarding cultural property by giving protected status to libraries, scientific collections, and works of art was first explicitly referred to in the Lieber Code of the U.S. Federal Army in 1863. It is still part of the U.S. military law and indicates when the military became a CPP stakeholder. The "Lieber Instructions" represent the first attempt to codify the laws of war. They were prepared during the American Civil War by Francis Lieber, a professor of Columbia College in New York, revised by a board of officers, and promulgated by President Lincoln. Although they were binding only on the forces of the United States, they correspond to other existing laws and customs of war. They strongly influenced the further codification of the laws of war and the adoption of similar regulations by other states. They formed the basis of an international convention on the laws of war presented to the Brussels Conference in 1874 and stimulated the adoption of the Hague Conventions on land warfare of 1899 and 1907.[100] The Declaration of Brussels of 1874 and the Oxford Code of 1880 mentioned cultural property but were not ratified by enough countries to be considered official international treaties.[101] In 1907, the Hague Convention on Land Warfare required parties to spare, as far as possible, buildings dedicated to religion, art or science, and historic monuments.[102] The 1907 Convention also indicated the different

---

99 ⟨http:/www.elginism.com/definition/⟩ [17 July 2011].

100 Source: Schindler and Toman 1988, pp. 3–23. Webpage ICRC, International Humanitarian Law treaties and documents. ⟨http://www.icrc.org/ihl.nsf⟩ [17 July 2011]. See also for Brussels and Oxford declarations.

101 Source: Boylan, Patrick pp. 43–108 in: Brodie N, and Tubb, K.W. editors 2002, *Illicit Antiquities, The theft of culture and the extension of archaeology.*

102 Hague Convention on Land Warfare Convention (IV) Respecting the Laws and Customs of War on Land 1907. Art. 27. ⟨http://avalon.law.yale.edu/20th_century/hague04.asp#art27⟩ [23 July 2011].

parties that still are today's CPP stakeholders.[103] Yet iconoclasm remained in practice for intentional destruction of certain groups' identities. Examples are the defacement and dismantling of monuments from Soviet-era Eastern Europe, many of which were destroyed in mass-participation spectacles, and the destruction of the Bamiyan Buddha statues in Afghanistan.[104]

Destruction of cultural objects became extraordinary devastating with the introduction of aerial bombing and long-distance weapons. World War I resulted in the destruction of many cultural properties in Belgium and eastern France.[105] World War II was even more traumatic, due to systematic aerial bombardments and export of cultural property from occupied territories.[106] After an appeal to President Roosevelt made by Pope Pius VII on 19 May 1943 to spare what was called "heritage of human civilization," the allies decided to avoid damage to religious and cultural buildings in Rome while liberating it from the Nazis. After the Allied landing in Italy in early 1944, the Italian cities were divided into three categories to be taken into account by aerial bombardments:[107] Category A (including Rome, Florence, and Venice), cities that under no circumstances could be bombed without consent of Supreme Headquarters.[108] Category B (including Ravenna, Assisi and Urbino) cities could be bombed if considered essential, and afterwards full responsibility would be accepted by Supreme Headquarters. Finally, Category C (including Siena, Pisa and Padua) cities were left on their own, since they had important military objects that had to be bombed in their vicinity, and as a consequence damage was acceptable.[109]

Several studies deal with this and other types of destruction in World War II such as *The Rape of Europa* by Lynn H. Nicholas, *The Concept of Cultural Property Protection in Times of Armed Conflict* from Patrick Boylan and Hector Feliciano's *The Lost Museum*.[110] They give a clear account of

---

103 Governmental organizations, political organizations, religion, science etc.

104 ⟨http://csmt.uchicago.edu/glossary2004/iconoclasm.htm⟩ [20 July 2011].

105 During World War I, the cathedral of Reims in France was damaged by aerial bombs and the library at the University of Louvain in Belgium was destroyed by fire. See also Pesendorfer and Speckner 2006. p. 81.

106 Source: Threats to cultural heritage in situations of international and non-international armed conflict—Real world and fictitious case studies, Michael Pesendorfer in Protection of CP in Peace Support Operations, international workshop Bregenz June 2006, ⟨http://www.bundesheer.at/cms/artikel.php?ID=2922⟩ [17 July 2011].

107 O'Keefe 2006.

108 This did not work out as perfect as desired for instance the papal basilica of San Lorenzo was hit and badly damaged.

109 Source O'Keefe 2006, pp. 72–73.

110 Nicholas 1994; Boylan 2002; Feliciano 1997.

London Daily Mail *cartoon, March 1944, responding to German art destruction propaganda (Cartoon by Illingsworth* © London Daily Mail)

Figure 8. Who's a Vandal? © Associated Newspaper Ltd/Solo Syndication.

offenses against cultural property as systematically committed by Nazi institutions like Hitler's and Goering's art collecting squads as well as the Soviets. Their Russian Trophy Brigades were ordered to retrieve "equivalents of the artworks destroyed or removed from Russia during the War as a form of reparation."[111] The Nazis were also in the business of stealing identities that were connected with cultural heritage as will be explained in the section on the sociology of cultural property protection and the military. A quite relevant aspect to address in the context of this book is the fact that the allies had their own CPP military capability in World War II, established in 1943 and called the Monuments, Fine Arts, and Archives (MFAA) program that fell within the Civil Affairs branch of the allied armed forces.[112] These MFAA

---

111 See: Akinsja and Koslov 1996. These equivalents included German state-owned cultural objects, cultural objects taken from churches and synagogues, as well as a great deal of private property that had been looted by the Germans from individuals. The art works taken back to the Soviet Union were held in relative secrecy for years, until the final years of glastnost (ГлаRсность). As European countries started to demand their cultural treasures and archives, Russian legislators passed a law that potentially nationalizes all cultural treasures brought to Russia at the end of World War II. In 1999 the Constitutional Court issued an opinion basically upholding the law. How do these actions comport with international law? What are the chances for restitution of these displaced cultural valuables? Source: Spoils of War versus Cultural Heritage conference, Harvard University February. 2008.

112 In June 23, 1943, President Roosevelt approved the formation of the "American Commission for the Protection and Salvage of Artistic and Historic Monuments in War Areas"

officers (also known as the Monuments Men) were cultural heritage professionals, most of whom were already serving in the military as either recruits or volunteers. Gathered in special teams, they were dedicated to salvaging, preserving, and, after the war, repatriating cultural property damaged or looted during the war.[113] Since this book is in a part based on information and experiences in theater gained during my time with the Dutch Armed Forces, I want to pay attention to one Dutch example of good CPP practice in the past. During and just after World War II, the Dutch MoD was more culturally proactive than today since the MFAA had one Dutch officer, Lt. Col. Alphonse Vorenkamp, who was a (probably reserve) Lieutenant Colonel in the Royal Dutch Army. He was the only known Dutch military CPP predecessor until CIMIC started to create a team in the beginning of 2000. Apparently, Vorenkamp worked in the United States in the late 1920s at Smith College in Northampton, Massachusetts, as an instructor in the art department. The College acknowledged his remarkable expertise in his field, Northern Art, and Vorenkamp became a full professor in 1939. Because of his familiarity with and knowledge of the Old Dutch and Flemish masters, he was uniquely qualified to lecture about them. During his first sabbatical, Vorenkamp completed his Ph.D. research under Prof. dr. Wilhelm Martin of Leiden University with a thesis entitled *Contributions to the Dutch Still Life in the Seventeenth Century*, a valuable resource for the study of still lifes. After World War II began, Dr. Vorenkamp helped Mrs. Jacques Goudstikker, widow of a Dutch art dealer, store sixteen of her spouse's paintings at Smith College from 1940 until 1946.[114] Vorenkamp served in the United States Army from 1942 to 1943; however, he never became an American citizen but kept his Dutch nationality. He returned to Smith College after an honorable discharge. In May 1945, he was granted a leave of absence when he was chosen by the Netherlands government for the task of identifying pictures and other objects of art, stolen and removed from the Netherlands by the Nazis. He was given the rank of lieutenant colonel in the Royal Dutch Army and was

---

known as "The Roberts Commission," after its chairman, Supreme Court Justice Owen J. Roberts. source: ⟨http://www.monumentsmen.com/the_heroes.php⟩ [20 August 2011].

113 Source: Corine Wegener, The 1954 Hague Convention and Preserving Cultural Heritage, October 19, 2010. ⟨http://www.archaeological.org/news/hca/3137⟩ [19 August 2011].

114 Much later the so-called Goudstikker case developed. U.S. heirs of Dutch Jewish art collector Goudstikker, who died in 1940, claimed that paintings seized by the Nazis during World War II were never returned to the family. They started a search and, after lengthy negotiations, they recovered or received compensation for a large part of the collection. Vital was a decision of the Dutch Government in 2006 to return 202 paintings to the family. ⟨http://www.nytimes.com/2006/03/26/arts/design/26ridi.html⟩ [19 August 2011].

responsible for the recovery of priceless treasures. Upon his return to the Netherlands, Vorenkamp was stationed in Amsterdam for a few months and worked at the General Commissary for Economic Interests in Germany (a program for the reclamation of almost everything, including paintings). Vorenkamp was the first to go, by invitation of the American authorities, to the Munich Collecting Point where stolen artworks were stored in the Führerbau for restitution. He remained in Munich from October 1945 to May 1946, and during this period, he identified for the Netherlands many private collections, including the Manheimer Collection, as well as other paintings that had been "obtained" for Göring and Hitler during the war. In the summer of 1946, he was knighted in the Order of the Dutch Lion. In late 1946, Vorenkamp participated in arranging an exhibition of forty-eight Dutch paintings that traveled across the United States as a gesture of appreciation on behalf of the Dutch government for America's role in recovering and restituting thousands of artworks stolen by the Nazis. The exhibit opened in December of 1946 at the National Gallery of Art, Washington, D.C., and then was on display at fourteen other museums whose staff had served with the MFAA section following World War II.[115] Many of the approximately 400 enlisted members and civilians of the MFAA went on to have fruitful careers. Largely art historians and museum personnel, they had formative roles in many of the United States' best cultural institutions, including the National Gallery of Art, the Metropolitan Museum of Art, the MOMA, as well as in museums and other institutions in Europe.

Finally, in 1954, developments lead to the creation of the first universal convention dealing exclusively with safeguarding cultural heritage: the Convention for the Protection of Cultural Property in the Event of Armed Conflict, better known as the Hague Convention of 1954, including a first protocol also listed as The Hague 14 May 1954. In the late twentieth century, identity-related matters, especially on individual levels, became more manifest because of the development of new social movements (many starting in the sixties) such as Black Power and Women's Liberation. This intensifying of identity gave an extra boost to identity related cultural property claims, some of the intangible kind, some deriving from an urge for individual distinction.[116] Concerns began to include the use and ownership of intellectual property in connection with the new information society as

---

115 This information is in large part an adaptation based on the section Biographies of the Monuments Men found on ⟨http://www.monumentsmen.com/bio.php?id=304⟩ [19 August 2011].

116 Bourdieu 1984.

well as the dematerialization of heritage.[117] On 26 March 1999, the Hague Convention of 1954 was strengthened by a second protocol applying to international and non-international conflicts and giving possibilities and regulations for enhanced protection and criminal responsibility as well as jurisdiction.[118]

Apart from these accomplishments that originate in the 1950s, little attention was paid to the issue in the period after World War II. Expertise and military capabilities like the Monuments Men, developed by the Allies during World War II, were allowed to disappear.[119] CPP had no priority within the respective defense organizations. This lasted until 2001 when the Bamiyan Buddhas were destroyed by the Taliban, who considered them irrelevant since they were pre-Islamic.[120] It illustrates how a geographical position and a regime or religion can influence the status and appreciation of cultural property. The Bamiyan demolitions led the protection of cultural heritage and its legal and ethical drivers to regain international attention.

Though lessons can be learned from history when it comes to the protection of cultural property in conflict, research shows that in spite of most efforts to promote the subject as being critical for military missions, many challenges remain.[121] All arguments used by (military) opponents range from "stuff happens" and low priority to mission creep.[122] Cultural property protection was and is, to an extent, perceived as less significant. At this moment, it seems that recent cultural disasters trigger a renaissance in cultural property protection including the military input. However, every rebirth appears to last shorter and CPP becomes increasingly dependent on economic circumstances. The wheel has to be reinvented repeatedly; the only firm solution is to make the subject sustainable by pointing out his-

---

[117] Brown 2005. p. 41. What in fact is meant is the rising salience of stories, designs, and information in discussions about CPP.

[118] For a commentary on the 1999 Second Protocol, see Toman 2009.

[119] See the webpage of the Monuments Men Foundation that aims to preserve the legacy of the Monuments, Fine Arts, and Archives (MFAA) section ⟨http://www.monumentsmen-foundation.org/about/⟩ [17 July2011].

[120] Different motives are given. The leader of the Taliban referred to a fatwa stating false gods or idols should be removed and claimed the act was necessary for the implementation of Islamic order. See also ⟨http://www.hazarapeople.com/buddhas-of-bamyan/⟩ [17 July 2011].

[121] Actually these efforts are part of the obligations under the 1954 Hague Convention see Article 25 and its Second Protocol see Article 30 Dissemination.

[122] This is the expansion of a mission beyond its original goals. The term often implies a disapproval of newly adopted goals by the user of the term. The term originally applied to military operations.

torical connotations and obligations, and by demonstrating projects and deliverables for all stakeholders.

The Sociology of Cultural Property Protection and the Military

One can see throughout history that the perception of cultural heritage and its potential to cause or contribute to conflicts appears to change over time. The status of cultural objects tends to follow alterations in society and politics and is therefore subject to continuous adjustments. For example, statues of Lenin and Stalin from the Soviet period were no longer considered relevant cultural heritage immediately following the disintegration of the Soviet Empire. Likewise, property such as the so-called memorial scapes or trauma scapes (e.g., former concentration camps and certain battlefields), have only recently been modified and adapted for incorporation in modern society thus becoming part of the heritage discourse.[123] Then there are objects and sites formerly not addressed as cultural property that are now treated otherwise. For example, identity-related values are currently attached to human remains (e.g., Indian burial grounds in the U.S.). Such areas are off limits to or of restricted use for military training and builders. Another recent development is that biological species and regional landscapes are sometimes claimed as cultural heritage.[124] Also within such contexts a constant factor remains, namely cultural property's availability for manipulation an aspect essential for the military. It indicates political and strategic values that can draw military interests. The triggered manipulations have different gradations. In the case of mild manipulation we can speak of creative use, or seen from an opposite fashion and as put into words by Nietzsche, this would be "creative forgetfulness," or, in other words, how the memory of some aspects of the past is predicated on amnesia about others.[125] This is, for example, the political use of archaeology, when it serves the design and construction of national identities or nationalistic interpretations of the archaeological record.[126] As mentioned in the preceding section,

---

[123] Rob van der Laarse, lecture given during the Cambridge seminar "Packaging the Past: The Commodification of Heritage." April, 2008.

[124] Brown 2005.

[125] Foner 2002, pp. xii–xiii. In this case U.S. historical consciousness on slavery before the 1990s was meant.

[126] Nationalism and Archaeology: On the Constructions of Nations and the Reconstructions of the Remote past, by Philip L. Kohl, *Annual Review of Anthropology*, October 1998, Vol. 27, Pages 223–246.

the Nazis made political use of archaeology to produce evidence for the evolution of a master race in Europe.[127] Another misuse of archaeology took place in the late 1960s by the white settler government of Rhodesia, now Zimbabwe, claiming a rather strange and false connection of the country with the Phoenicians.[128]

The location or even character of objects in art history can be manipulated too. A well-tried method is taking a cultural identity and adding it to your own group, as did the Nazis when classifying Rembrandt as "Nordic and Germanic," and thus part of the German culture.[129] More recent examples of vital identity associations of monuments that show what can go wrong if such qualities are not recognized include: the (re)moved statue of a soldier of the Red Army in the capital of Estonia Tallinn causing deadly riots in April, 2007; the still-ongoing temple dispute between Thailand and Cambodia that involves the Preah Vihear site; and the case of the Jewish heritage from Iraq addressed in the section dealing with the influence of the media.[130]

Motives for the destruction of cultural objects are not a constant factor; in other words, they are not time-resistant. Modern iconoclasm can be seen in former Yugoslavia and Afghanistan (e.g., the destruction of Bosnia's national library in 1992, the 1993 shelling of the Mostar Bridge, and the demolition of the Bamiyan Buddhas in 2001).[131] These actions aim at identity destruction as has occurred repeatedly in antiquity. However, in the past (e.g., the Middle Ages), cultural objects were rarely a direct source of identity-related conflicts unless religion was at stake. Commonly speaking, cultural property and (national) identity were not considered important enough to protect and ownership was not particularly disputed.

National identity or nationalism developed in Western Europe after the French and American Revolutions when it replaced theology and dynasticism as the primary instrument used by the state to justify its power. In fact, this invention of nationalism gave way to the development of different types of group-related identities linked to cultural heritage and cultural properties.

---

127 Arnold 1990 and Kohl 1998.

128 Garlake 1973.

129 See Nicholas 1994. *The Rape of Europa.*

130 ⟨http://preahvihear.com/⟩ [17 July 2011].

131 On 25 August 1992, Bosnia's National and University Library, a Moorish-revival building built in the 1890s on the Sarajevo riverfront, was shelled and burned. Some 1.5 million volumes, including over 155,000 rare books and manuscripts; the national archives; deposit copies of newspapers, periodicals and books published in Bosnia; and collections of the University of Sarajevo were lost. Source: András Riedlmayer, Erasing the Past 1995.

The changing perceptions and appreciations of cultural property occur throughout military history too, but are not closely related to the civil concept of identity as to the military way of thinking. Adjustment of military mindsets is an ongoing process influenced by circumstances as described in the previous discussion of looting and poverty. Soldiers used to loot but have now transformed into protectors of (cultural) property. This transformation of the military way of thinking from legitimizing plunder and destruction of cultural property to actively preserve and protect heritage was stimulated by different social factors. Examples that were instrumental were the development of international legislation, increasing awareness of cultural property protection in support of the military missions, and the identity aspect of CPP that is important for the distinctiveness of (local) populations involved.[132] The element of supporting the mission needs some clarification; CPP provides for better relations with local populations, stimulates economy via tourism, restrains illicit traffic of artifacts, and by doing so diminishes financial resources of opponents. Finally, the development of tourism should be mentioned. Thanks to Thomas Cook, who in 1841 organized affordable excursions in the UK, this concept evolved into the modern (mass) tourism industry. Through tourism, cultural property has gained value as a means to generate jobs and income.

The facts described above support the thesis that in order to improve the quality of the military role within cultural property protection, it is indispensable to keep track of military attitude toward cultural heritage. Such implications can be either positive or of an unethical nature. The latter can occur when CPP, in a military context, engages in, or is perceived as being part of, counterinsurgency operations (COIN). Before going into this, it should be explained that in the United States, counterinsurgency is a wider construct than in Europe. One can say that in Europe, COIN has more negative connotations, while in the U.S. winning the hearts and minds of local populations and force acceptance are considered part of COIN. In Europe, COIN is a subject that is perceived to be directly related to undercover missions, espionage, and commando operations. Therefore, international discussions about military involvement in CPP sometimes create misunderstandings. Still, structural relations between military-initiated cultural property protection and the more drastic COIN applications have to be, and can be, avoided since CPP officers must act according to international

[132] CPP supports the mission because it fosters better relations with local populations, stimulates economy via tourism and restrains illicit traffic of artifacts, thereby diminishing financial resources of opponents.

legislation such as the Hague Convention of 1954. Having said this, a quote from Charles Garraway comes in mind: "Counter-terrorism lies on the borderline of differing legal regimes and we need to use all the legal tools in our toolbox."[133] To show what can happen in practice, a case example can be found in the section on the media regarding involvement of social scientists in the COIN-related so-called Human Terrain Systems.

It must be emphasized that this study is not intended to give an ethical or technical judgment about COIN. It is not my area of expertise and is essentially a subject for publications on military science. In itself, COIN is a tool that has been in military use for some time.[134] International humanitarian law, and sometimes national caveats, apply to these types of operations. However, at present, there is a tendency to involve cultural awareness, and especially Human Terrain Systems, in the "kill the enemy" type of COIN as opposed to its current position in the more "hearts-and-minds" orientated COIN.

Nevertheless keeping track of new insights, preferably those in tune with military traditions, codes, and cultures, can lead to finding connections and opportunities for the integration of cultural protection activities. To judge all parameters including civil matters, an accurate picture of the playing field and the players, such as the media, science, religious institutions, the military, non-governmental and governmental organizations, international organizations, restoration and conservation institutions, and commercial parties who claim, protect, use, and misuse cultural property, is needed.

This taxonomy can serve as a starting point for further research and makes matters more accessible from an analytical perspective. Therefore, Chapter 2 has provided an oversight of key players involved in CPP. Through examples and observations, a picture of the respective stakeholders has been drawn and the ways they experience their input and responsibilities, taking into account related problems and challenges from their differing points of view. Since they are introduced as key players, emphasis has been placed on the military. The categorization is meant to be as universal and international as possible. However, since I am Dutch I took the liberty to, as far as appropriate, explore the situation in the Netherlands a bit further.

---

133 Garraway 2010.

134 Counterinsurgency (COIN) warfare. The ultimate goal of COIN warfare is to "build (or rebuild) a political machine from the population upward." Source: David Galula, Counterinsurgency Warfare: Theory and Practice (New York: Frederick A. Praeger, 1964, reprinted 2005).

In the Netherlands MoD, the state of affairs can be described as problematic. CPP as a phenomenon is slowly developing in a complicated environment. Behaviors within the complex of parties involved are dominated by a constant struggle between cultures, identities, interest, funding issues, and competencies as will be illustrated in the case studies, and background sections of this study. In the meanwhile, implementation of the subject is personality-driven and depends largely on the determination of those proactively involved. The quality of cultural property protection seems to be in the lap of the stakeholder. There is no proactive nor even a reactive approach towards CPP. For now, raising awareness on the subject in the Netherlands and the majority of European countries appears to be subjected to the following analysis from Arthur Schopenhauer: "All truth passes through three stages. First, it is ridiculed. Second, it is violently opposed. Third, it is accepted as being self-evident."[135]

---

135 Attributed to Arthur Schopenhauer (1788–1860).

CHAPTER THREE

CASE STUDIES

As indicated in the preface, initially not many sources were available that contained "recent" experiences and lessons suitable for interpretation and of benefit for the planning and execution of coming operations. Consequently there was not sufficient material for scientific research. Luckily, since my investigations began, the number of sources has grown, although there is still a need for practical perspectives to gain knowledge that can serve as a basis for improvement and adaptation of current practices. Therefore, and to contribute to the production of knowledge about CPP, I wish to present, in chronological order, a number of case examples. At the end of each case, key issues and dilemmas are addressed and discussed. Hopefully this will help to put these cases in the broader perspective of arguments presented in this publication and will trigger further discussion and facilitate the development of these cases into "lessons learned." A number of cases have already been published in previous publications by the author of this study.

An Ethnographical Museum for Afghanistan

In answer to requests and after necessary research and consultations of experts and parties involved, the Cultural Affairs unit of CIMIC Group North designed the following proposal and plan with the title: An Ethnographical Museum for Afghanistan.[1]

Since the expulsion of the Taliban in autumn of 2001, international and Afghan organizations and experts started making plans for the resurrection and reconstruction of the Afghanistan National Museum. The Taliban destroyed part of the collected objects of this world-famous museum in the spring of that year. Previously, in the early 1990s, a substantial part of the collection was already stolen and the building itself seriously damaged by

[1] Based on a document prepared on 20 August 2002 by Willem Vogelsang with contributions and editing by Joris Kila in order to satisfy the request from the Afghan authorities for support.

different bombardments and mortars. The museum's collection consisted in large part of archaeological objects discovered in Afghanistan from as early as the beginning of the last century. Most objects dated from the country's pre-Islamic period, or more exactly, before 800 AD. Many items represented Buddhist and Hindustan periods, and the Taliban especially selected these objects for destruction.

Archaeological activities in Afghanistan have been linked strongly to the build up of Afghanistan as a nation, a process that started in the first half of the twentieth century. The same goes for the establishment of the National Museum. The ruling elite that was striving for the creation of a secular-based nation was trying to demonstrate by utilizing archaeological projects within the Afghanistan borders to show that an old and rich culture existed long before the Islamic period. Archaeology, as well as the National Museum of Afghanistan, served as a means for the country's ruling parties to secure their own and their nation's position.

The ordinary Afghan's resentment for the above-mentioned political strategy became apparent when in 1929 the ruling monarch was impeached and replaced by an Islamic-fundamentalist ruler who immediately ended the policy of reform that was implemented at that time. All archaeological projects in Afghanistan had to stop while the new regime destroyed monuments and objects dating from pre-Islamic periods. The cultural property destructions in 1929 showed similarities with the recent Taliban vandalism. The destruction of the famous Buddha-statues of Bamiyan in the spring of 2001 also fits this *modus operandi*. The Taliban, supported by many other Afghans, cannot relate to an era in which the inhabitants of the country did not convert to Islam. The reconstruction of Kabul's archaeological museum, however good in its intention, therefore raises a number of questions. Is this really what the Afghan people want? Is this what they need? Is it not possible to spend allocated funds in a different and better way? Is the rebuilding of the museum not part of the wish list of foreigners accompanied by western-orientated leaders that want to give priority to the rebuilding of the museum? It is remarkable that the ethnological collection of the National Museum almost entirely survived the civil war as well as the Taliban regime. This is, of course, not without reason. The surviving objects relate more directly to the lives and customs of the average Afghan; therefore, they remained almost undamaged. It is easy to draw a conclusion from this phenomenon. Plans have been initiated by independent experts for the establishment of an Ethnographical Museum in Kabul. Such a museum should focus on Afghanistan's contemporary history presenting visitors with an image of the country traditional and modern life using daily objects, tools, photographs, etc. In short, the museum should give the visitor an impression of the Afghan identity in the context of daily life. The exhibitions on display should not only stress differences between existing ethnic and religious groups within the society, but should also explore themes such as water management, the climate, clothing and costumes, village life, etc. It seems also logical that Islam would have a prominent position within this approach.

The museum must not function as a mere storage for old objects but has to serve as a dynamic location with changing exhibitions, workshops, lectures, and a cinema theater. An example demonstrating these qualities is the head office of the Iranian Cultural Heritage Organization in Teheran. It is of the utmost importance that the Ethnographical Museum be designed, constructed, and the interior decorated by Afghans themselves. They must execute all construction work since these activities concern their museum, their culture, their country, and their future.

The president of the intermediate government of Afghanistan, Hamid Karzai, indicated in the beginning of 2002 that the establishment of an Ethnographical Museum in Kabul is a high priority. The president even suggested a particular building in the outskirts of Kabul as a possible location for the museum. The earlier-mentioned independent experts have been talking about the subject with UNESCO representatives in Kabul; with the Afghan Minister of Information and Culture; with his deputy minister who is especially in charge of national museums; and with the director of all national museums in Afghanistan. There is an agreement on subjects such as the necessity and exact nature of a new Ethnographical Museum. The building suggested by Hamid Karzai is probably not very suitable for the museum; however, this has to be determined during a fact-finding mission. As a good alternative, there is a complex of buildings located near the center of Kabul. These buildings are almost undamaged and are presently owned by the Afghan Ministry of Defense. It is of course necessary to find funding for this project and, apart from this, the buildup of relevant expertise is very important. In late July of 2002, it was agreed in Kabul that the UNESCO representation in Afghanistan would be responsible for the design of a complete plan; henceforth this plan would be presented to several potential donors in order to acquire financial support. Concerning possible involvement of the Netherlands, conversations took place with Dutch representatives in Kabul and Islamabad as well as with staff members at the Ministry of Foreign Affairs in The Hague. Support for this project has to be multinational in order to prevent chauvinistic implications. Concerning the build up of expertise, it seems easy to use several functional specialists of CIMIC that are particularly qualified for this project. Apart from this, they can offer possibilities for Afghans to take training courses to become ethnographical curators in the new museum or somewhere else. Of course, funding is also needed for these activities.

Possible Dutch support for this initiative cannot be viewed separately from the general need for international involvement in the development in Afghanistan. In the short term, a complete plan is expected regarding the museum as well as a European visit by the Afghan Director of National Museums. It is highly recommended that CIMIC execute a fact-finding mission on relatively short notice in order to speak to all parties involved to examine, with the help of a qualified architect (functional specialist of CIMIC Group North), the possible locations suggested for the museum. CIMIC's involvement will primarily concern the adjustment and repair of the building as well as basic training in museum-related skills and the creation of a depot and basic laboratory with acceptable climate conditions. The exact terms of reference for the project have to be determined during and following the fact-finding. The proposed project is 100% politically correct. The activities involved will generate a substantial amount of force protection since kick-off results will be directly visible. Splitting activities and taking part in one or more phases is simple. Sustainability is guaranteed because of UNESCO participation. For follow-up and transfer of knowledge apart from the deployment of functional specialists, it is also possible to request the cooperation of the Netherlands Institute for Cultural Heritage (ICN).[2]

This proposal was supported by UNESCO who also requested a fact-finding mission to be carried out by military cultural specialists from CIMIC Group North[3] and the Afghan Academy of Sciences, who wrote a separate request to the ISAF headquarters in Kabul (see Figure 9).[4] The plan/proposal was submitted to the Dutch authorities as well as to NATO.[5] Finally, the

[2] As of 2011, this no longer exists independently, but is part of the "Rijksdienst voor het Cultureel Erfgoed."

[3] Letter from UNESCO to the Commander CIMIC Group North dated April 23, 2003 signed by L. Levi-Strauss, Deputy Director Division of Cultural Heritage.

[4] Letter from the Afghan Academy of Sciences dated 10-8-2002, No. 45, signed by Abdul Bari Rashed.

[5] NATO did not respond and Dutch authorities initially delayed a response and later declared that the plan did not support the mission. The "low priority" argument in the case of culture is often used when there is no specific knowledge about the Hague Convention and other relevant treaties.

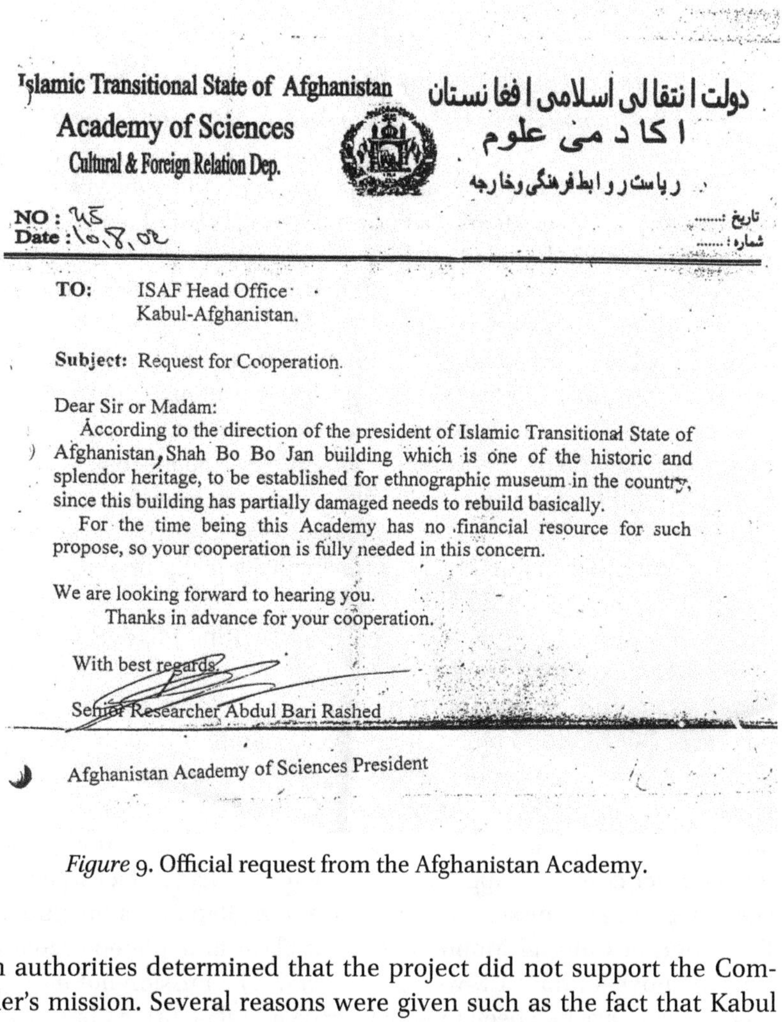
Islamic Transitional State of Afghanistan
Academy of Sciences
Cultural & Foreign Relation Dep.

دولت انتقالی اسلامی افغانستان
اکادمی علوم
ریاست روابط فرهنگی وخارجه

NO : ۴۲۵
Date : ۱۵،۸،۰۲

تاریخ :......
شماره :......

TO: ISAF Head Office
Kabul-Afghanistan.

Subject: Request for Cooperation.

Dear Sir or Madam:

According to the direction of the president of Islamic Transitional State of Afghanistan, Shah Bo Bo Jan building which is one of the historic and splendor heritage, to be established for ethnographic museum in the country, since this building has partially damaged needs to rebuild basically.

For the time being this Academy has no financial resource for such propose, so your cooperation is fully needed in this concern.

We are looking forward to hearing you.

Thanks in advance for your cooperation.

With best regards

Senior Researcher Abdul Bari Rashed

Afghanistan Academy of Sciences President

Figure 9. Official request from the Afghanistan Academy.

Dutch authorities determined that the project did not support the Commander's mission. Several reasons were given such as the fact that Kabul was outside the Dutch AOR and culture has low priority.

Key issues and dilemmas found in this case concern:

- International cooperation;
- Risk avoiding behaviors of parties involved in CPP;
- Cultural property as part of identity, here not part of religious identity;

- Funding; and
- CIMIC and CPP in support of the COM's mission versus obligations deriving from The Hague Convention of 1954.

Iconoclasm in the Orthodox Monastery of Matejce in Macedonia: The Creative Use of Damaged Cultural Property

The monastery of St. Bogorodica Matejce is situated near the village of Matejce, approximately 40 kilometers north of the Macedonian capital, Skopje. The monastery was founded by the Serbian Emperor Dusan and completed in 1355 by Empress Jelena and her son, the Serbian Emperor Uros. Forming part of the monastery is the Church of St. Bogorodica. Armed conflict in the Republic of Macedonia commenced at the beginning of 2001 and the monastery was occupied by the Ushtria Çlirimtare Kombëtare (UCK-National Liberation Army), who operated in the Republic of Macedonia in 2000 and 2001, who used it as their headquarters and arsenal. The Macedonian civil and religious authorities feared that the monastery had suffered damage. Early action to assess and possibly restore the suspected damage was financially supported by the Dutch Embassy in Skopje. The first report (6–7 July 2001) included a photographic record of the Church of St. Bogorodica provided by staff of the EU Monitoring Mission. The pictures indicated damage to the roof and UCK graffiti on some of the church mural paintings, but not on the fresco paintings. The report recommended that no one be permitted to touch or remove the graffiti from the mural paintings since that would cause more extensive and irreparable damage to the fourteenth-century Byzantine murals. The report also recommended that only Macedonian and international experts should undertake any treatments. Later it became apparent that the frescos had in fact suffered damage. A fact-finding mission by experts from the Republic's Institute for the Protection of Cultural Monuments took place in September 2001 at the time members of the UCK were still *in situ*.[6] The mission not only discovered that damage had been inflicted on the mural paintings, but that owing to "cleaning" work being carried out, contrary to the earlier recommendations, some paintings had been destroyed. The report of this second mission also noted the urgent need for the temporary repair of the damaged roof in the southeastern corner to prevent further damage to the interior,

[6] Nicolik-Novakovic 2004.

Figure 10. Damaged mural in Matejce. Photo by Joris Kila.

which contained valuable fourteenth century mural paintings, and, as a high priority, the cleaning of the church and the repair of damaged mural paintings.[7]

One of the first projects to be undertaken by the newly formed Cultural Affairs functional specialists' network from CIMIC Group North (CGN) was an assessment mission to Macedonia, where the Dutch led the NATO operation "Amber Fox." CGN was a dedicated CIMIC capability at the time based in the Netherlands, affiliated with NATO, and consisting of five other participating nations: the Czech Republic, Denmark, Germany, Norway, and Poland. It contributed CIMIC support units and, where possible, functional specialists to be active in the areas of civil administration, humanitarian aid, civil infrastructure, economy and commerce, and cultural affairs. As CGN's network manager for cultural affairs, I went to Matejce in the last week of August 2002 as part of this assessment mission. I arrived at the monastery accompanied by two Macedonian colleagues from the National Museum

[7] When reading the ICOMOS Macedonian Committee report, one gets the distinct impression that matters were considerably delayed by the highly bureaucratic procedures that followed. Numerous institutions were involved, such as ICBS, ICOMOS, UNESCO and the State Institute for the Protection of Cultural Monuments (RZZSK).

in Skopje. The monastery and surroundings were apparently not yet completely cleared of mines and the complex was still in use by the UCK, which presented some difficulties, but we found several instances of damage as described above. I saw murals destroyed because someone tried to remove the graffiti using steel wool scouring pads soaked with soap normally used for cleaning dishes. On closer inspection of the graffiti, we saw that some murals had been sprayed with green paint, whereas others had been drawn upon with what looked like a black felt-tip marker. I took samples of very tiny fragments lying on the floor, which came from parts of the mural-free wall. Undecorated areas of the wall had also been sprayed and written upon, so I was able to take samples of this wall surface covered with the green paint and black ink. The paint in most readily available spray cans is based on two types of binding agents, acrylics and alkyd. Subsequent laboratory tests revealed that by using acetone and wadding it was easy to remove the paint, implying that acrylic paint had been used for the green graffiti in Matejce. After testing the samples of the black marker ink used on the painting of St. Peter, we discovered that we had to be careful: the difference between the green paint and the black marker ink is that the black ink used color pigments that directly dissolved in the basic acetone liquid. Therefore, their application was more deeply intrusive. In addition to the challenge of dissolved pigments, other chemical processes could take place during attempts at removal, such as the chromatographic reaction that causes the separation of color pigments. Tests showed that alcohol was not effective in removing the ink. However, acetone and ethyl acetate did the job, at least in the laboratory. Therefore, it was decided that the best way to operate would probably be to use a gel instead of a liquid to prevent the cleaning agents from damaging additional layers.

Carved and scratched murals such as the painting of Georgios Okrites (Figure 12) are best treated by carefully filling and retouching them. Following the laboratory tests, CIMIC Group North's specialists offered to restore the damaged mural of St. Peter (Figure 4) by removing the graffiti and applying a non-intrusive protective layer that would facilitate the removal of future graffiti should it be targeted again. However, to our surprise, the party responsible for the mural saw its defaced state as excellent public relations and asked us not to restore it until a peace agreement was signed. For the moment, they were quite happy with their "treated" mural, which made a powerful statement. Later, the whole project involving the specialists of CIMIC Group North was stopped by the Dutch MoD owing to the withdrawal of Dutch troops.

Figure 11. Matejce Monastery. Photo by Joris Kila.

Figure 12. Georgos Okrites, probably an Archbishop or St. George damaged mural in Matejce. Photo by Joris Kila.

This Macedonian example raises a question over how situations like these should be interpreted. Is this example a misuse of damaged cultural property as propaganda? Is someone trying to create a win-win situation? Of course, art historians, politicians and all the concerned parties should consider these issues. However, in the meantime, it remains a rather confusing matter for the military, who have to distinguish between cultural property and damaged cultural property. By means of comparison, one can consider what the difference is between the damaged St. Peter (the Maradona) and a conceptual piece of art like Marcel Duchamp's L.H.O.O.Q., see pictures 3 and 4 page 25.[8] To an outsider they both look like vandalized paintings; however, Duchamp's picture is actually in itself a creation of Marcel Duchamp, rather than Da Vinci's Mona Lisa damaged. His aim was to attack the eternal values of western culture. Note the fact that the UCK members, who were unlikely to be trained in art, used graffiti symbols derived from western mass culture such as Ray Ban sunglasses, soccer trophies, and Diego Maradona, while at the same time attacking Christianity, which they perceived as equivalent to western culture. How, therefore, can the military recognize cultural objects, and damage to them, and ask for advice based on a rudimentary iconographic description to be judged by so-called "reach-back capabilities" (scholars, research institutes, etc.) who are not present and may be thousands of miles away? What is damage in this context: Is it the destruction of art or of identity, and who is the vandal?

In the Matejce example, a number of key issues and dilemmas can be identified, including the military perspective on conflict comprising changing military approaches to current types of conflict and changing military attitudes toward issues such as cultural property. Issues and dilemmas are the role of parties involved, such as functional specialists and NATO; international cooperation; legal obligations within international humanitarian law and the legal status of parties involved especially the UCK; the status and definition of cultural property as perceived by the military; changing aspects such as the international political environment; heritage as a means of identity and distinction; heritage used for propaganda and manipulation, and finally, religion.

Though it is a unique case, the range of parties involved in the Matejce case gives an indication of the complexity of implementation of CPP and how many different stakeholders are involved frequently in CPP activities.

---

[8] See p. 25, footnote 58.

All of the following took some part in, or had a view on, the Matejce case study.

- Military: CIMIC Group North, Functional Specialists, Netherlands Armed Forces.
- Militant armed forces from the UCK.
- International Organizations: NATO, UNESCO, ICBS, ICOMOS.
- Religious institutions in Macedonia.
- Governmental institutions: Macedonia: Institute for the Protection of Cultural Monuments of the Republic of Macedonia, Ministry of Culture Macedonia, and National Museum Macedonia. Netherlands: Royal Netherlands Embassy in Skopje, Instituut Collectie Nederland Amsterdam, MoD the Netherlands.
- Individual Art Historians and Restorers.

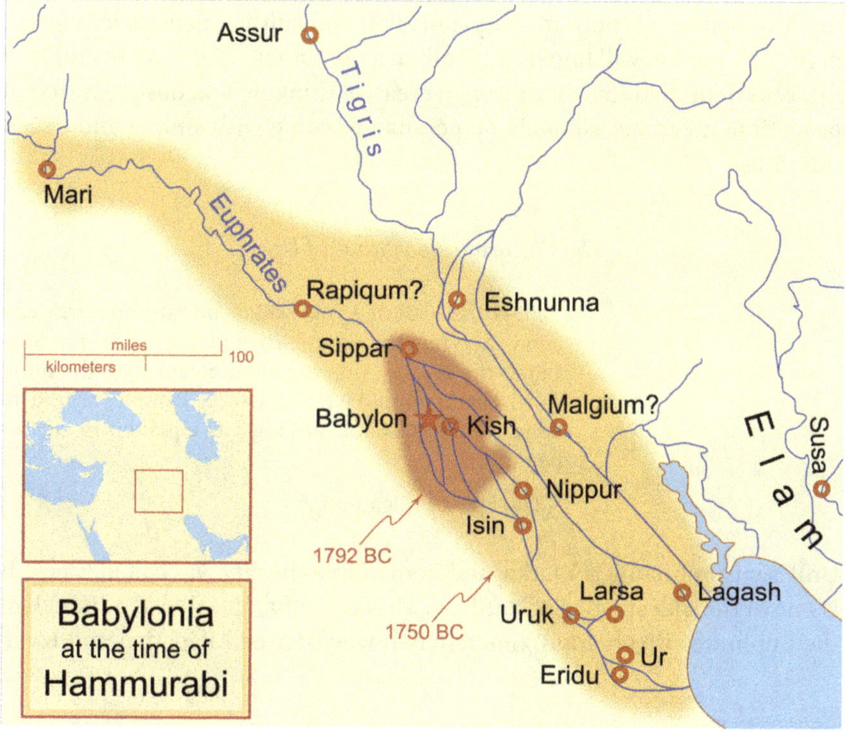

Figure 13. Map of Iraq (public domain).

Saving Uruk from Looting

The subject of this case is the Iraqi archaeological site of Uruk (today Warka) and its safeguarding from looters. I will start with an introduction followed by a narrative part based on my own experiences in theater. The case study gives an impression of the variety of parties involved in an attempt to safeguard cultural property in a conflict situation and reveals a number of key elements. Following the case, a more in-depth analysis of these elements is presented including a number of basic challenges to be met when trying to protect cultural property in times of conflict. These dilemmas will be more closely studied while making comparisons where possible using sources from field research, existing literature, historical parallels, and implications of a legal, social, military, political, economical and anthropological nature. Although I am no legal expert (my background is in archaeology and art history), it is important to make a contribution that can help legal (both military and civil) and cultural experts join forces in the debate that will hopefully result in a permanent dialogue. In addition this case demonstrates that through creative thinking and desk research in peacetime it can occasionally be possible to come with simple and cheap solutions.

The Cultural Importance of Uruk[9]

> This is the wall of Uruk, which no city on earth can equal. See its ramparts gleam like copper in the Sun. Climb the stone staircase more ancient than the mind can imagine, approach the Eanna Temple, sacred to Ishtar, a temple that no king has equalled in size or beauty.
>
> – The Epic of Gilgamesh.[10]

Uruk's current name is Warka, and in the Bible the city was called Erech. It is one of the oldest cities of southern Mesopotamia, situated at a branch of the Euphrates River, approximately half-way between Baghdad and Basra

[9] Sources used: information from dr. M. van Ess DAI institute Berlin and the DAI website ⟨http://www.dainst.org/⟩, information from Prof. dr. Wilfred van Soldt, University of Leiden., The Oxford Encyclopedia of Archaeology in the Near East vol. 5, New York 1997., Kila 2008a., *Alle Hens*, magazine from the Royal Netherlands Navy Marine Corps, March 2004.

[10] Mitchell 2006.

in Iraq. Uruk is the largest tell in this area; the site measures approx 400 hectares.[11] Excavations have exposed part of the city. The most important period in Uruk's history was without any doubt the era of so-called "high civilization" between c. 3400 and c. 2800 BC. This period saw the construction of major buildings that could only be realized within a highly organized administrative system, and the invention of cuneiform—humanity's earliest known writing system. The city remained important throughout the twenty-seventh and twenty-sixth centuries BC. This was the time of the great kings such as Enmerkar, Lugalbanda and, most famously, Gilgamesh. During the Parthian era (second and third centuries AD), the city flourished again but was probably deserted shortly after its inhabitation came to an end sometime during the Sassanian period (224 to 633 AD).

History of Excavating Uruk

Sir William Loftus executed some minor explorations between 1850 and 1854 on the most prominent mounds, finding clay-tablets and clay-coffins and uncovering the famous colored clay mosaic cone wall. It was not until 1856 that Sir Henry Rawlinson, famous as the decipherer of Assyrian cuneiform, visited the site. He became convinced that he had found the biblical site of Erech, in his words, "the mother of all cities." However, it took more than fifty years before the first systematic excavation of Uruk was conducted, between 1912 and 1914 AD, by a German team led by Julius Jordan for the Deutsches Orientgesellschaft. After the First World War, the excavations resumed from 1928 to 1939. They were stopped by the Second World War and started again from 1953 to 1989 under the aegis of the *Deutsches Archaeologisches Institut* of Berlin (DAI). The political situation followed by the First Gulf War prevented continuation. Therefore the thirty-nine campaigns of German excavations came to a halt in 1989. Only in 2001 and 2002 did a team directed by M. van Ess return to Uruk to begin mapping the site using subsurface magnetometry, a method used to see what is under the surface without digging.

---

[11] Many of the oldest cities in the world are called tells. The word "tell" is from Arabic, meaning mound or mount. Ancient cities experience disasters such as fires, earthquakes, and assaults from enemies. If a city's structures were demolished, there was no way to remove all the demolition rubble; people built right on top of the ruins. ⟨http://archaeology.about.com/od/archaeology101/qt/buried_city.htm⟩ [15 August 2011].

Figure 14. Uruk at the time of the Dutch Military Patrol's visit. Photo by Joris Kila.

Military Cultural Intervention

When a Battle Group from the Dutch Army (Marines) took over Al Muthanna province from the Americans in the summer of 2003, I learned through information obtained from Professor MacGuire Gibson of the Oriental Institute of the University of Chicago that Uruk was situated in the Dutch area of responsibility. During a Civil Theater Assessment mission on behalf of the Dutch Ministry of Defense (MoD) that addressed the key Civil Military Coordination functional areas (including Cultural Affairs), I was in a position to visit the site (see pictures 14, 16 and 17) with a patrol of the Dutch Military Police (Marechaussee) and thus discovered that Uruk was one of few Iraqi sites that had not yet been looted.[12]

According to information from the German archaeological experts, Uruk was formerly guarded by a local Bedouin tribe acting as guards for the

[12] Iraq Civil Assessment Al-Muthanna, Internal report October 2003 Dutch MoD.

German Archaeological Institute, the concession holders for excavating the site. It had been necessary for the German scientists to stop their work when the situation in Iraq had deteriorated. After the start of the war the payments to these Bedouins guards initially staggered, and finally ceased in the spring of 2003. The German Archaeological Institute (DAI) provided me with the name of the head of the tribe, Muhhar Rumain, and gave me a letter of introduction in Arabic. Before involving members of certain tribes in guarding archaeological sites or monuments, extensive research and the checking of credentials should take place as existing or potential conflicts between different tribes can create big problems. The same goes for the involvement of tribes or clans that are not originally from the area where the monuments or sites are located. At the site, I met Muhhar Rumain's son. He explained that Uruk belonged to his clan, the Bedouin at-Tobe, by virtue of an agreement with the tribes who ruled over other parts of Al-Muthanna. I was told that they still wanted to safeguard the site, but after the German payments had stopped, their capabilities were limited due to lack of means of transport and money to buy food and water. It was arranged that the Dutch Army and the DAI should pay a modest sum of money (approx. U.S. $200) to the tribe every three months through Dutch military channels allowing them to continue their work. Following an agreement with the Dutch MoD these payments continued until the Dutch forces withdrew from Iraq.

At the end of January 2004, a patrol from the Dutch Marines visited Uruk. While receiving a guided tour from Muhhair Rumain himself, they saw people digging in the far distance. Muhhair told them that these were plunderers. The patrol and the Bedouin guard rushed to the area, arrested the thieves, and returned the stolen goods that had been taken from an illegally opened grave (see Figure 15). Only minor damages were reported. As far as we know, this was the only incident involving looters that took place at Uruk. The Dutch troops left Al Muthanna and Iraq in March 2005.

As I received no permission from the Dutch MoD to revisit Uruk, there was no handover of the military cultural property protection activity to either a succeeding force or a civilian party. According to the DAI in Berlin, contact was made in May 2007 with the Bedouin guard and everything appeared to be in order in Uruk at that time. In addition, some recent pictures of the expedition house, taken by members of the Iraqi State Board of Antiquities, became available. Except for some foreseeable erosion in the expedition house and in the ruins themselves, everything seemed fine. Nevertheless, the bad condition of some ancient buildings in Uruk will become a major problem in the near future and is currently the biggest danger to the site. In June 2008, a field trip was made by John Curtis (British Museum), Elizabeth Stone (Stony Brook University), and Margarete Van Ess (DAI). This resulted in the report "An Assessment of Archaeological Sites in June 2008: An Iraqi British Project."[13] According to this report, the on-site guards (now joined by fifteen Special Protection Force members) were still present in Uruk and there were no signs of looting. The fence that surrounded the site was renewed in 2006 with Japanese funding. The DAI still manages to make payments for the on-site guard. U.S. Army archeologist Laurie Rush was able to visit Uruk in April 2009. This visit enabled her to set straight an example of a potentially good activity, based on inaccurate information. It concerns a replica of a fragment of a stone cone mosaic tower from Uruk. Such replicas are in use as avoidance targets on Fort Drum's Adirondack Aerial Gunnery Range 48. The idea is utilizing mock ups to train pilots on avoiding cultural objects and sites that vary from mosques and cemeteries to archaeological remains. Nevertheless, the mock up is modelled after the picture of the fragment from the original cone temple wall that, as the pictures in the paragraph on teaching and training show, is still *in situ* in Uruk.

At the time the replica was made nobody checked, or was able to check, the real measurements *in situ* probably because of safety concerns due to the unrest in Iraq at the time. In April 2009, when Laurie Rush was able to visit Uruk, she found that the scale was completely wrong. It is an excellent lesson learned emphasizing the argument that specialists, in this case academics, have to be consulted whenever possible. See more in the paragraph on training and education.

Key Elements for an Effective Cultural Property Protection Strategy Found in This Case

The Uruk case study contains several important elements that play a role when implementing cultural property protection in the context of military operations. These elements apply for preparations in peacetime as well as when the troops are in theater. I will mention them and explain their role in the case study as well as their relevance for the military implementation of cultural property protection in general. The essentials identified are civil military cooperation; cultural property officers; handover procedures;

---

[13] See ⟨http://www.britishmuseum.org/PDF/Iraq%20Report_with%20images.pdf⟩ [21 August 2011].

Figure 15. Looted Grave in Warka, January 2004. Photograph reproduced with permission from the Royal Netherlands Navy Marine Corps.

legal obligations and implications that can include the aspect of military necessity; economic implications; military incentives when implementing cultural property protection; looting, illicit traffic and the link with security; financing and training and education.

Figure 16. The Dutch Patrol including CIMIC team members on site in Uruk, September 2003. Photo by Joris Kila.

Figure 17. Dutch CIMIC Cultural Property Officers in Uruk, at the top of the big Ziggurat. Photo by Joris Kila.

CPP and Civil Military Cooperation

In theater, cultural property protection and cultural emergency response in times of conflict (and sometimes disaster) take place, for the large part, in a civil-military context. In Uruk, the military worked together with local civilians—a form of civil-military cooperation (CIMIC). However there are legal implications when combatants work together with non-combatants since they both differ in status under the Geneva Conventions. More research by both civil and military legal experts is desired on this matter. In general, countries attempt to implement cultural property protection through civil-military cooperation or civil affairs branches, which both traditionally operate mainly on a tactical and operational level. So-called "functional specialists" can be deployed when expertise that is not available within the standing armed forces is needed, as in the case of cultural property protection. In Uruk CIMIC functional specialists were used by the Dutch armed forces. Both Iraq and the Netherlands are parties to the Hague Convention of 1954, so there was a legal obligation for cultural property protection in line with international humanitarian law.

Cultural Property Officers

Implementation of cultural property protection through Civil Military Co-operation (CIMIC or CA) brings restraints. Due to the NATO AJP-9 CIMIC doctrine, any implementation must be in support of the (field) Commander's mission. However, cultural property protection is always mandatory under IHL. This discrepancy can give rise to conflicts of interest: some commanders tend to use the military necessity excuse for not paying attention to cultural property protection or consider it a good career move to only make high-visibility quick-impact project statements (painting schools) instead of implementing measures for the protection of cultural property. Such conflicts of interest can be avoided by giving cultural property protection a permanent, dedicated position within the Ministry of Defence. Personnel that fill such positions should be involved, or give at least advice, in planning procedures and be an integrated capability linked to operations and coordination with civilian institutions. A good example of ministry-wide implementation of cultural property protection by "official cultural property" officers is found within the Austrian Federal Army "Bundesheer": the Cultural Property Protection Officer (CPPO). The Austrians describe the CPPO as being in accordance with a provision in their Ministry of Defence for experts and services referring to articles 7 and 25 of the 1954 Hague Convention.

The tasks of this CPPO include securing and keeping respect for cultural property among the military, acting as a commander's cultural property protection advisor and expert, providing training for troops and commanders, and liaising with civilian institutions and experts that deal with cultural property. Furthermore, the CPPO gives advice during planning and is in control of the tactical measures concerning cultural property protection in critical areas. The CPPO is also an advisor and consultant to civil authorities and gives a situation report in his capacity as a member of staff.[14] In the Austrian example, an overall incentive is the fact that all information and recommendations produced are meant to raise awareness and to start debates among military planners, post-war planners, policymakers, military lawyers, academia, and governmental officials.

Handover Procedures

After a military mission, or following the end of a mandate, cultural property protection activities must be properly handed over to local authorities, NGOs, or succeeding military forces as appropriate. The military from a certain country may be redeployed to a different area before the situation is stable enough to hand over to proper civilian bodies and agencies. This has been the case in Iraq. A political decision brought about the redeployment of the Dutch Battle Group from Iraq's Al Muthanna province. As a result, all personnel had to leave but the Dutch military cultural expert who set out the cultural strategies was not allowed by the Dutch MoD to return for a proper handover. Procedures must be developed to hand over cultural rescue activities either to military successors or local authorities when such events occur.

Legal Obligations and Implications

> Manches Herrliche der Welt ist in krieg und Streit zerronnen. Wer beschützet und erhält, hat das grösste Los gewonnen.
>
> Johann Wolfgang Goethe (1749–1832)

Military necessity is often cited as a reason, or excuse, for cultural destruction. The Second Protocol of the 1954 Hague Convention (Article 11-2) states

---

[14] Information from a brochure made in cooperation with the National Defense Academy of the Austrian Armed Forces in Vienna and the Austrian Society of Cultural Property ⟨www.kulturgueterschutz.at⟩ 2006.

that immunity granted to cultural property can be lifted in "exceptional cases of unavoidable military necessity." While such military necessity did not play a role in Uruk, it is still useful to mention it here for the more general role it played in Iraq. For instance: minarets such as those in Samarra were used by snipers, and monuments were utilized to store weapons and keep hostages.[15] The vibrations caused by demolition of Saddam-era ammunition by U.S. soldiers had dramatic effects on the temple complex of Al-Hatra, although in a later stage expert advice helped to lessen the impact of these explosions.[16] Obviously, the problem as to how military necessity is defined, or rather interpreted, remains.

Uruk is an important site of global significance. Sitting at the heart of the Mesopotamian "cradle of civilization," Uruk is considered the birthplace of writing, and of the Epic of Gilgamesh, found on clay tablets in the city. Potentially, Uruk is capable of attracting tourism. The current inhabitants have a different appreciation. For them Uruk is a plot of land that is "owned" by a certain Bedouin tribe that has successfully claimed it through an agreement with other local tribes. Though the head of the tribe realizes the historic importance of his land, it is predominantly seen as a home to the tribe and for small scale agriculture and cattle-breeding. In Al Muthanna most of the inhabitants are Shiia, and the population consists of a mix between Bedouins and farmers and some city folk. Every inhabitant is linked to a tribe (approx. fourteen tribes in total) and every Iraqi owes loyalty to his clan or family before the tribe and the local government. Tourism is not yet seen as a source of income due to the length of Saddam's regime resulting in reluctance among tourists to visit Iraq and the country's political isolation. However, through the German excavators the Bedouins in Uruk/Warka for many years had a regular income working as excavation assistants during the dig season and as site guards throughout the year.

This economic incentive illustrates to a local population the relevance of protecting the site for future excavations and thus keeping options open to generate a more or less stable source of income. Apart from ethical considerations implying that it is wrong to damage national cultural heritage

---

[15] The pinnacle of the minaret was damaged April 1, 2005 by a bomb reportedly placed by insurgents in response to U.S. forces prior use of the minaret as a sniper's nest as from September, 2004; March, 2005, Iraq State Board of Antiquities ordered U.S. forces to vacate the Minaret. ⟨http://www.cemml.colostate.edu/cultural/09476/iraq05--060.html⟩ [10 August 2011].

[16] Stone, Farchakh 2008.

(linked to a national or regional identity) it became clear in my talks with the inhabitants that they were aware that financial rewards for looting were quite meager and unsustainable. In general locals normally get very low prices for antiquities.[17] In this context it was a good decision to continue paying "salaries" for the protection of the site through military channels. In fact this way a win-win situation was created; the locals experienced sustainable income including future perspectives concerning jobs when the excavations are resumed in the future. For civilian military cooperation, the (project-based) financing was legitimized because funds were provided to be spend on food and water and earned by locals guarding cultural property. Finally, the military followed the 1954 Hague Convention since Iraq is a State Party to the Convention and its First Protocol both were ratified by Iraq in December 1967.

Looting, Illicit Traffic and the Link with Security

> Antiquities are the most precious relics the Iraqis possess, showing the world that our country ... is the legitimate offspring of previous civilizations that offered a great contribution to humanity.
>
> – Saddam Hussein in a 1979 speech[18]

Dealing with looting, stealing, and trafficking of cultural objects and subsequently the protection of sites and monuments including preparations in peacetime has to be looked at from multiple angles.[19] Given most recent cases, protection seems only possible with the use of armed civil or military guards combined with technical solutions such as cameras or even satellite observation. Most solutions rely heavily on the military not the least because of military logistics, tools, and access to conflict areas plus (classified) data such as aerial photography. The idea of involving contractors (in these case, mercenaries) as guards has been discussed in a number of expert panels like the yearly military CPP panel at the AIA conferences. However, this idea has been rejected by many for legal and financial reasons. Legal refers to matters of authority in conflict areas and financial refers to the fact that many MoDs and other stakeholders like UNESCO do not

---

[17] Stone, Farchakh 2008, pp. 135–141.

[18] Eakin, Hugh. The Devastation of Iraq's past. July 27, 2008. ⟨http://www.internationalnews.fr/article-21591970.html⟩ [10 August 2011].

[19] Mac Ginty 2004.

have the financial resources to hire contractors. Identification of effective strategies for protection can be hindered by the fact that, especially in troubled times, specific cultural objects are looked upon as national- or group-related and become targets for opposing forces. Here the subject touches the realms of military intelligence and security because as established trading of looted artifacts in war-stricken areas is not seldom practiced by opposing forces. Large numbers of artifacts originating from war areas are looted often commissioned by insurgents.[20] Smuggling routes can be the same as those used for trafficking insurgents, weapons, drugs, and for the export of stolen artifacts. The link with criminality and opposing military forces is good reason to inform all military personnel involved in missions in sensitive areas that buying artifacts is strictly forbidden. At present, the United States uses small illustrated pocket cards with instructions on how to recognize such objects; there are also cultural property playing cards both in the United States and the Netherlands and an Arts, Monuments, and Archives Guide created by the U.S. Civil Affairs.[21] As a general rule, military personnel entering or leaving a mission area are checked by military police.[22]

Looting manifests itself in a variety of guises such as mob looting, systematic looting, and flash looting. All have different causes and catalysts. In the case of Uruk the economical incentive was neutralized by offering (minor) payments for local guards. Looting has a military parallel too; already the Romans allowed their soldiers to plunder as a form of wages, even today the traditional tribal militia in Afghanistan and Pakistan the Lashkar are not paid salaries but share in loot captured from the enemy. They are an exception since modern operations and legislation forbid this form of pay. The whole complex of the looting, stealing, and smuggling of artifacts is, of course, market-driven and based on the international rising demand for antiquities. Since there is only a finite supply of legal objects that are available for trade, any increase can only come from illegal sources.[23]

---

20 A recent example are the looted and stolen objects from Afghanistan, often commissioned by the Taliban, that are smuggled out through the Kandahar Military airport and end up in expensive antique shops in Brussels, Belgium.

21 Heritage Preservation, Pocket Guide for Military personnel, Draft 04-09-07. See also Rush 2010.

22 Olbrys 2007.

23 O'Keefe 1999.

Figure 18. Tools and stolen artifacts from arrested looters in Uruk, January 2004. Photo courtesy of Royal Netherlands Navy Marine Corps.

Financing

In peacetime assessments should be made to allocate funding or detect governmental as well as private possibilities to finance training and research as well as preparations in peacetime for military cultural intervention such as building networks and reach back capabilities. In general, it remains to be determined whether or not the military in charge of certain areas of responsibility have funds at their disposal to spend on the protection of cultural property when operations actually take place. The U.S. military have the U.S. Commanders' Emergency Response Program (CERP) funds and Ambassador's funds; other countries might for example use local embassy funds if they have embassies in countries where operations are carried out. A case of good practice dates from 2004 and took place in Baghdad. Several collections of documents from the Iraqi Libraries and Archives had been damaged during the war. When Baghdad was still relatively secure, civilian experts managed to deep-freeze the objects, which had suffered water and mould damage. Freezing is a commonly used protection technique that preserves documents for final conservation under better circumstances. Apparently the collections started to deteriorate at a certain stage due to electricity failures causing the documents to defrost. Cultural property officers, after assessing the situation, asked for support. As a result, the U.S. Army used CERP funds to provide equipment in the form of a generator-powered freezer truck, and the objects were refrozen in this vehicle. However, civilian military cooperation/civilian affairs (CIMIC/CA) officers and cultural property officers are sometimes confronted with serious criticism from NGOs, IOs and governmental decision makers.[24] Some NGOs consider military emergency aid to be false competition plus they claim that (already earmarked) money that was originally meant to be spent on NGO activities is used. I do not know if this is true for other CIMIC/CA disciplines, but such arguments carry no weight in the case of cultural property protection. Apart from this there are only a limited number of civilian organizations dealing with cultural heritage protection, and on several occasions (Iraq, Afghanistan) security conditions have compelled these organizations to ask for the assistance of militarized experts.

Currently a big challenge for implementing military cultural property protection is the fact that cuts on financial spending appear to be used as an excuse not to implement cultural property protection. This is not only against international (customary) law but also demonstrates the low priority the subject has with some MoDs and military organizations.

Conclusions Concerning the Uruk Case

The case study shows that international cooperation is important for the safeguarding and protection of cultural property. If the information concerning the exact coordinates of Uruk had not been supplied by a civilian stakeholder, in this particular case MacGuire Gibson from the University of Chicago, it would not have been possible to convince the military to pay attention to the site. Of course, coordinates and even aerial pictures are available to the military, but this material is often treated as classified. An admittedly expensive way out might be data supplied by space organizations. Even so, it is expected that in the near future GIS data from the websites of IMCuRWG and the U.S. Combatant Command Historical/Cultural Action Group will be available to selected parties. Utilizing cultural military experts in times of cultural emergency proved to be a good solution since

---

24 Kila 2008, p. 201.

they, unlike civil parties, are less restrained by security or logistic issues. This was clearly the case in the province of Al Muthanna where Uruk is located. At the time of the case study the so-called Coalition Provisional Authority had just started. Consequently, there was no Iraqi government and no law enforcement (apart from tribal local laws). Civil or even national cultural experts are not able to function in such situations.

In addition, the Uruk case shows the need for assessments and desk research prior to launching cultural property protection activities as part of a mission. On top an overview of funding possibilities both external and internal for projects such as Uruk is useful. Financing is currently even more of a problem for Ministries of Defense; for example, the Netherlands MoD regrettably stopped all cultural property protection initiatives including training and education as proposed after a seminar held in The Hague in 2009 under the excuse of financial cutbacks.[25] Since the costs especially when working together internationally are quite low, one can wonder if the real reason is not lack of appreciation and understanding of the subject. Recent events where at this moment cultural heritage is in danger show that it is realistic to prepare for emergencies and civil and military aid to safeguard and protect where possible and in accordance with international legislation.

The Polish Approach in Iraq

Poland deployed militarized archaeologists in Babylon, Iraq.[26] The Polish Multinational Division Central South (MND CS) was alternately based at the site of the ancient temple of Babylon and at the Tell al Uhaimir-Tell Ingharra

---

25 A report was written on the seminar's outcomes including a description of the status of CPP in the Dutch Armed Forces as well as recommendations for the way ahead. Valuable contributions were given by Professor Peter Stone from Newcastle University. The report was meant for the Dutch Chief of Defence. The most significant conclusions were the need for international cooperation and the creation of a small team embedded in the Dutch MoD to assess and implement CPP policies. There has been no follow-up.

26 The information used is based on several talks with a former CIMIC commander of the MND CS, Colonel Knoop (lent out by the Dutch army) and for a substantial part an adaptation of the article of Miroslav Olbryś, Archaeologists on Duty in Iraq, Olbrys 2007, that I reviewed. It is curious that at the time the Polish experts were active in Iraq there apparently was no communication between them and other militarized cultural experts (such as from the Dutch army). I found out much later which experts were active for the MND CS and what they were doing, although they were part of a CIMIC unit lead by a Dutch commander. This demonstrates the need for continuous international communication on the subject, especially with the military.

site. In southern Iraq, MND CS was present near the Tell el-Muqayyar site (ancient Ur).

The Polish zone covered five provinces: An Najaf, Al Qadisiyah, Babil, Karbala', and Wasit. Polish archaeologists have been present in Iraq since November 2003 as civil specialists of the CIMIC unit of the Polish military contingent in Iraq to document and protect archaeological sites and monuments located within the MND CS area of responsibility.[27] The archaeologists cooperated with their Iraqi colleagues and the MND CS staff on issues concerning preservation and maintenance of excavated and partially reconstructed monuments.

The conditions of several archaeological sites were determined by experts embedded in military helicopters and through the use of military satellite photographs. Whenever possible, aerial and ground reconnaissance of archaeological sites was carried out. Aerial inspections of the Babylon site took place in July and November 2004. In February 2005, reconnaissance of archaeological sites located in the southeastern part of Al Qadisiyah province and in the western part of Dhi Qar province was conducted to assess the condition of sites like Shuruppak, Adab, Kisurra, Umma, Zabalam, and Isin, Sumerian cities that had been heavily looted. Other archaeological sites in the region, like Nippur and Tell es Sadoum (ancient Marad), were visited in convoys.

Babylon suffered from damage caused by heavy vehicles and the storage of containers in the immediate neighborhood of its monuments. This damage was done by coalition forces. The most famous example involved military personnel who indiscriminately loaded huge bags with rubble from the site, and then used them for enforcements for the camp. Cultural affairs units could have helped avoid this had military planners been trained in this subject matter in peacetime and had more cultural units been available in wartime. Another mistake was the enlargement of the existing helicopter landing ground, in which the leveling work affected an area with ancient remains. In addition, pits dug into tell slopes to obtain sand needed in defensive constructions resulted in irreversible stratigraphical destruction. Because of the construction of watchtowers, part of the terrain was leveled. Fuel tanks were dug into the ground near the Greek theater. Other military fortifications included the digging of ditches near the ziggurat of Babylon

27 From November 2003 to April 2005, six Polish archaeologists worked in Iraq on six-month contracts in agreement with the Polish Ministries of Culture, Foreign Affairs, and Defence. Through a bilateral request, the CIMIC unit had two Dutch commanders successively lent out as augmentees.

Figure 19. Babylon from a military helicopter
January 2004. Photo by H. Knoop.

in February 2004. MND CS military camps experienced problems with military personnel involved with illegal trading in ancient objects; actions were undertaken in cooperation with the military police to prevent illegal sales to military personnel. Archaeologists advised on checking baggage of military and civil personnel returning home.

Polish archaeologists and military specialists published a report in November 2004 assessing the condition of monuments in Babylon.[28] From December 11–13, 2004, a meeting of the International Audit Commission took place at the Babylon site in order to assess its condition, based on the report prepared by Polish archaeologists. Participating in the meeting were representatives of Iraq's Ministry of Culture headed by Mr. Borhan Shaker; Dr. Miriam Omran Mousa of the SBAH (State Board of Antiquities and Heritage) Babylon Regional Office; Dr. John Curtis, an expert on Mesopotamian

[28] Miroslav Olbryś, T. Burda, and A. Dolatowska, "Report on the current condition of the Babylon archaeological site (the military Camp Alpha site)," ⟨http://www.mk.gov.pl/website/index.jsp.catId=340⟩. The report was also published on CD (Warsaw 2005).

archaeology from the British Museum; representatives of the multinational forces in Iraq; and the MND CS. Dr. Curtis was invited by the Ministry of Culture and prepared a report on his observations.[29] The document also served as a starting point for handing over the site to Iraq's Ministry of Culture. The MND CS troops left Babylon on December 22, 2004. A document for transferring the former Camp Alpha to the Ministry of Culture was signed in Baghdad on December 31, 2004. From that date, Iraqi archaeological police were in charge of site security, utilizing part of the military infrastructure that was donated and left behind, such as the habitable containers, watchtowers, and fencing.

In 2005, archaeological assessments were carried out in the eastern part of Al Qadisiyah province. This province was secured from September 2003 until April 2004 by a Spanish brigade that was part of MND CS forces. Major archaeological sites in the region, mainly of Sumerian and Babylonian date, were inspected, with large-scale devastation observed at Ishan Bahriyat (Zibliyat).

In March 2005, the condition of archaeological sites in the province was assessed and proposals for immediate and long-term protective actions were written.[30] Aerial reconnaissance confirmed the looting of many archaeological sites. The ruins of Tell Fara (Shuruppak), Ishan Bahriyat (Isin) and Tell Abu Hatab (Kisurra) were found to be full of craters from continuous and methodical illicit digging that neither coalition forces nor the local antiquity service were able to prevent.[31] Cultural institution infrastructure and documentation had been destroyed. In general, Iraq lacked a credible database containing information on monuments, precise locations, and general descriptions. The Al Qadisiyah Regional Office of the SBAH was understaffed and almost unarmed. The local archaeological police had very limited resources at their disposal to patrol the entire province and faced the same problems as the SBAH. Consequently, operational effectiveness was low. A follow-up inspection of the Nippur archaeological site revealed that the introduction of protective measures by the Spanish brigade at the

---

[29] See John Curtis, "Report on the meeting at Babylon 11th–13 December 2004," British Museum, ⟨http://www.britishmuseum.org/the_museum/museum_in_the_world/middle_east_programme/iraq_project/babylon_report_2004-5.aspx⟩ [18 August 2011]. Curtis 2004.

[30] Miroslav Olbryś, Raport otwarcia: Stan dziedzictwa kultury i jego ochrony w prowincji Kadisija, Irak, oraz propozycje działań pilnych i długookresowych [Opening report: The Status of Cultural Heritage and its Protection in Al Qadisiyah Province, Iraq, and Proposals of Urgent and Long-Term Activities], (typescript paper submitted to the MND CS command, March 2005).

[31] Cindy Ho, "Heritage Lost: Looting of Archaeological Sites Continues in Iraq," Saving Antiquities for Everyone, Blog (first published in 2004), ⟨http://www.savingantiquities.org/feature_page.php?featureID=7⟩ [18 August 2011].

end of 2003 eliminated plundering and illicit digging. The entire site had been encircled by more than four miles of wire entanglements. Twenty-four police officers were stationed in a new police station and have been patrolling the site twenty-four hours a day. Finally, five police stations were built for the archaeological police in Al Qadisiyah near the American Mission excavation house. Helicopters of Spanish and Polish coalition forces flew regularly over the site. Helicopter flights over endangered archaeological sites have proven to be one of the most effective measures for preventing illicit digging.

Polish archaeologists at Camp Alpha undertook several projects in cooperation with Iraqi experts from the SBAH and Babil University in Al Hilla and Al Qadisiyah University in Ad Diwaniyah. Most activities were financed from the MND CS CERP. Since early 2004, they have also been involved in the reestablishment of the Iraqi archaeological police (i.e. Facility Protection Service, or FPS).[32] This resulted in Babil and Al Qadisiyah provinces in the creation of archaeological police units with 350 and 100 men respectively by early 2005. The archaeological police are intended to support a system of civil unarmed guards (*haras*, in Arabic), recruited from among local communities and living on or nearby the sites that they are supposed to guard. The Department of Museums supervises this new unit.

Meetings with archaeological police unit commanders in several provinces helped to identify essentials, like training and the need for means of communication, cars, uniforms, and weapons. New and restored police stations were also marked as indispensable.

Archaeological sites were assessed in terms of priority. A list of twenty-eight sites in the provinces of Babil, Al Qadisiyah, Karbala', and Wasit was prepared in cooperation with Iraqi archaeologists. The most important sites were fenced off and further protected by occasional military patrols. In December 2003, provisional barbed wire fences were installed around the most important monuments of the part of the Babylon site located inside Camp Alpha. Following consultation with the SBAH office for Babil province, the damaged and partly torn down fence around the archaeological site at Tell al Uhaimir was rebuilt in July 2004. Warning signs were also installed as well as a habitable shelter for the guards. Shelters and temporary protection installations were set up around the ruins of the Summer Palace of Babylon at Barnum. At the Birs Nimrud site, observation towers were erected in late 2004. Installation of a barbed wired fence around the

---

32 Olbrys, 2007.

western part of the site and a shelter to serve as a police station at Tell es Sadoum took place in spring 2005.

Projects aimed at restoring the infrastructure of museums and local antiquity inspectorates were implemented in the Babylon Museum, the Hammurabi Museum, and the SBAH office for Babil province. Further activities included equipping the SBAH offices with computer hardware and software (an Iraqi priority request). Twenty Iraqi workers were trained in basic computer operation. Additionally, the SBAH office in Babil received a professional theodolite and a set of multimedia equipment (a digital video camera, notebook, and multimedia projector) to facilitate inventory work. The Department of Archaeology at Babil University in Al Hilla was provided with similar equipment. Several projects were realized to supply a detachment of the archaeological police in Babil province located at Babylon with individual equipment, including uniforms, helmets, bulletproof vests, metal detectors, and walkie-talkies. In the spring of 2005, archaeological police in Al Qadisiyah province were in the progress of being supplied with basic equipment.

There is still a debate on the question of whom or what caused certain damages inflicted on the Babylon site. Both the Polish and the U.S. Army deny responsibility, but archaeologists from the United Kingdom and Poland found damage they claim was military in nature. Furthermore, considering that McGuire Gibson had attempted to supply the Pentagon with a list of important cultural heritage sites in Iraq prior to the war, had the U.S. military and coalition forces used this list, it would have known that the sites in question were historically and culturally sensitive. Had there been international military cooperation on cultural affairs issues between the Poles and the United States, for example then they could have agreed upon a standard operating procedure. Unfortunately some events played out as they did due to a lack of coordination between the different international units and a lack of education, awareness, and training in issues regarding archaeology, history, and cultural heritage protection.

A Case Example of (Unintended) Violation the Hague Convention: Hescos

The practical example described here is a violation to the Hague Convention: Article 3. Safeguarding of cultural property Article 4. Respect for cultural property Article 5.2 Occupation Article 7. Military measures and the Geneva Convention IV articles 33 and 53.

The problem is the use of so-called Hescos, which are large bags that are filled with sand/rubble to serve as barriers for military camps and fortifications they are also known as Concertainer™ Barriers and made by the UK Company Hercules Engineering Solutions Consortium; in short, HESCO.

Cases are known that these bags were filled with deposits from archaeological sites containing pottery sherds, bones, etc. The soil in an archaeological site represents all kinds of important data that are only useful when extracted by experts from their original context.

For instance, earth layers can give information through stratigraphical data, for example, pottery fragments can serve as an important dating tool when found in the original context of the soil. When such deposits are used for filling hescos the context of the site is disturbed and it is very difficult or even impossible to be used for archeological research. Even worse were cases where after a complaint was made about the use of archaeological deposits these deposits were replaced and dumped on another archaeological site thus causing a second disturbing the context. John Curtis Keeper of the department of the Ancient Near East at the British Museum gives examples in his *Report on Meeting at Babylon 11th–13th December 2004.*[33] According to different sources including Dr. Curtis the military detachment at Babylon in June 2003 was small but continued to grow through the second half of 2003 and the first part of 2004 so that, by the summer of 2004, it occupied an area of 150 hectares and housed 2000 soldiers.[34]

In preparation for the meeting the three archaeologists attached to the Polish forces Miroslav Olbrys, Agnieszka Dolatowska and Tomasz Burda had prepared a document entitled *Report Concerning the Condition of the Preservation of the Babylon Archaeological Site*. As the title suggests, this document is essentially a condition report, and it contains many photographs that provide an invaluable record of the state of the site in November 2004. Therefore, Curtis sometimes also refers to the "Polish Report" as a source to verify his observations. I will quote some segments of Curtis' report dealing with the misuse of deposits in hescos in Babylon. Apart from the hesco issues, Curtis found that large areas of the site had been covered in gravel brought in from the outside, compacted, and sometimes chemically treated to provide helipads, car parks, and accommodation and storage areas. In addition, there are reports that places were damaged by the use of (later

---

33 Curtis 2004.

34 Curtis 2011.

Figure 20. Militaries preparing hescos. Photo © Hesco Bastion Ltd.

Figure 21. An aerial view of Babylon in 2004 on the left parts of the military camp. Photo by H. Knoop.

removed) concrete slabs; other damages are described in the paragraph on the Polish approach. The status of future information about these damaged areas is seriously compromised.

Babylon is undoubtedly one of the most important archaeological sites in the world, and was the capital city of two of the most famous kings of antiquity, Hammurabi (1792–1750 BC) who introduced the world's first law code, and Nebuchadnezzar (604–562 BC) who built the Hanging Gardens of Babylon, one of the Seven Wonders of the World. In the report the condition of several parts of the site are investigated they bear sometimes modern names like the Reno Gate, Warsaw Gate, and Tent City.

"Reno Gate"

[...]

3. To the west of the Reno Gate there is a trench *c.*30 m × 10 m, up to 2 m deep, that is said to have been dug to fill conix containers (HESCO bags).
4. There are further large cuttings to the south of the barbed wire perimeter that we were not allowed to visit.
5. To the south of the Reno Gate for a distance of about 200 m the road is lined by HESCO bags that have clearly been filled with deposits from the Babylon site, containing sherds, bones, etc.

Tent City #2

In the northern part of Tent City #2 there is much disturbance in an area used as an ammunition store. What remains is a horseshoe-shaped berm made up of deposits emptied from HESCO bags. These deposits clearly come from archaeological contexts. Much sand, said to have been brought in from the desert, has also been deposited in this area. See the *Polish Report*, figure on p. 31.

"Warsaw Gate"

1. Outside the so-called Warsaw Gate, which is in the north-west corner of the camp there are 2 trenches, each *c.*20 m long. See the *Polish Report*, figure on p. 16. In the piles of spoil alongside the trenches there are many fragments of brick, some with inscriptions of Nebuchadnezzar.
2. About 200 m south-west of the Warsaw Gate are HESCO bags protecting an open storage area with floodlights that are filled with earth containing many fragments of brick, some inscribed ...

Around the site, there are thousands of sandbags and HESCO barriers/conix containers. Originally, these sandbags and HESCO barriers were apparently filled with earth scooped up from the Babylon archaeological site, and the presence of potsherds and bones in the bags is a testimony to the archaeological nature of the deposits used. I was informed that on 3 November 2003, an order was issued requiring that the bags should only be filled with sand and earth brought in from outside Babylon, but this is in effect substituting one problem for another. By bringing in large quantities of sand and earth from elsewhere (some of these probably in themselves archaeological deposits), the deposits at Babylon will be irrevocably contaminated.

John Curtis Keeper, Department of the Ancient Near East, The British Museum.

The Hesco problem can be solved by good training in peacetime and by including cultural experts in assessment missions prior to a military mission and by (temporarily) including military cultural experts in a mission. The problem should be addressed in military field guides and training.

The Case of the Iraqi National Library

An example of what can go wrong with libraries and military is the following case that took place in Baghdad on 8 August 2007.[35] According to the director of the Iraqi National Archives and Library (INLA), a group of Iraqi national guards broke into the National Library and Archive's main building. In doing this they violated the instructions of the Council of Ministers, which clearly assert that Iraqi security and armed forces cannot enter any state-run institution without a prior approval of the government and the concerned authorities. The national guards acted without consulting the director Dr. Saad Eskander and entered the building by force. Because there was a four-day curfew period, the director was not able to go the INLA to speak with the INLA's own guards, who did not know how to react. Dr. Eskander talked to the commander of the national guards by phone, asking him to leave the building immediately. He refused to evacuate the building, claiming that he had orders from his superiors and the Americans to

[35] Sources: email from Jeff Spurr Harvard university to the author dated 8 August 2007, letter to Spurr from Saad Eskander director Iraqi National Library and Archive's dated 8 August 2007, Looting Fear as Iraqi State Library seized in the Guardian 10 August 2007.

occupy the INLA. The commander also stated that the national guards wanted to protect Shi'í visitors of the holy shrines of al-Kadhimiyah, which is situated thirty kilometers away from the INLA. Apparently, according to Dr. Eskander on Monday (6 August), a U.S. military patrol entered the INLA's main building also without his permission. The commander of the patrol interrogated the INLA's guards and ordered them to show their IDs. In July, U.S. soldiers entered the INLA three times. Obviously, the actions of U.S. soldiers have encouraged Iraqi national guards to do the same, that is, entering and then occupying the building by force.

U.S. authorities in Baghdad were contacted indirectly with the request to stop the violations and the unlawful actions of both U.S. soldiers and Iraqi national guards against the INLA and its staff but showed no interest in the matter according to Dr. Eskander who asked for support from his international colleagues asking them to protest on the matter to all authorities.

This is an example of a situation that can happen when there is no or bad communication between the military, governmental, and civilian parties. First, there is the fact that apparently Iraqi militaries used their U.S. colleagues as an excuse to achieve their own goal that in this case involved a cultural property. Second, both U.S. and Iraqi military violated the Hague Convention by invading the cultural property mentioned. Third, there was apparently no military necessity proven. The only excuse was protection of Shi'í but this was not very likely considering the distance from the holy shrines. Probably there was a strategic interest concerning the building or the status of the INLA's own guards. However, matters could have been solved through good liaison with the U.S. militaries. It is remarkable that in this case a situation arises where cultural heritage matters are mixed with ethnical and religious as well as military matters. This shows the complexity of CH protection and how important it is to organize training and develop procedures and good contacts already in peacetime.

Egypt February 12–16th 2011

In January 2011, turmoil started in Egypt. Large demonstrations took place in the Tahrir Square in Cairo. After many years of authoritarian ruling and inspired by the Tunisian uprisings, the Egyptian people were fed up and wanted to get rid of Mubarak and his clique and their corruption. At a certain stage, the headquarters of President Mubarak's National Democratic Party headquarters went up in flames and people started to worry about the

Figure 22. Al-Watan, Saudi Arabia, 31 January 2011.

adjacent National Egyptian Museum that fortunately seemed to have been spared by the flames.

However quite unexpected and unforeseen by the international archaeological community, rumors started to appear about lootings in the National Museum and damaging of antiquities and archaeological sites. These reports triggered reminiscences of the Iraq lootings that are addressed in the introduction and first part of this book.

Several cultural experts from within the international community that had been involved in Iraq were afraid that the Iraq disaster would repeat itself in Egypt. This could only be prevented or at least controlled and registered if this time the international cultural heritage community would act. Via all sorts of entrances and routes, attempts were made to contact high officials in institutions that are considered to be first responsible to take action in the spirit of the 1954 Hague Convention. The International Military Cultural Resources Working Group (IMCuRWG) and ANCBS succeeded to send a direct appeal to UNESCO's Assistant-Director General for Culture who is also director of the World Heritage Centre. The urgent request to UNESCO was to immediately set out an assessment mission to Egypt or at least support or strengthen such a mission if this would be initiated by

IMCuRWG and the ANCBS. Though it was checked and confirmed that the message was received and read, no answer was given nor any mission undertaken by UNESCO. This corresponds with the presumptions stated in this research in the paragraph on international organizations relating to the apparent inability or unwillingness of UNESCO to act in what is generally considered an effective way during cultural crises.

Due to UNESCO's silence, and also because of the time pressure, IMCuRWG and ANCBS decided to take immediate steps by sending out a mission to assess the situation and register possible damages. A second objective was to give a signal from the international community that criminal offenses against cultural property in times of turmoil in a (relative) power vacuum would at least be registered. The official report of the mission is included as Appendix 6.

Since rumors and reports about theft and lootings not only increased but also seemed to extend to the entire country it was opportune to travel to Egypt within the shortest notice possible. On February 5, it was decided to start the assessment on the 12th of February, meaning that there was only one week to make preparations. Both the insecure circumstances and the goal of the mission necessitated a small team that could travel low-profile and, due to its size, was flexible. In this perspective, it seemed good to have the mission conducted by cultural heritage experts with military expertise. Two persons qualified: Karl von Habsburg the President of the Association of National Committees of the Blue Shield (ANCBS) and Joris Kila, chair of the International Military Cultural Resources Work Group (IMCuRWG). Thomas Schuler, who is chair of the Disaster Relief Task Force (DRTF), acted as reach-back capability (see Part I for more about the reach-back system). In practice, this meant media research, liaising with academics and keeping the team informed. He operated from Berlin.

Still it was difficult to estimate the situation on the ground because of the short time available for preparation and since, as reported, the circumstances were chaotic. Many embassies in Cairo issued travel warnings and many foreigners were evacuated. In addition, there were practical implications, for example, strong rumors that all cameras would be confiscated upon arrival. This raised the question whether to travel as tourists, scientists, or civil military experts. No clear answer to this question could be found, therefore the team improvised while relying on their own contacts and assistance from the Austrian diplomatic representatives in Cairo including the Austrian Defense attaché.[36]

---

[36] The Dutch defense attaché did not respond.

The Austrians provided the team with an Egyptian driver who could be trusted and would provide for pick up from the airport. In addition, a "safe" hotel was booked in Dokki a part of Cairo away from the Tahrir Square. The team left from Vienna on February 12 and with the intention to stay in Egypt until February 16 2011 unless changes in the situation would necessitate a longer stay.

Before departure, some appointments were made in advance with Egyptian connections within the respective networks. Among them an Egyptian affiliate from WATCH and the office manager of the Netherlands Flemish Institute in Cairo; the institute itself was still closed at the time the mission was planned. The Austrian Embassy invited the team for a gathering with both the Ambassador and cultural experts from the Austrian Institute of Archaeology in Cairo.

The very evening before the team (to be referred to as we) travelled to Egypt, Hosni Mubarak stepped down as President, the Parliament was dissolved, and the Constitution declared invalid. This relieved the tensions somewhat and made arrival easier. In fact, upon arrival all power was with the military, making the head of the Armed Forces Supreme Council, Field Marshal Tantawi, the actual ruler of the country.

From the perspective of this publication, this was an interesting situation since it is argued that in a situation of conflict, the military are in charge or the first present also when it comes to protecting cultural heritage. Furthermore, strategies discussed in the first part of this book include building networks and reach-back in peacetime to be utilized in times of emergency as well as during theater assessments. Consequently, the Egypt case was a test case to see if and to what extent certain mechanisms described function in practice.

Nevertheless, conditions were unsafe; the security system in Egypt was still not really in place. The police in Cairo had literally vanished after the beginning of the demonstrations. Reasons mentioned in the press varied. According to some the police were identified with the former regime; some also argued was that they were on strike because of long time underpayment. Police functions were, to a certain extent, taken over by the military and by spontaneously created neighborhood watch groups.

Though the team wished to investigate as much as possible, there were limitations both timewise and due to actual conditions; for example, all sites and museums were closed. Therefore, the team did not inspect the National Museum at Tahrir Square. Many international and national experts as well as the press were already all over the Museum case; besides, the team members did not want to repeat what happened in Iraq where everybody

Figure 23. The author at the Tahrir Square in Cairo the evening of 12 February 2011. Photo by Karl von Habsburg.

concentrated on the looting of the National Museum in Baghdad while in the same period a large number of archaeological sites were looted.

Kila and von Habsburg arrived in Cairo in the afternoon of February 12. In the evening, the area of the Egyptian Museum and Tahrir Square was visited to get an impression of the situation. At the time, a night curfew still existed and the area of the museum was packed with military and tanks.

The next day, February 13, the Dutch Flemish Institute was visited. Although it was officially closed, a small emergency staff was still present. From the Institute it was possible to reach an official of the Supreme Council of Antiquities (SCA) in Saqqara, who confirmed attempts of looting but denied anything had been stolen. An attempt was made to obtain solid information about the situation in the Kharga Oasis where supposedly a lot of street fighting and looting was going on. No details were known. Later communication with experts in the Dakhla Oasis, which is close to Kharga, confirmed that nothing serious happened in Kharga. In fact, the team was repeatedly confronted with a constant stream of contradictory information about the cultural heritage situation. Many stories appeared to be driven by complex theories, fantasy, or propaganda. Clearly to obtain objective high quality information it was necessary to concentrate on the archaeological sites around Cairo that had mostly not been visited by independent experts since the beginning of the unrests. The idea was that less information of of good quality is more effective than more information of a dubious nature. A first trip was undertaken to Memphis for which occasion the team was joined by the Director of the Austrian Archaeological Institute in Cairo, Dr. Irene Forstner-Müller, who is an Egyptologist.

A car with diplomatic number plates from the Austrian Institute was used, which could be of help to gain access to closed sites. Actually, this was an encouragement to visit Saqqara as well. Saqqara is in the same direction as Memphis though a bit further. The team first arrived in Saqqara or in fact in front of the entrance of the necropolis. However, armed guards prohibited entrance and the team was sent away. "Do not try Memphis" was the advice, "you will not be allowed access." This did not prevent the group from going there anyway, and miraculously they succeeded in talking themselves into the open-air museum mainly because of the official car and the Arabic language skills of Dr. Forstner-Müller.

The museum was supposed to be looted, but, fortunately, no visible signs of damage or theft were found. This was confirmed by the fact that the souvenir shops on the museum terrain were intact without any traces of disturbance. Much later there was a report about a warehouse near the museum complex that could have been looted, but this looting could not be checked nor confirmed.

While still in Memphis, an email from the Minister of Antiquities, Dr. Zahi Hawass, arrived. Von Habsburg and Kila were invited for a meeting that same day. This more or less came to the mission's rescue because without any permission from high-ranking officials it would be virtually impossible to get access to the sites that definitively had to be checked; any permit had to come from Dr. Hawass. After rushing back to Cairo, von Habsburg and Kila went to the Supreme Council of Antiquities (SCA) building that still served as the office of Dr. Hawass who was the former head of the SCA. Surprisingly there were massive demonstrations going on around the building, so the team had to use a small side entrance, and even there they had to squeeze their way in through angry demonstrators.

In the waiting room of the minister's office, a television crew of Sky News was met and the team was interviewed on the activities of ANCBS and IMCuRWG. Then a short meeting with Dr. Zahi Hawass took place; he asked for the team's wishes and it permission was granted for visits to Saqqara, Dahshur, and Abusir. Immediately a connection was made with the head

Figure 24. Memphis open air museum with intact souvenir shops. 14 Feburary 2011. Photo by Joris Kila.

Figure 25. The office of the SCA besieged on 13 February 2011. Photo by Joris Kila.

inspector of SCA for the Saqqara region, who happened to be in the ministry. It was agreed to meet the next day at ten o'clock in the morning at his office in Saqqara.

The next day started with a bit of frustration since it was impossible to find an Egyptologist to accompany the group as a specialist. Dr. Forstner-Müller had to leave for Aswan, so she was not available. Apparently the Egyptologists that normally would have been around either had left with the political turmoil, were somewhere else in Egypt, or were not willing to come. Luckily, the best replacement one could wish for was found. The Office Manager of the Dutch Institute, Tilly Mulder, accompanied the team. Her command of the Arabic language is almost of a native speaker. In addition, the driver was critical to the purpose of the mission; he was always sitting on the outside with the guards and listening to their version of events. This type of cooperation is important to consider for future missions.

After arriving at the entrance gate to Saqqara, similar problems occurred as the day before. The head inspector that supposedly would be there to meet was not present and was not expected to come, either, since it turned out to be a holiday. Luckily, his mobile number was at hand; when he was called, he turned out to be still sleeping. Nevertheless, after waking up he directed the team to the inspector in charge of the Saqqara site office, who, after a long palaver, received the group. It was difficult to convince this inspector that there were no journalists or tourists in the team. He was presented with the cultural heritage card decks and then became much more open and forward. The inspector revealed information about several break-ins that happened in Saqqara; it was a first-hand account since he had already stayed overnight in Saqqara for a certain period. Apparently, the break-ins started in the night of Saturday 29 January when the police had left and about 100 people, mostly local youngsters, forced their way in and started to force open locks. Some intruders were armed while the guards had no weapons since they normally rely on the police to take care of matters.

Apparently, these guards receive a salary of 270 pounds, or about thirty-eight euro, per month; they are not motivated to risk their lives for such low salaries. According to the inspector's account, the looters forced the locks of the tombs of Nefer and the two brothers. The doors of the pyramid of Pepi I had also been forced. During the following two days, the lootings went on, usually between five o'clock and nine o'clock in the evening. Finally, on January 30, the military came, but just to secure the storage area, especially Storerooms 1 and 2, which contain the most valuable pieces. The police only returned on February 12. According to the inspector's account, the Imhotep museum located next to the ticket office stayed untouched. This could not be checked since it was closed; the same was true of the storage area next to the main office complex of the inspectorate. The SCA inspector reported that at the French excavation premises the perpetrators broke through a new wall instead of the door, but the excavation stayed untouched. After this briefing, the team went into the necropolis to see things for themselves.

The Necropolis of Saqqara; An Introduction

Courtiers of the First Dynasty pharaohs started a cemetery consisting of mastabas on the northern tip of the Saqqara plateau.[37] From the Second Dynasty on, royal tombs were constructed at Saqqara as well. Not much is known of these subterranean structures. The last king of this reign was buried in Abydos like First Dynasty pharoahs, but he still constructed a rectangular enclosure at Saqqara. This set the example for his successor Djoser of the Third Dynasty (c. 2630–2611 BC); his funerary complex comprises a similar enclosure. In its center is located an architectural innovation: the Step Pyramid, made of six mastabas piled up on top of each other. The rest of Djoser's enclosure contains temples and dummy buildings. After Djoser, step pyramids rapidly developed into what we call normal pyramids. Simultaneously, the enclosures became smaller and merely surrounded a pyramid temple joined to a valley temple through a sloping causeway. Most kings selected other Memphite cemeteries for their pyramids like Giza and Abusir north of Saqqara or Dahshur and Meidum to the south. Still, Saqqara features the remains of the step pyramid of Sekhemkhet (Third Dynasty), the mastaba tomb of Shepseskaf (Fourth Dynasty, 2472–2467 BC), the proper pyramids of Userkaf, Djedkarê, and Unas (Fifth Dynasty, 2465–2323 BC), and all the kings of the Sixth Dynasty (Teti, Pepi I, Merenrê, Pepi II, 2323–2150 BC). The latter five monuments contain samples of the oldest religious texts from ancient Egypt, the so-called Pyramid Texts.

By the time of Pepi II, many areas of the Saqqara plateau were already lined with mastaba tombs of Memphite courtiers and officials. During the Middle Kingdom (2040–1640 BC) and New Kingdom (1550–1070), both the capital and the major cemeteries moved further south. Only two more mud brick pyramids were built at Saqqara in the Thirteenth Dynasty. Large-scale construction at Saqqara was not resumed until the middle of the

[37] The pharaohs of the first Egyptian royal Dynasty (c. 3000–2800 BC) chose to be buried at Abydos in Upper Egypt. The historical information about Saqqara used here is an adaptation from the historical section on Saqqara to be found on the website Saqqara.nl that is an initiative of the Friends of Saqqara Foundation in the Netherlands.

Eighteenth Dynasty (from about 1400 BC onwards) when the pharaohs again devoted more attention to Memphis. High officials, priests, and artisans built tombs dispersed all over the plateau. These were of a new type: a freestanding chapel or temple, sometimes with open courtyard and pylon gateway, with rock-cut burial chambers deep underground. There are also completely rock-cut tombs along the edge of the Saqqara escarpment. After two centuries, attention shifted to the new capitals in the Nile Delta. During the last millennium BC, a great number of shaft tombs were cut, until the whole substructure of the desert was honeycombed. The same period witnessed religious activity on the Saqqara plateau. The site developed into a place of pilgrimage centered on the burial place of the sacred Apis bulls of Memphis (the Serapeum). The latter consists of vast underground galleries with burial chambers for the individual bulls. Similar galleries were cut for more animal cults, for example, cows, baboons, cats, dogs, and ibises. This upsurge of the traditional Egyptian cults was followed by Christianity, which brought several monastic communities to the desert of Saqqara. After about 850 AD, the plateau was deserted and most of its monuments were gradually covered by drift sand.

The Saqqara terrain is quite large and difficult to explore and assess for those not experienced and familiar with the site. This and the fact we had no Egyptologist accompanying us made matters difficult. However, there was no alternative and only limited time, therefore we proceeded and did the best we could given the circumstances. From the Dutch perspective, there was special reason to go to Saqqara. The "Leiden" excavations at Saqqara were reported to have been looted.

According to the leader of these excavations, which are carried out by the Leiden Museum and Leiden University, some doors of warehouses had been damaged in attempts to force them or break them open. Supposedly, these doors were repaired using new wooden planks. The Dutch excavation leader Dr. Raven thought that the looters would have created a mess when surging for treasures.[38] He explained that the smaller corner and center chapels of the tombs were partly restored with new bricks, doors, and locks and currently used as on site warehouses. Dr. Raven presumed that the intruders most probably created a mess by emptying baskets containing pottery and pottery sherds as well as skeleton fragments and other small objects. He added that some of these will probably have been stolen during the burglary

[38] Source: correspondence of the author with Dr. Raven dated 9 February 2011 and several phone conversations.

and admitted that most objects were already studied and registered. In that case, the damage is less since the real important finds such as fragments of sculptures and reliefs were taken some time ago to the central warehouse near the Imhotep museum that was supposed to be untouched. Still when materials not registered nor studied are thrown aside and mixed with other objects by intruders, the archaeological context in which they were found and kept is lost and they become scientifically worthless. It is of utmost importance that nobody but the excavators does the cleaning or tidying because they are the only ones to judge if at least some of the objects remained in their original context. The Leiden team especially feared for the tomb complex of Maya that comprises beautiful colored reliefs. It took four years to restore these and reposition them in a concrete cellar under the courtyard.[39]

First, the assessment team visited the tomb of Mere Ruka and found it undamaged. Actually, this could be verified by Joris Kila who had been there not too long ago in 2009. Next was the tomb or actually the collapsed pyramid of Teti: the team went via a corridor to the antechamber and the burial chamber and it looked undamaged. Then the tomb of Ka-Gmni was passed—the door was opened by vandals, now it is welded shut; supposedly there is no damage, but this could not be confirmed.

Our next stop was the Unas Pyramid, figure 27, which was especially opened for the mission. It had obviously been closed for at least a year or so. The shaft that leads to the entrance door was filled with garbage and rubble. It looked undamaged and nothing seemed changed since Joris Kila was there in 2009.

On the way to the Maya complex the tomb of Isisnofret, granddaughter of Ramses II, was passed. The burial place was closed, the door was welded, and the tomb supposedly unharmed. When we arrived at the Maya complex, figure 28, we saw that though the warehouse chapels had clear signs of vandalism such as broken locks and broken pieces of wood, it did not give the impression of being heavily nor systematically looted. This was in correspondence with the information Leiden supplied. Interesting to note is that the mission members were told it was impossible to visit the tomb of Maya since everything was locked. However when they came *in situ*, the door was secured with a piece of wire. The entrance to the famous underground reliefs was sealed with an SCA seal, so they could not be seen. The inspector guaranteed that they were in perfect order. There is no real reason to doubt

---

[39] They could not kept safe in their original spaces some 22 meters deep due to moist and danger of collapse.

Figure 26. Tomb of KA-GMNI. Photo by Tilly Mulder, 15 February 2011.

that since all reliefs above ground generally were left in order. The general impression is that Saqqara was vandalized instead of looted. This probably happened out of anger with the system, low wages, unemployment, and bad management.

Figure 27. Unas underground burial room.
Photo by Joris Kila, 15 February 2011.

Figure 28. Forced and repaired door at the Maya complex. Photo by Joris Kila, 15 February 2011.

Figure 29. The Tomb of the Two Brothers, forced door welded shut and with new lock. Photo by Joris Kila, 15 February 2011.

Next to Maya is the tomb of Tia. The cupboards to protect the reliefs were not locked, the reliefs looked untouched, and some cupboards were sealed. Later Leiden confirmed that most cupboards were not meant to be locked since they served as part of an exhibition for the public. The adjacent tomb of Horemheb appeared to be untouched as well. Then the Mastaba of Niankhkhnum and Khnumhotep, also known as the tomb of the two brothers, was checked as far as possible since the team could not go in; the doors had new locks and were welded shut. There were clear signs of a break-in. The same applies to the tomb of Nefer and his family members: new locks, doors welded shut, the team could not go in.

The SCA inspector of Saqqara handed the group over to the local SCA head of Abusir who would accompany the mission to Abusir and Dashur. Abusir is a large site, and the team had to choose which part to check due to the time limits. The Abusir inspector mentioned that a lot of illegal digging had taken place on the premises of the complex. Supposedly, the diggings were without results and the holes were already filled in. These digs were said to be in the desert at remote distance of the main parts of the site so the team did not go to check the closed holes. To give an impression of Abusir: it was the main royal necropolis during the Fifth Dynasty. There are in total fourteen pyramids in Abusir, all smaller and inferior in construction to the pyramids of the Fourth Dynasty like Khufu or Cheops, Snofru and Khephren. Most of the Abusir pyramids were built as step pyramids. In South Abusir is the cemetery of lower-ranking officials of the Old Kingdom including the important tomb of the priest Rahotep. The team only visited the Mastaba of Ptahshepses, see figure 30, who was the vizier and son-in-law of king Niuserrewhich. The mastaba, is part of the Czech excavation; they hold the concession for the whole site. The Ptahshepses complex cannot be locked. According to the inspector, people were spotted on the site, but we could not establish any harm while we were there, which does not mean that there was no damage.

Later reports, dating from after the assessment mission to Egypt, confirm that approximately 200 illegal pits were dug on the site (in a more remote area). Some of the holes of four to five meters deep contained ancient tombs that were now left empty by the robbers.[40] A portion of the false door was stolen from the tomb of Rahotep and, according to Czech reports, the tomb is also damaged. To make matters worse many objects stored in the expedition's on-site warehouse are permanently damaged.

In the meanwhile, the team received an urgent message concerning an appeal made by Dr. Dieter Arnold from the combined Metropolitan Art New York and German DAI institute from Berlin project. An urgent request was made to check an apparent break-in and looting of the so-called De Morgan excavation warehouse where part of the objects of their Dashur excavation are stored.[41]

The team headed to Dashur to get into problems at the entrance to the site. The SCA inspector of Dashur was not present, so he was contacted. He wanted to come, but his car broke down. The team's car was sent to pick him up. When he finally arrived on the spot, a great conflict with the police (or some guards) broke out. They did not want the team to go to De Morgan. Numerous reasons were given such as the car could not make it, there was too much sand, you need a four wheel drive, etc. Finally, after long discussions, the team drove there accompanied by a police car and the SCA inspector.

---

[40] Sources: ⟨http://egyptology.blogspot.com/2011/03/news-re-looting-at-abusir.html⟩ [17 July 2011], the blog of Zahi Hawass: ⟨http://www.drhawass.com/blog/further-updates-state-egyptian-antiquities⟩ [17 July 2011].

[41] Named after French archaeologist Jacques de Morgan (1857–1924) a former Director of Antiquities in Egypt.

Figure 30. The Ptahshepses Mastaba, part of inner courtyard. Photo by Joris Kila, 15 February 2011.

Later, back in the Netherlands, I found an announcement from al Ahram online (a big Egyptian Newspaper) with the following: Minister of State for Antiquities Zahi Hawass announced that an inventory carried out at Dashur storage gallery, known as De-Morgan's by the site inspectors, reveals that there are eight missing amulets. A huge iron gate is to be erected around the gallery in an attempt to tighten security.[42]

When the team arrived, there was no iron gate, but De Morgan was practically sealed. Doors and windows were bricked, but the mortar was still wet, see figure 31. According to the on-site guard, it was bricked the day before so we could not check inside. The roof was checked and found intact, and some ammo shells were found around the compound.

According to the guards, the main looting took place on the 13th at 4am, two days before the assessment. Two armed groups came from different sides, told the guards to stay put if they wanted to stay alive, and broke in.

[42] Source: ⟨http://english.ahram.org.eg/NewsContent/9/40/5593/Heritage/Ancient-Egypt/Looted-artifacts-from-Egyptian-museum-found.aspx⟩ [17 July 2011].

After an hour, one of the guards managed to sneak to the neighboring oil facility plant and asked the staff to switch on their searchlights, which they did. This urged the looters to leave because they thought there were cars coming. We were told that the last person that had been inside De Morgan before they bricked the warehouse up was Mr. Kamal Wahed, the person who was assigned by Zahi to help us and who was asleep in the morning. We decided to call him again to ask him for his comment. He confirmed the case and said that some small pieces had been taken; the most important pieces were brought to a safe warehouse. He said for the exact details one would have to talk to Zahi Hawass. Later contacts with Dieter Arnold, the leader of the New York Metropolitan Art Museum's excavations in Egypt, learned that he considered the looting of the Morgana warehouses a loss but not a big one "it is more like we suffered a black eye." This is because important objects had already been moved to Cairo, and the smaller objects that were kept in the facility were already studied and registered.[43] By that time, the team was almost in the middle of a sandstorm and had to leave. After a very brief visit to the Red Pyramid of Snofru, the mission members returned to Cairo.

On 16 February, the mission explored further possibilities to support training of military cultural heritage protection staff in Egypt and left for Vienna in the afternoon.

Conclusions from the Egypt Looting Casus

The above account supports suppositions presented in this study. For instance, several mechanisms that already became manifest in Iraq such as looting the national museum and, in the slipstream, archaeological sites, (alleged) political manipulations of cultural property, and economic implications of conflict-related heritage destruction are common. It was especially worrying that both in Egypt and in Iraq all media attention was first drawn to lootings in the respective national museums since in the time attention is focused on such iconic objects, it is relatively easy to loot other sites without being watched. Just like in Iraq, information about missing and damaged objects was kept vague. Most probably this had to do with avoiding responsibilities, but there were also rumors that the old regime in Egypt staged the museum looting to blame the protestors. True or not, these are methods or strategies known in history, for example, Nazi Germany, Iraq, and Afghanistan.

---

[43] Source: telephone conversation between the author and Dr. Arnold on 17 February 2011.

Although there are considerable interests for the Egyptian population regarding tourism as a source of income directly related to the country's cultural resources, this did not stop certain groups and individuals from looting. As discussed in the paragraph about looting and poverty in the introduction of this book, there seems to be a direct relation with locals suffering of poverty. Moreover, it was established that guards and SCA staff are not motivated to do their job under threat of violence due to their low salaries.[44] The latter is not only related to economic circumstances but also to certain governmental policies since it was reported that these people are already underpaid for years. The Egyptian emergency assessment mission brought the unique opportunity to test an important argument made in this study, namely, that military should implement CPP and its preparations in peacetime to avoid cultural disaster in times of conflict or turmoil. When the rules that are laid down in the 1954 Hague Convention and protocols both signed and ratified by Egypt should have been followed, the army or a special department from the Egyptian MoD would have had emergency preparedness plans in place to undertake immediate action. Other implications argued in this study played a role as well. Implications included issues caused by political and cultural differences, for example, the Egyptian MoD refused to be trained by Americans, an opportunity offered during the Bright Star exercise of 2009.[45] As a result, Egyptian military were not trained (in peacetime) to safeguard their cultural heritage when turmoil started in 2011, and consequently they did not act or did too little too late. Other premises given in this study like the influence of the media were also confirmed to a certain extent. The media, including the social networks, played a significant role in the Egyptian revolution; they were of influence to the behaviors of political and military stakeholders not only concerning the overall situation but also regarding the cultural heritage issues since there was a constant flow of looting reports. Aspects of manipulation with cultural property played a role too. There were, for instance, strong rumors about political manipulation in connection with the (according to some) staged looting of the Egyptian Museum. Supposedly, the idea behind this was to create an excuse to crack down on the protesters that were on the Tahrir Square. Then there was the inadequate response of UNESCO. The

---

44 The majority of guards we spoke to complained about this.

45 Laurie Rush describes in Archaeology, Cultural Property and the Military that the Egyptians pointed out that people responsible for destroying Babylon should not be teaching anyone about CPP. See Kila 2010b. Laurie Rush, Teaching Cultural Property Protection in the Middle East, p. 103.

organization did not answer appeals made by those who were willing to take risks and initiate an emergency assessment. More than a month after the mission's return and still without any consultation or communication with the team that already visited Egypt, UNESCO set out a mission to Cairo. The team visited the sites that were already checked by the emergency assessment mission. There is no feasible explanation for UNESCO's attitude.

We can find a more theoretic analysis of how CPP stakeholders or parties involved can behave in a presentation by U.S. Colonel Mark Yanaway called "Balancing Stakeholders in Babylon."[46] His account is interesting for multiple reasons: first, it is a direct military source and second, he draws a parallel with the original paradoxal trinity of von Clauzewitz.[47] Third, his contribution is important since it demonstrates that military science opens the door to reflect on CPP. For the purpose of his lecture, he used a military attempt to protect the cultural property of Babylon in Iraq as a case example. Yanaway compares the stakeholders of this situation, namely, the government, the army and the people, with the Clausewitzian Trinity. Clausewitz mentions three elements in his trinity: violence that Yanaway substitutes by the people, chance substituted by the military, and reason substituted by the government. Without going deep into the question how Clausewitz Trinity is applied in classic and modern military operational theory, it can be said that the people, the military, and government are in fact the three contradicting elements within the Egyptian casus. This became very clear in the Egyptian Museum looting in which the people stand for the demonstrators at the Tahrir Square; the Military as second party were in a paradox with the two other parties whereas the third was the Government or the regime also in paradox with the other two.

Another thesis discussed in the paragraph on looting is the connection with poverty.

In Egypt, the looters were local gangs and certain guards acted driven by poverty. Other aspects described in this book were present too, such as potential or actual illicit traffic of stolen artifacts, the lists of missing objects that were made, and alerts that were given to the Customs and Interpol. Then there were the usual funding problems. It is a pity that initiatives to undertake cultural emergency missions have to rely on private

---

[46] COL Mark Yanaway, CA, USAR, Civil Affairs Planning Team Chief, presentation January 8th at the AIA Annual Meeting 2011 CHAMP Workshop in San Antonio, TX, United States.

[47] Clausewitz 1968.

Figure 31. The damaged de Morgan storage facility Dashur with bricked doors. Photo by Joris Kila, 15 February 2011.

Figure 32. The burnt out Institut d'Egypte with scaffolding on 17 January 2012. Photo by Joris Kila.

funding by individuals. There are organizations with budgets for emergency operations; however, when armed conflict is at stake, no organization wants to fund or cooperate except after a successful emergency operation, to share in the success. A crucial element of the mission proved to be the reach-back capacity at the home base (office of Dr. Thomas Schuler in Chemnitz, Germany) that was constantly furnishing the newest information and coordinating contacts. This tool is explained in the section about the different CPP parties.

Egyptian Epilogue

Unfortunately history is repeating itself.[48] On 17 December 2011 the following incident took place in Cairo involving the "Institut-d' Egypte," see figure 32. CNN reported: "The library was a scene of intense confrontation Saturday (17 December). A dozen men dressed in military uniform were positioned on the library roof and threw cement blocks and rocks on the protesters and sprayed them with water hoses to push them away from the building. But protesters hurled back rocks as well as Molotov cocktails. Then a massive explosion erupted, apparently originating from inside the building, and black smoke billowed."[49]

The following impression of the situation is based on email updates from Dr. Thomas Schuler of the German Blue Shield, sent to the author.

> The fire started on the lower floors of the building, located on Qasr al-Aini Street in central Cairo, but later reached the higher floors. The fire brigade is located in the same street, but the firemen arrived very late and initially could not control the fire. The Egyptian Newspaper "Al Wafd" published a video on YouTube showing the seven minutes immediately after the fire had broken out. It proves that there had been several persons on the roof of the building; they seem to throw something down on the protesters, and they continued their activities despite the growing smoke and flames. This video does not show any activity of a fire brigade.[50]
>
> Both sides blame the other. The army blames the protestors for throwing a Molotov cocktail into the building. Eyewitnesses were reported to have seen protestors throwing a Molotov cocktail at stone-throwing soldiers at the

[48] This casus is based on several email messages to the author from dr. Thomas Schuler referring to different news paper articles and web blogs and a visit to Egypt by the author in January 2012. Dr. Schuler placed a detailed report on the website of the German Blue Shield. ⟨http://blueshield.de/institut.html⟩.

[49] http://edition.cnn.com/2011/12/17/world/africa/egypt-unrest/index.html.

[50] http://www.youtube.com/watch?v=Hcg3VHAqP6c&feature=related.

Shura Council building, but the projectile missed the intended target and instead landed in the Egyptian Scientific Institute.

The protestors claim that the army was using the building as a base from which to attack them, and some have even suggested that the fire may have been started deliberately by the army to discredit the protests. Le Monde reports on theft of manuscripts from the ruined library: there might be some confusion of witnesses that mix up theft with the rescue attempts by protesters and other people around (and the delivering of rescued books to the army). Nevertheless, a public call has been issued to bring back any books taken from the library.[51]

The first monitoring and relief activities:

Al Ahram reports: "Minister of State for Antiquities Mohamed Ibrahim assigned today an archaeological committee led by Mohsen Sayed, head of the Islamic and Coptic Antiquities Department, to inspect the Geographic Society in downtown Cairo after the building housing it was burned amid escalating clashes between protesters and the Egyptian military."

Update 20 December.

– The Sheik of the Sharjah Emirate and the French Government offered their assistance in reconstructing the building.

– 16 truck loads of (wet) books and manuscripts have been salvaged and moved to the National Library.

– The copy of "Déscription de l'Egypte" (one of eleven existing worldwide) is safe. Some volumes show damage to its covers, but can be restored.

Zein Abdel-Hady, who runs the country's main library, is leading the effort to try and save what's left of the charred manuscripts. "This is equal to the burning of Galileo's books," Abdel-Hady said, referring to the Italian scientist whose work proposing that the earth revolved around the sun was believed to have been burned in protest in the 17th century. Below Abdel-Hady's office, dozens of people sifted through the mounds of debris brought to the library. A man in a surgical coat carried a pile of burned paper with his arms carefully spread, as if cradling a baby. The rescuers used newspapers to cover some partially burned books. Bulky machines vacuum-packed delicate paper. At least 16 truckloads with around 50,000 manuscripts, some damaged beyond repair, have been moved from the sidewalks outside the U.S. Embassy and the American University in Cairo, both near the burned institute, to the main library, Abdel-Hady said. ⟨http://hosted.ap.org/dynamic/stories/M/ML_EGYPT_BURNED_ARCHIVES?SITE=FLDAY⟩

Lisa Anderson, president of the American University in Cairo (AUC) which has a campus near the institute, says the Dar al-Kutub, the National Library

---

[51] ⟨http://www.lemonde.fr/afrique/article/2011/12/18/l-incendie-de-l-institut-d-egypte-une-catastrophe-pour-la-science_1620245_3212.html⟩.

and Archives, is leading a rescue effort by scholars, library specialists, and archivists. AUC is providing student and faculty volunteers and supplies from its own rare books library. "It is impossible at this point to estimate what is lost, since some books and other materials were rescued by private individuals, and we do not know where they are," she says. "Presumably they will begin appearing, either delivered to the Dar al-Kutub or in the used books markets, over the next weeks and months."

Anderson called the event "a terrible tragedy for the historiography of Egypt," adding that "the response of the scientific and scholarly community has been very heartening."

Bernard Valero, the French minister of foreign affairs spokesperson, called the destruction a "cultural catastrophe" and urged the Egyptian government to begin an exhaustive and transparent investigation, in order to find and punish those responsible. He added that France would consider any request from Egypt to help rehabilitate the gutted institute.

⟨http://news.sciencemag.org/scienceinsider/2011/12/egypt-institute-burns-scholars.html⟩.

Egyptian media said that more than 35,000 manuscripts and books had been rescued from the flames, although their condition remains unclear. Anderson expressed hope for the collection, which she characterized as "a wonderful, somewhat eccentric, irreplaceable archive of mostly 19th century history and geography—books, manuscripts, and maps."

⟨http://news.sciencemag.org/scienceinsider/2011/12/egypt-institute-burns-scholars.html⟩

Preventing Illicit Traffic, William J. Kopycki, Field Director, Library of Congress—Cairo, Egypt, U.S. Embassy posted images of Library stamps from the Institut d'Egypte with the hopes that it would be useful should any of the Institut's holdings be spotted in the antiquarian bookmarket. This is merely a precaution and should not be construed as anything being reported missing.

http://ancientworldbloggers.blogspot.com/2011/12/library-stamps-from-institut-degypte.html

Update 22 December

"Every now and then the armed forces tell us that the conditions are stabilized enough for us to go search for more of Egypt's historic books under the ruins of the complex," Saber al-Arab, secretary general of the Dar al-Kotob publishing house and the committee formed to measure the damages, said. He added that the armed forces deliver the books to the library and a group of the library's employees looked for books under the wreckage. "Alsosome protesters call us if they find any book or document that was inside the complex," he said pointing out that it is difficult to retrieve the books due to the ongoing clashes.

⟨http://www.thedailynewsegypt.com/books/70-percent-of-books-destroyed-in-fire-says-dar-al-kotob-head.html⟩.

> Cooperative efforts are running now to restore the saved items. American University in Cairo (AUC) and Bibliotheca Alexandrina are participating effectively.
>
> Saber al-Arab, secretary general of the Dar al-Kotob publishing house and the committee formed to measure the damages, said that Dar Al-Kotob is salvaging the books through two steps: "There are some books, documents, records and manuscripts that are totally damaged and unfortunately cannot be retrieved. For those we can work on, we start by drying and sterilizing them in dry vacuum packing bags to reserve it from mold," he said.
>
> The second step, Arab said, is to start restoring the books to their original form.
>
> "We use specialized restoration labs for this process, but we cannot start doing it before collecting all the books we can," he added. ⟨http://www.thedailynewsegypt.com/books/70-percent-of-books-destroyed-in-fire-says-dar-al-kotob-head.html⟩.

Conclusions

The casus of the Egyptian Institute compares to other case examples described in this book such as the Jewish Archives and Baghdad Museum cases from Iraq. To mention a number of equal aspects and mechanisms, in all events there were no or insufficient risk preparedness measures, military involved did not receive any or at least inadequate training about the protection of cultural property, it appeared that the monuments involved were used by military thus making the objects military targets at least in the legal sense, there were links to identity of groups or nations, several parties claimed to be of help, the media played an important role, and politics (was at least accused to have) played a role.

Libya

In this book, various aspects connected with cultural property are described that recur throughout history such as manipulation of heritage for political, propaganda or military purposes. The cases from the last war in Iraq confirmed this directly. Matters at stake like low priority and lack of transport for CPP officers as addressed clearly by Lynn Nicholas in her study of what happened in World War II reoccurred for instance, in the Dutch AOR in Al Muthanna.[52] Yet, history also repeats itself in the phenomenon that certain

---

52 Nicholas 1994.

sites unfortunately are repeatedly at risk in different conflicts; the recent uprisings in Libya and the fact that the Leptis Magna is endangered again speak for themselves.

The following section is an adaptation of Robert Edsel's description in his book *Monuments Men*.[53] In January 1943, the battle between British and Axis powers that was fought out in the North African desert lasted already three years. In October 1942, the situation started to change in favor of the British when Italian-German forces were defeated at the Second Battle of El Alamein. The British, who began to push towards Tripoli, broke through the Axis lines. "By January 1943, they had reached Leptis Magna, an extensive Roman ruin some sixty-four miles east of Tripoli. It was here that Lieutenant Colonel sir Robert Eric Mortimer Wheeler, Royal Artillery, British North African Army, and an Archaeologist beheld the majesty of the imperial city of Emperor Lucius Septimius Severus containing the impressive basilica gate, the hundreds of columns that marked the old marketplace, the giant sloping amphitheater, with the Mediterranean in the background. At the height of its power at the turn of the third century AD when Emperor Severus had invested much money into his hometown in an attempt to upgrade it to the cultural and economic capital of Africa. Leptis Magna had been a port, but in the last seventeen hundred years, the harbor had silted up and become a hardpan of clay, a dull and empty world. Here, Mortimer Wheeler thought, is power and a reminder of our mortality."[54]

The British had lost the ruins of Cyrene on the East Libyan coast two years before in 1941 to the Italians led by the German General Erwin Rommel. The Italians had published the propaganda pamphlet *Che cosa hanno fatto gli Inglesi in Cirenaica*—"What the English have done in Cyrenaica."[55] The propaganda piece showed images of defaced walls at the Cyrene Museum, smashed statues, and damaged artifacts. The Italians claimed that British and Australian soldiers did this damage. Another historic example of the misuse of cultural property for propaganda and political manipulation. The British discovered these claims were false when they recaptured Cyrene, four hundred miles east of Leptis Magna. According to a different source, another archaeologist, Lieutenant Colonel John Ward-Perkins, accompanied Wheeler and both tried to prevent damage by the army as they moved in and through the ruins. In London, their reports ended up with Sir Leonard

---

53 Edsel 2009.

54 Ibid., p. 33. After serving in World War II, Wheeler was made director general of archaeology for the government of India (1944–1947).

55 Roma 1941.

Figure 33. Leptis Magna Theater, 29 September 2011. Photo by Joris Kila.

Woolley, an archaeologist, friend of Lawrence of Arabia, and Architectural Advisor to England's War Office, who worked with them to prepare preservation plans for all of Libya's ancient sites. In October 1943 Woolley, acclaimed for his excavations in Ur (Mesopotamia), was appointed head of a Monuments and Fine Arts Branch in England, which worked closely with the Roberts Commission, and, with the help of English experts, compiled similar lists of monuments, collections and sites requiring protection in both Europe and Asia.[56]

Although the Italian claims had been false, the British had spent two years defending themselves with little proof to contradict the claims. It was Mortimer Wheeler, learning from the mistakes of Cyrene, who ensured that Leptis Magna was preserved. The current threats for Leptis Magna are discussed in the paragraph on follow-up activities to safeguard heritage in

[56] A recent presentation by (Judge) Arthur Tompkins from New Zealand ⟨http://art-crime.blogspot.com/search/label/Judge%20Arthur%20Tompkins⟩ [26 August 2011]. President Roosevelt established in 1943 a special commission, naming Owen J. Roberts, the Chief Justice of the Supreme Court, as chairman. The name of the commission was the American Commission for the Protection and Salvage of Historic Monuments in War Areas.

Libya.[57] It should however be noted that the historical context as described in this paragraph fed discussions about the status and identity of heritage overseas of certain countries such as Italy. Questions that arise for today's restorers include how to select heritage and whose heritage and consequently whose (historical) identity is preserved or how to stay objective in such matters. As stipulated earlier in this book, emergency operations should be first carried out before considering strict rules (probably still to be developed).

The Current Conflict in Libya

Beginning of March 2011, unrests started in Libya. They quickly developed into a full-fledged inter-state conflict. At this moment (end of July 2011), the fighting is still going on while bombardments and shelling are carried out by the warring parties along with aerial strikes and a no-fly zone operation by NATO. Libya is since 1957 a party to the 1954 Hague Convention for the Protection of Cultural Property in the Event of Armed Conflict, and signed the Second Protocol of this convention in 2001.[58] Libya has five World Heritage sites, designated by UNESCO: the ancient Greek archaeological sites of Cyrene; the Roman ruins of Leptis Magna; the Phoenician port of Sabratha; the rock-art sites of the Acacus Mountains in the Sahara Desert; and the old town of Ghadamès, an oasis city.

An Introduction to the Libyan World Heritage Sites

- Cyrene was one of the principal cities in the Hellenic world. It was Romanized and remained a great capital until the earthquake of AD 365.
- Leptis Magna was enlarged and embellished by Roman emperor Septimius Severus, who was born there. It was one of the most beautiful cities of the Roman Empire, with impressive public monuments, a harbor, a market place, storehouses, shops, and residential districts.
- Sabratha was a Phoenician trading post that served as an outlet for products of the African hinterland.

---

57 ⟨http://projectpatrimonio.wordpress.com/2011/06/14/leptis-magna-at-rist-history-repeats/⟩.

58 Source for much of the historical information in this paragraph is the U.S. Committee of the Blue Shield thanks to Cori Wegener. ⟨http://www.uscbs.org/⟩ [17 July 2011].

- The rock-art sites of the Acacus Mountains are in the Sahara Desert. This rocky massif has thousands of cave paintings in different styles, dating from 12,000 BC to AD 100.
- The old Town of Ghadamès known as "the pearl of the desert" stands in an oasis. It is one of the oldest pre-Saharan cities and an excellent example of a traditional settlement with a special style of domestic architecture. Ghadamès is listed on the World Heritage List of UNESCO since 1986. On 11 June 2011, the Libyan Rebels reported that the town was bombed by Kadhafi's troops.[59]

On 14 June 2011 the Director-General of the UN Educational, Scientific and Cultural Organization (UNESCO), Irina Bokova, called parties involved in the armed conflict in Libya to ensure the protection of the World Heritage site of the Old Town of Ghadamès and its immediate surroundings. She also appealed to the parties involved not to expose the world heritage site of Leptis Magna to destruction and damage. Besides the world heritage sites, there is the Libyan coast that has a rich underwater cultural heritage. It consists of numerous archaeological and historical sites from pre-historic times to the Second World War. This cultural heritage is hugely important in developing the understanding of Mediterranean history. Other important cultural heritage sites in Libya include the Jamahiriya Museum; this is Libya's national museum and contains an extensive collection of history and archaeology. It is located in Tripoli's Assaria al-Hamra, or Red Castle/Fortress, the Museum of Libya on the Algeria Square in Tripoli, the Medina (Old Quarter of the city of Tripoli) and the Libyan Archives.

Follow up Activities to Safeguard Heritage in Libya

Some 200 coordinates referring to cultural heritage sites and museums from Leptis Magna and Tripolitania (the area north-west of Libya) were gathered through the international networks, workgroups and institutions that are discussed in Part I. Through these international both civil and military cultural networks, coordinates were given to military targeteers in the U.S. Several people contacted the involved American military commands, AFRICOM and CENTCOM, about the Libyan sites. As was confirmed via military contacts, the targeteers were informed about the sensitive areas to avoid. The United States had certainly shared the site coordinates with the

59 ⟨http://www.volkskrant.nl/vk/nl/5444/VK-Dossier-De-opstand-in-Libie/article/detail/2444334/2011/06/11/Eerste-aanval-op-werelderfgoed-in-Libie.dhtml⟩ [17 July 2011].

NATO command. Cori Wegener of the U.S. Blue Shield (USBS) is reported to have been in touch with NATO representatives working liaison in Washington, D.C. and they seemed to understand the issues.

The Chair of IMCuRWG Dr Joris Kila shared the data with a Staff Officer of the Strategic Plans and Policy department of NATO's Allied Command Transformation Center (ACT) in Norfolk, Virginia. The UK MoD had, via different routes, also been provided with all of the information given to the United States. Several lists with cultural sites and properties compiled by Prof. Andrew Wilson (Chairman, Society for Libyan Studies; Professor of the Archaeology of the Roman Empire, University of Oxford, UK), Dr Philip Kenrick (Honorary Treasurer, Society for Libyan Studies, UK), Dr Paul Bennett (Head of Mission, Society for Libyan Studies, UK), Prof. David Mattingly (Professor of Roman Archaeology, University of Leicester, UK), Katia Schörle (University of Oxford, UK), Charles Le Quesne (RPS, UK) and Dr. Hafed Walda (Kings College) were forwarded to the Joint Staff, and the Joint Staff Legal forwarded them to the targeteers. Dr Laurie Rush and other members of the Combat Commands Cultural Historical Action Group (CHCAG) were engaged in disseminating lists and information to several parties through the USAF/Air Combat Command.[60]

IMCuRWG provided the operational staff of the Dutch Armed Forces with the coordinates and extra information. The Netherlands took part with F16s under NATO command in imposing the no-fly zone over Libya backed by the United Nations Security Council. Though asked for by IMCuRWG during handover, the actual use of the data was not confirmed by the Dutch MoD.

In June 2011 NATO announced (via CNN) that the UNESCO heritage site, Leptis Magna, could be at risk should NATO forces receive evidence that Kadhafi was hiding military equipment amongst the ruins. It was said that Rebel forces claimed that Kadhafi was using the site. Commander Mike Bracken, a representative for NATO, said it "would be a concern for us that Kadhafi and pro-Kadhafi forces would choose to contravene international law in hiding themselves in such a location."[61] There is a very interesting aspect in the situation that confirms a number of suppositions

[60] Other U.S. experts involved were Prof. Susan Kane (Oberlin College, USA) and Dr Sam Carrier (Oberlin College, USA) while Dr Tom Elliott (Institute for the Study of the Ancient World, NYU) was instrumental in collating and deduplicating the data and preparing the list submitted to the DOD.

[61] Sources ⟨http://projectpatrimonio.wordpress.com/2011/06/14/leptis-magna-at-rist-history-repeats/⟩ [26 August 2011]. ⟨http://edition.cnn.com/2011/WORLD/africa/06/14/libya.war/index.html?hpt=hp_t2⟩ [26 August 2011].

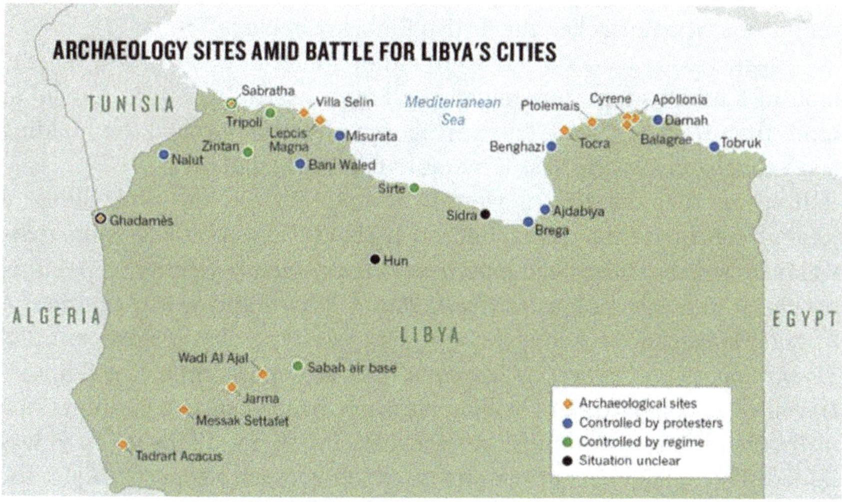

Figure 34. Map of archeological sites in Libya. From "Libya's 'extraordinary' archaeology under threat," at nature.com. Published online 2 March 2011. http://www.nature.com/news/2011/110302/full/news.2011.132/box/1.html.

made in this book about possible manipulation, misuse, and military connections to cultural property. The point is that if NATO would not say "we will attack" the site of, in this case, Leptis Magna, then the opponent would surely use the premises to hide weapons and people. Of course, at the time of the announcement no evidence could be given to underpin this, but history showed later it was not true as confirmed by the Blue Shield/IMCuRWG team's assessment. Contributing to this was the fact that Kadhafi was not very interested in archaeological sites. In fact it is said he considered archaeology a colonial activity. Still, some cases of looting in Libya that fit the patterns described in this book can already be mentioned here. When on 23 August the first footage was shown on television about Kadhafi's compound in Tripoli being overtaken by rebel forces, it was curious that immediately a form of looting took place similar to what happened in Iraq after Saddam's fall. Trophies such as the head of a statue of the dictator and his Colonel's hat were taken and statues and other objects smashed and burned. Several characteristics of looting as mentioned in the paragraph on looting, poverty and the Egyptian casus seem to apply for Libya.

Another example of pillaging and perhaps illicit traffic happened in the British Embassy in Tripoli. According to the Daily Mail of 15 June 2011, "various irreplaceable paintings worth £130,000 were stolen by Gaddafi supporters who ransacked the British Embassy in Libya."[62]

In fact unique works of art were either stolen or destroyed when the mob of Kadhafi supporters raided the Embassy. The paintings, valued at more than £130,000, were taken while the attackers torched the building and vandalized a World War II memorial on the first of May.

It seems that the actions were in revenge for the apparent killing of Kadhafi's son and three grandchildren in a NATO missile attack. Among the works believed to have been looted was an eighteenth-century oil painting by Philip Reinagle called *Harrier Killing a Bittern* and worth £60,000. A £35,000 landscape in the style of Italian painter Salvator Rosa, entitled *Mountainous Landscape with Travelers*, has also gone missing. And Edmund Havell's £20,000 portrait of William Stratton, head keeper to Sir John Cope of Bramshill Park in Hampshire, was also in the residence when it was raided. The overall cost of the attack, which is much higher than just the cost of the paintings, will not be revealed until British officials are able to return to Tripoli.

Taking into account the deadline for this book, the following information had to be limited, but it concerns two emergency assessment missions executed by IMCuRWG and ANCBS to check what happened with Libya's cultural heritage through 17 November 2011.

The recent conflict in Libya called for an emergency assessment to determine the cultural heritage situation. Since no independent confirmation about damage and looting was available thus far, and no immediate missions were planned by the International community or relevant international stakeholders, two organizations involved in international protection of cultural heritage, Blue Shield and the International Military Cultural Resources Work Group, organized a visit to meet with Libyan officials and get a first hand impression of the situation.

Due to time and safety concerns the visit was initially limited to the Tripolitania area.

The planning for the first mission began early summer 2011 but commenced after the cessation of most active hostilities in Tripoli. There were a number of problems to be solved with regard to official approval from the Transitional Government for the team to travel to Libya, not to mention the logistical difficulties of travel to and within Libya. The team flew to Djerba, Tunisia, on Tuesday, 27 September and on the 28th they managed to cross

[62] Source: Mail Online (Daily Mail UK) 15 June 2011.

the Libyan border and traveled by car to Tripoli. On 30 September the team returned by the same route.

The team consisted of Karl von Habsburg, President, Association of National Committees of the BlueShield (ANCBS), Dr. Joris Kila, Chairman, International Military Cultural Resources Work Group (IMCuRWG) and University of Amsterdam, Dr. Hafed Walda, archaeologist from Misurata (Libya) and King's College in London. The Reach Back Capability (background research, coordination, communication) was provided by Dr. Thomas Schuler, President, Disaster Relief Task Force (DRTF) International Council of Museums who operated from Berlin.

The mission visited the National Museum in Tripoli as well as two world heritage archaeological sites: Sabratha and Leptis Magna. All three mentioned are currently closed to the public, but appeared to be well-guarded. The team was impressed by the excellent precautionary measures of local museum professionals and archaeologists. The most important pieces were brought into storage rooms or hidden vaults. Welding exterior doors proved to be much better protection than locks. Very important at the large archaeological sites was the intense collaboration with the local population, for example, sheep herders provided for herds of sheep grazing in Leptis Magna (normally not allowed of course); that way intruders and booby traps were detected or avoided.

Some results are listed:

- The National Museum in Tripoli: no losses, nearly no damage.
- In Leptis Magna Kadhafi militia tried to take control of the site, but without success; currently everything is safe.
- In Sabratha the Army Brigade 219 occupied posts from early July until the 17th of August. This caused minor damage from small arms and anti aircraft fire and from the use of heavy equipment on site. The perimeter fence was broken down in many places.

Reports from other places in Libya were mixed. Among the bad news was the report that the museum in Misurata had been severely damaged, but it was not known if pieces were missing. The museum director was kidnapped by the Kadhafi militia shortly before the collapse, and he is believed to be dead.

Overall, it can be stated that there was no evidence of organized looting in the museums or sites of Tripolitania. The final detailed and illustrated report is published online on the web site of Blue Shield Austria: http://www.blueshield.at.

Figure 35. Members of the team in Tripoli 28 September 2011. Left Dr. Walda, right Dr. Kila. Photo by Karl von Habsburg.

A second Civil-Military Assessment Mission to Libya also executed by ANCBS and IMCuRWG was undertaken from November 12 to 16 in 2011. This operation was aimed at the Benghazi area. The objectives of this visit and the first Libyan emergency assessment mission went beyond mere damage inspection. Both also focused on typical post-war problems such as illegal digging and illicit traffic of cultural property. International, timely, and independent missions of the kind described provide support on the general level while at the same time giving a midterm perspective. In addition, they demonstrate international concern and solidarity.

Since the Libyan uprising against, civil society and the military is now (end November 2011) in fact process of fundamental transformation, it was vital to be in contact with those who are currently responsible for Libya's heritage. This way assistance is given to raise awareness on the protection of cultural property, and international professional support is offered and discussed on a personal and direct level.

On the morning of 12 November, the team for the second mission arrived in Benghazi, Libya, via Istanbul. There was one serious problem: almost no functioning means of communication were available in this area. Ahmed Buzaian, an experienced archaeologist, met the team at the airport. First a visit was paid to a warehouse where, at the onset of the revolution, a good part of the archive of the Department of Antiquities (DoA) in Benghazi had been hidden for safekeeping. The next stop was the bank, from which the famous Benghazi Treasure (a collection of coins and artefacts from different time periods) was stolen. This bank is close to the Freedom "Tahrir" Square where the Libyan revolution started and is situated behind the building of the former intelligence service. The building was burned down very early in the conflict, and many people assume the fire was intentionally started in order to rob the treasure—pointing to an inside job. The treasure was never on display and only partly photo-documented.

It is usually impossible to get access to the bank, but it was opened up especially for the mission. The thieves had drilled a hole from the cashier room right into the safe—through the floor of approximately seventy centimeters of steel-reinforced concrete, see figure 36. The hole was so small that the thieves had to use somebody extremely small or a child to climb down and get the treasure. It must have been very noisy to drill that hole, and several people must have been involved. The only way for the team to get to the lower level to have a look at the safe door was to climb down through the burned-out elevator shaft, making their way through piles of soot and debris. The timeline, though, is shocking: the bank was burned down at the beginning of February 2011 while the responsible senior inspector, Youssef bin Nasser, was trapped in Ghadames because of the revolution. It took him two months to make his way via Algeria, Tunisia, by boat to Egypt and then over the border back to Benghazi. When he arrived and heard that the bank burned down, he immediately inquired about the treasure. The bank only acknowledged the theft in writing on 25 May. So the exact date of the robbery cannot really be established.

After visiting the bank, the team went to Youssef bin Nasser's office. There he showed several unprovenanced objects such as pottery and a ceramic figurine, stolen in the area and brought over the border to Egypt where the items were sold. They were bought by a Libyan benefactor, who recognized and returned the items.

The Benghazi museum was torn down in 2006. It was demolished by order of the (at the time) Libyan prime minister, supposedly since the museum was blocking a clear view of the lighthouse. Some of the objects are currently stored in Youssef bin Nasser's office. He has installed a secure fencing system in his office at his own expense for maximum protection. Of interest was that Youssef showed pictures from the south of Libya close to

Figure 36. Joris Kila in front of the hole drilled in the floor of the Benghazi Bank to rob the "treasure," 12 November 2011. Photo by Karl von Habsburg.

the Sudanese border (near Al Khofra) of graves containing mummies. The graves had suffered from looting and vandalization during the revolution. This is surely something that needs further examination when the situation permits.

After a meeting with the DoA controller of Benghazi, Mohammed Attiatallah, the team drove to a Roman settlement area called Umm al Shuga, few kilometers from Dariana. This site has been seriously damaged using heavy equipment. Before the revolution a massive building programme was under execution to create irrigation channels in the area. When the fighting started, the workers deserted this heavy equipment. The tools were taken over by thieves and used to illegally "excavate" a group of settlements. It is likely that nothing was found, but the destruction is vast. There are holes five meters deep and twenty by ten meters wide; also many Roman walls have been destroyed.

Next day's first destination was Tokra, one of the five cities of the Greek Pentapolis. The site was not harmed during the revolution but was used to store (and hide) many materials from the cathedral and the museum in Benghazi. It is important to note that the first Interim Council was created in Tokra at the beginning of the revolution. This council put the protection of the site very high on their agenda. This implies that the local population was again very involved in the safeguarding of cultural heritage, a very positive local approach found in Libya. A big threat to the site, particularly for the section on the Mediterranean shore, is coastal erosion. The sea has encroached on the archaeological site by four meters in the last twenty years.

The following stop was Tolmetha (Ptolemais); the museum was opened especially for the team, and looked not harmed as was confirmed by the staff. The only damage occurred to the Polish archaeological mission home. This house is currently occupied by armed squatters. They have not given access to representatives of the Department of Archaeology and have illegally sold several pieces that were in the house. Luckily the objects were recently recovered. It is dangerous to approach the house. The team drove by to have a look. Over the compound wall, many pieces originating from excavations on site can be seen lying around in the courtyard. Supposedly there are some important mosaics on the premises, but they were not visible, so they could not be inspected.

While speaking to local experts the team tried to get information concerning sites in the south of the country. There was encouraging news from specialists who recently visited the Jofra Oases and Djerma. The sites seem to be intact. It is however not possible yet to get any information on Acacus as the security situation in that region is too dangerous to allow a survey.

From Ptolemais the team drove to Qasr Libya. Neither the museum nor the site suffered any damage. We decided to open up the museum for the first time since the revolution. This necessitated cutting open the metal doors that were welded. Inside is a beautiful small museum containing mosaics with Christian motives. In addition the church next door was opened. Present in Qasr Libya was also the DoA controller of Cyrene, Nasser Abdu al Jalil, who accompanied the team during the next part of the mission.

The following stop was Cyrene (see gallery). In the "modern" city, a lot of battle damage is visible. A military camp right next to the entrance appeared to have been the scene of a lot of fighting, which luckily had no immediate effect on the archaeological site. Still, many surrounding buildings were burned down. First a museum was visited of which the entrance doors had been welded and specially opened. The spectacular collections of Cyrene are grouped in Archaic, Hellenistic, Roman, and Byzantine departments. In the entrance space is the statue of Venus of Cyrene (repatriated from Italy). The team visited a specially locked small reserve that contains some important statue heads and several boxes containing coins.

The diligence of the guards at Cyrene has to be particularly commended. They moved away from their families for periods of weeks in troublesome times in order to protect the site. also the DoA controller showed great courage. On March 9, at the height of the conflict, he learned of some illegal digging. First he sent out the guards to check the situation but they reported that they could not find anything. The next day he inspected the location personally and ran straight into the looters. They had just dug up a torso and he demanded that they hand it over. The group was composed of eight well armed men and he was alone and unarmed. After an exchange of words the situation became physical and they throttled him until he was unconscious and also stole his phone and keys. Later he called his stolen phone and started negotiations with the looters for the return of the torso. Alas the stolen objects have not yet been recovered, although some of the looters are in jail.

On site we visited the famous mosaic of the four seasons in the Jason Magnus palace. In the days leading to the revolution this monument was vandalized and two of the emblems depicting the seasons were stolen, creating a lot of damage. We also visited the ethnographic collection, housed in one of the warehouses; it was inspected and found unharmed.

At the following meeting the controller Nasser Abdu al Jalil explained the timeline. When the first demonstrations started in neighboring Egypt, the regional members of the Department of Antiquities met to talk about contingency plans. Nothing had, as yet, been foreseen. They decided to remove the archive from the site so the most valuable books and several boxes containing artifacts could be brought to a secure and well guarded hiding place. On 16 February, the Controller of Cyrene contacted the Director of Antiquities based in Tripoli, Saleh al Agaab, for instructions. Dr. Saleh al Agaab authorized him to take any necessary measures for the protection of the cultural heritage should communications fail, which was soon the case. The controller instructed the six local offices to individually take measures for protection of the antiquities. This happened with varying success. Since the Transitional Government was not able to help them, the guards decided to keep on working without pay and organized to get provisions locally. So for three weeks the site was guarded by local armed volunteers.

The next morning the team visited the library of Cyrene, one of the oldest in Libya, founded 1914. The buildings are in an abominable state but most of the valuable books had been stored safely at the onset of the revolution. The head of the technical department provided several photos of the vases that have been stolen in Apollonia, which was visited by the team next. Apollonia used to be the harbour for Cyrene and is at a distance of roughly fifteen kilometers.

About half the city of Apollonia disappeared in the earthquake of 365 AD and the tsunami that followed. The outline of the harbor can still be seen through the position of some rocks protruding from sea. The site is also very important for underwater archaeology.

The team visited the Appolonia museum, where a break in occurred on 25 July. The looters forced the bars of an office window with direct access to the museum. They had obviously targeted what they were taking since they smashed a show case containing the four vases and left a fifth behind. After that the team visited the on-site warehouse that contains some of the valuables. Amongst them are rare Panathenaican amphorae and the fifth vase that had been in the show case with the ones that were stolen from the museum. The warehouse seemed reasonably safe.

A visit to the temple district of Cyrene and a stop at the temple of Zeus, which was destroyed 117 AD and later partly rebuild by Italian archeologists, rounded up the day.

In the morning the team drove to Darnah. This town was not in a good state and looked rather neglected. Darnah got severely damaged during the revolution but the charm of the city center was still amply evident.

The Darnah museum is located in a (now) burned out building. The first floor was used as the local tax office and therefore felt the brunt of the revolution. Museums and government offices apparently do not mix well in times of crisis. The museum's archive and its most important objects were brought to a safe place at the beginning of the revolution and the entrance doors to the museum were welded shut. The looters broke a hole in the door and stole a computer and an antique vase. Later the door was welded again.

From the closed museum, the team drove to the palace of King Idris. This rather small building is in a desolate state and is occupied by armed squatters who did not allow access. A plan exists to bring the museum to the King's palace. The palace is nevertheless owned by the heirs of King Idris and any new use requires their consent. Kadhafi tended to burn land registers when he wanted to conceal property belonging to the former king's family. He attempted the same in Darnah, but the original state was reconstructed from copies of the register.

After returning to the museum, the doors were opened with an angle grinder. The inside of the building was a mess. There were burned pictures of Kadhafi, broken show cases, but also some good pieces that were collected by the officials of the Department of Antiquities and brought to a safe place.

Next the team drove to Ras Hilal to visit the ruins of an early Christian church ca. 5th or 6th century. It is in an acceptable condition. Back in Al Bayda, its oldest mosque Zauia, was visited. A former school is attached and the local dignitaries would love to see it revived. They would also like to see the mosque listed as cultural heritage site. On the way back, shortly before Benghazi, the team stopped at a Roman settlement, Ten Saluh, that was damaged by illegal digging prior to the revolution.

In the evening the team received valuable information. Eight coins from the Benghazi treasure had been offered for sale to a journalist, who informed the authorities. Those coins were later retrieved from the Benghazi market by a DoA official.

In addition, the team had a meeting with Proferssor Abdulla Rhaibi of the University of Benghazi who, two weeks before, had visited Sirte to assess the situation at both the museum and the old Islamic site. The site is several kilometers away from the town and had not been harmed. The rest house was slightly damaged and the stores were broken into and part of their content stolen. Currently work is underway to quantify the damage. In Ajdabiya, the artifacts of the museum were taken by a number of private persons for safekeeping and were subsequently returned to the controller. A number of meetings with Libyan scholars concluded the mission to Cyrenaica. There is still a need to visit the cultural heritage sites in the south and in Ghadames. However, there are grounds to believe that they are largely unharmed.

Lessons Learned

Both missions were necessary and very well received as was demonstrated by the encouragement of Cultural Heritage officials as well as local staff on site. The two missions would not have been possible without the specialized knowledge and the many contacts of Dr. Hafed Walda and his communication with the Transitional Government and the specialists and academics in place especially Dr. Adel Al-Turki. In a country with only a very basic political structure, no confirmed government and a tribal- or regional-based security system, local contacts are always of special importance; in this case such contacts were instrumental to achieve the objectives of both missions.

Another basic condition for a successful operations was the willingness of the participants to go and take certain risks without waiting for insurances. Disappointment that other (big) NGOs and Governmental Organizations dealing with Cultural Heritage had not yet managed to send experts or assistance to Libya could be heard from all sides.

Epilogue:

From March 8 to 13 2012 a team from the University of Amsterdam (UvA) paid a visit to Tripolitania the goal was to assess possibilities for a cooperation between the UvA and the Department Of Antiquities (DOA) in Libya. This trip was a direct result of the visit a Libyan delegation paid in November 2011 to the UvA. At that time the Libyan delegation talked to UvA-archaeology, museology, cultural heritage, conservation and restoration experts. A Dutch team was invited and Dr Joris Kila appointed by the UvA to coordinate both the assessment as well as possible projects. The following locations were visited by the UvA team:

- Leptis Magna (including a designated building to house a restoration laboratory).
- Villa Silin
- Sabratha
- Tripoli: Archaeological Museum

Special attention was given to the Villa Silin. This Roman Villa was discovered in 1974 and has been dug up and restored by Italian archaeologists. The site contains 46 spaces many of them decorated with fresco's, and mosaics. Currently Villa Silin is in a bad state due to the limited sustainability and sometimes wrongly executed restorations. To give an example the application of armed concrete under the mosaics led to large damage because of corroding iron in the concrete. A roof has been constructed using the wrong

Figure 37. Fragment of floor mosaics in Villa Silin in March 2012. Photo by Joris Kila.

materials there is leakage and rust water sipping through damaging murals and walls. The DOA and UvA are currently (end March 2012) preparing a plan to solve many of the problems in different phases (emergency solutions first). Funding has to be found to start the work. This project is a direct result of the emergency mission undertaken during the Libyan conflict.[63]

---

[63] The latest news (May 2012) is that the DOA signed a contract with the Italians for emergency restorations on Villa Silin. Curious is the fact that the same Italian experts apparently did a bad job in the first place causing the current bad condition of Villa Silin.

CHAPTER FOUR

THE WAY AHEAD

Balancing the Interests

The Hague Convention of 1954 was designed as an instrument to diminish and control the tensions that naturally appear between those taking care of cultural heritage and those whose core business is armed conflict. To put it more simply, the treaty aims at maintaining a proper balance between cultural heritage and warfare. Obviously, the term proper as used in this context is subject to trends, insights, and historical and political circumstances as described. The stakeholders from all sides are also portrayed in the first part of this study.

When looking at then cases and examples described in Chapter 3 of this book, it seems that the convention is not reaching its objective and that it has created more tensions in the playing field. All interests at stake seem to be to a certain extent mutually exclusive or at least not in balance with each other. This instability has different origins including personal, bureaucratic, ethnic, or political situations, to mention a few. For example, one can think of tensions between groups supporting archeological sites preservation versus those who give priority to exploitation of cultural heritage for tourism. Other cases of friction relate to cultural resources management involving federal versus provincial control and national versus international authority, not to mention collective interests versus individual interests.[1] In the case of ownership of property, tensions can occur related to private possession of cultural heritage versus community owned properties. Chapter 3 not only shows the development of this research via a collection of published and peer-reviewed articles but also contains case studies that illustrate different interests, behaviors of parties, tensions, and mechanisms as they occurred in practice especially during the period this research was executed. In all cases presented, the balancing of interests appears to be a key factor for effective future realization of CPP methods and strategies.[2] Since

---

[1] In the Netherlands activities are often blocked by the head of the cultural awareness dept. (CAI) due to personal competence issues.

[2] A source of benefit especially for the use of the term balancing the interests was a

no legal framework seems to be effective enough to achieve this, new opportunities and creative solutions must be identified. In the current situation it looks like these solutions will have to come from those not afraid of taking risks and willing to handle bureaucratic rules and formats with flexibility.

Educational materials and research results that illustrate different perspectives as well as possible (military) incentives play a role in the (re)balancing process. The following paragraphs, while taking into account outcomes of this study and lessons learned from case examples, will identify and investigate a number of vital restraints and challenges. While doing so, there is room for legal considerations, unpredicted opportunities, research, education and training methods, clear cut solutions, and other strategies.

Identified Dilemmas or Challenges Standing in the Way of CPP Implementation

Several identified dilemmas are mentioned in sections of Chapter 2, e.g., the paragraphs explaining the different parties involved. Practical cases that include such dilemmas were also given, for instance concerning the media (the Jewish archives, Baghdad museum) and religion (Bamyian and the Israel Temple Mount). A number of vital challenges will be further explained and summarized while suggesting solutions. Some issues are of a juridical nature. Let me stress that I am not a juridical expert and therefore approach the fundamental juridical implications from a more or less multidisciplinary position in fact, as it normally happens in practice when a commander has to interpret advice given by experts from different disciplines to make a decision. Judgments and conclusions are not mentioned without consulting juridical experts but some issues that go naturally for legal experts are discussed from a non-juridical point of view. The research shows that military CPP is often mixed up or too closely linked with military Cultural Awareness (CA). Recent discussions, like the one at the World Archaeological Congress in Dublin in 2008 that is addressed in the paragraph about the media, and several publications confirm this.[3] In fact this is an issue between some of the stakeholders addressed in this study, namely, science, the media, and the military.

---

presentation by Colonel Mark Yanaway at the AIA conference that took place in San Antonio, TX, in January 2011.

[3] E.g. Umberto Albarella, Archaeologists in Conflict: Empathizing with which Victims? Heritage Management Volume 2, Issue 1 (Spring 2009) Forum.

To avoid all kinds of sometimes-unexpected confusion and unwanted synergy it is better that CPP officers are embedded in a military organization separate from cultural awareness experts. Activities aiming at raising awareness through supplying information and training should include clear explanation of the fact that CPP and Cultural Awareness are two separate disciplines. Of course, they are related to each other, but in the same way as a dentist is linked to a cardiologist: both work in the medical field. Nevertheless even the vaguest relationship can potentially cause legal implications because of the legal and consequently ethical framework CPP officers should work within, the Hague Convention of 1954. Implications could arise in the case CPP that touches specific areas within the field of counterinsurgency; for instance, when attempts are made to decrease illicit traffic of artifacts in a conflict zone. Again, it should be emphasized that in this context reference is made to the European civilian perception of the term counterinsurgency. This argument needs clarification. It was brought to my attention on several occasions that European civilian social scientists and for that matter the general public tend to perceive COIN as secret operations aimed at destroying opponents. The Americans, including the U.S. public, use a wider construct of the term and recognize all activities that are in support of a military mission, or, in other words, create a force multiplier such as CPP as a tool to be used against the opponent. If CPP through COIN gets mixed up or confused with something that is understood as intelligence operations aimed at destruction or at physically disabling the enemy, we get situations like what happened in Dublin or even worse, resulting in limited opportunities to carry out what IHL wants with respect to cultural property protection.

This example shows that confusion about certain matters can partly be influenced or triggered by factors of social, geographical and cultural descent but also by an individual's or group's professional expertise and environment. Apart from these, there are other vital aspects, for instance, the fact that the multi-disciplinary nature of CPP and this investigation makes it difficult for the non-juridical trained to use and interpret juridical data and issues. On the other hand, it makes it suitable to fit in other comprehensive models like the 3D concept. As discussed earlier, CPP not only fits perfectly in this so-called 3D approach used especially in peacekeeping and stabilization operations, but CPP actually belongs in all military operations. The 3D or diplomacy, defense, and development formula is in the Netherlands presented as the Dutch approach, implying it is a Dutch invention. In practice its implementation and consequently development remains somewhat behind and vague since the Dutch MoD suffers from

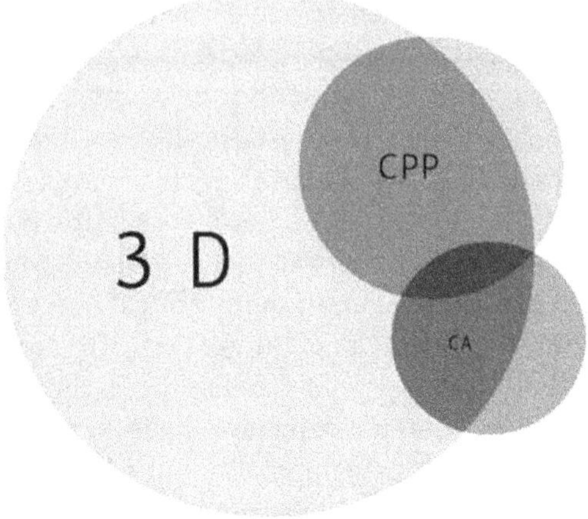

CPP Mandatory under International Humanitarian Law (IHL)
3D approach Defense Diplomacy and Development
CA There is a relation with CPP but CA is not mandatory under IHL

Figure 38. 3D approach. © Joris Kila.

major financial cut backs not allowing them to fully educate and train troops and specialists on topics and expertise vital to really realizing the 3D format. It is, however, possible to illustrate the positions of CPP and CA within this 3D context; see Figure 38. It is interesting to take into account that in this 3 D method, several stakeholders introduced in Chapter 1 take part: governmental institutions (ministries), the military, and NGOs; in addition to these, advisory groups, scienctific organizations, and international organizations can be involved.

A big restraint to point out is the general lack of mutual understanding and coordination between the different parties that should carry out what is stated in the 1954 Hague Convention and other relevant legislation. The deficiency of common sensibility is seriously hindering implementation of activities. Varying opposing factors instigate this, but an overall issue is the apparent difficulty for the civilian side to understand military conditions and culture and vice versa. Conditions are worsened by the fact that the military are not showing much interest in the subject. In many countries, lack of interest and awareness cause the military not to object when CPP is not dealt with in their organizations. There are even cases where the existence of cultural awareness programs is used as an excuse not to implement CPP. Egypt is a recent example of this phenomenon and shows what the devastating results can be if a country's armed forces are unable to act when police protection of sites and museums suddenly disappears. In fact, we are talking about bad cooperation between CPP stakeholders (military, government, juridical and civil cultural experts) as identified in Chapter 2. This is even more reason to identify common denominators. On top of all this there is a trend started by a small number of individuals that appear to invent and introduce less relevant ethical aspects thus contributing to restrain cooperation between civil experts and military. Their arguments are often unfounded because they are made without real knowledge about the military and legal perspectives. Moreover, such opinions are beside the point because if all parties stick to the legal framework provided by the 1954 Hague Convention, there cannot be an ethical problem. It can even be argued that ignoring cooperation and resolutions as mentioned in International Humanitarian Law is un-ethical. This ethics trend has as a consequence that the scarce number of experts (often reservists) that try to function in between the civil and military spheres and have knowledge of and experience with both "cultures" are prone to suspicion from scientific peers as well as from professional military colleagues and are at risk of being marginalized. One more major challenge for meeting the obligations as laid down in the 1954 Hague Convention is the lack of funding. The bad economical situation giving low priority to subjects as CPP and in civil society culture in general is often referred to as an excuse, but it in fact it indicates low appreciation of the relevance of dealing with CPP. Because of this attitude, Europe and the Netherlands in particular stay behind with implementing CPP strategies for military organizations as required by the 1954 Hague Convention.

Different examples have shown that training of the military is held up by conflicts of interests as well as by contradicting powers and arguing factions within circles of stakeholders.[4] These can be called identified dilemmas and are often based on oppositions and constraints linked to strategic cultures.[5] They occur on different levels and involve diverse parties, disciplines, and issues. Balancing the respective interests is again a pre-requisite for success. Following are more examples, after each identified predicament

---

[4] E.g cultural awareness specialists versus CPP specialists.

[5] Strategic Culture is that set of shared beliefs, assumptions, and modes of behavior, derived from common experiences and accepted narratives (both oral and written), that shape collective identity and relationships to other groups, and which determine appropriate ends and means for achieving security objectives. Source: Comparative Strategic Culture Syllabus, Jeannie L. Johnson and Jeffrey A. Larsen, Fort Belvoir, Virginia, 2006.

a clarification with a reference to a thesis and case used in this study is given: a classic dilemma from the juridical sphere is balancing between cultural property protection and military necessity. This is a basic conflict of interest between the cultural expert's desire for conservation and preservation of cultural belongings and the military aim to reach a conflict's end state as soon as possible. A famous case dates from the Second World War namely the case of Monte Cassino.[6] Out of such dilemmas, more contradictions become apparent such as the desire to achieve military results against the apparent constraints of international humanitarian law (IHL). Here it becomes tricky for people not educated in the law. IHL is incorporated into military law and is also known as the Law of Armed Conflict (LOAC). While human rights law applies in peacetime and subject to derogation, in times of armed conflict, IHL/LOAC only applies in armed conflict. As with all international law, the laws of armed conflict are based on treaties and customary international law. Of course, military law is at the same time a body that contains directives and rules for the military. It is critical to distinguish the multiple layers and applications of such juridical instruments. All play a role in the CPP complex though intermingled with different political, technical, or cultural elements. Obviously more research as well as cooperation between civil and military legal experts and cultural experts is needed to keep all elements under control while giving expert advice to commanders. For that matter, cases and problems mentioned in this study have to be checked for their juridical implications while asking what problems can derive from such cases. This is especially important since it is not apparent to civil CPP stakeholders when or under which circumstances the accomplishment of military objectives prevails over allowing for directives of national laws or international humanitarian law on protecting cultural property. Situations obviously cannot be judged without the advice of legal experts, but these experts are normally not educated about archaeological, cultural, and preservation aspects, to mention a few. This example points out the difficulties of establishing cooperation between parties representing the law, the military, and science.

Apart from existing issues there are matters to be considered and researched that contain new implications (or opportunities) linked with CPP such as the environmental angle. This link has, for instance, not been checked for probable legal consequences deriving from environmental rules

---

[6] In 1944, the Abbey of Monte Cassino was bombed based on the fear that it was being used as a lookout post for the Germans; this proved later not to be the case.

and laws. For that matter, possibilities to undertake emergency assessment missions for working groups as IMCuRWG and their status in the field have not been investigated from the legal perspectives that are valid in conflict and foreign diplomatic situations. A final relevant issue to mention is the fact that tensions exist between instrumental parties with financial resources to protect CP such as governments and intrinsic parties that have the expertise but lack financial resources; this is the case in the Netherlands.[7] An important but inconsistent relation exists between civilian experts and military- or militarized experts. Problems range from ranking concerns as addressed in the CIMIC paragraph including financial and hierarchy consequences to legal implications such as legal status issues when noncombatants and combatants work together in theater.[8]

The above is a selection of contradicting forces that are always present. Their respective influence is illustrated in the cases used in parts one and two of this book. Nevertheless, within the context of this study the legal aspects, like the classic and crucial contradiction involving military necessity already mentioned, need more elucidation. The latter concerns two elements of international humanitarian law (IHL), namely, the principle of military necessity that is in fact a restriction on the conduct of hostilities addressed under Hague Law versus the obligation to protect cultural property as codified in the 1954 Hague Convention.[9] It is useful for non-juridical experts to get an idea of the lawful context in which certain aspects function and correlate when CPP is at stake. Such a closer look is necessary to put matters in perspective while describing the legal environment connected with war. At that point it may be possible to understand the concepts of proportionality and what some consider the ill-defined principle of military necessity.[10] Moreover, a comparison is made between different interpretations from juridical experts.

[7] Feil 2008, pp. 219–220.

[8] Both have a different status under military law and IHL.

[9] Present-day international humanitarian law has grown from two main sources: the Law of Geneva, i.e. a body of rules protecting victims of war, and the Law of The Hague (or Hague Law), i.e. those provisions which affect the conduct of hostilities, source: ICRC Resource Centre, 31-12-2001 Article, International Review of the Red Cross, No. 844, by François Bugnion.

[10] See: Thurlow 2005, pp. 164–166.

Legal Aspects to Consider When Implementing CPP

> "The law is an arcane subject. It was once said that international law is at the vanishing point of law—and the law of armed conflict is at the vanishing point of international law!"[11]

> "The laws of war are as vague as you can get but they are getting more defined," as was said by Antony Dworkin.[12] Some countries are using them to try to alter the notions of war, combatant, and battlefield. Charles Garraway disagrees to a certain extent by stating that some laws of war are very specific. However, he agrees that a few are not as clear as one might like because diplomatic conferences draft them and everything drafted by multiple entities is a compromise. On the other hand, Dworkin argues that one can look at the history of the laws of war as a battle between making them more precise and more defined versus making them vaguer. This process is in fact in line with other examples of contradicting forces presented in this publication including juridical elements of CPP. One of the most amorphous is the principle of military necessity.

> "We are bound to respect monuments as far as war allows. If we have to choose between destroying a famous building and sacrificing our men, then our men's lives count infinitely more and the buildings must go. However, the choice is not always so clear-cut as that. In many cases, the monuments can be spared without detriment to operational needs. Nothing can stand against the argument of military necessity but the phrase is sometimes used where it would be more truthful to speak of military- or even personal convenience."

> *General Eisenhower, 29 December 1943.*[13]

Of course, the statement of General Eisenhower is almost 70 years old and the situation has changed since. Important areas in the law of armed conflict were subject to alterations while codifications of restrictions on the conduct of hostilities sometimes changed by building in specific exemptions such as using terms like "imperative" as an adjective to necessity. In that case, necessity can be considered a high test while the addition of "imperative" or other adjectives makes the test even higher. More differences that are

---

[11] Lauterpacht 1952, pp. 360–382.

[12] Antony Dworkin is the web editor of the Crimes of War Project, a site dedicated to raising public awareness of the laws of war. This quote comes from the Seminar War Reporting and War crimes in the Aftermath of 9/11, London October 2002.

[13] Allied General Order issued by General Eisenhower. Source: Report of the American Commission for the Protection and Salvage of Artistic Monuments in War Areas 48–49 (Washington, D.C.: U.S. Government Printing Office, 1946).

basic developed in the last seventy years; they concern aspects like the type of weapons used, the kind of targets that can legitimately be attacked, and alterations regarding international criminal liability.[14] When focusing on the term military necessity, for a nonprofessional it reads as a need for the military. There is civilian legal notion of necessity, but this cannot be compared to the notion of military necessity. A good definition is that military necessity is an exception to a prohibition in international humanitarian law (IHL).[15] In 1863 Francis Lieber described military necessity as "those measures which are indispensable for securing the ends of war, and which are lawful according to the modern laws and usage's of war."[16] This implicitly suggests that the definition of military necessity is always connected to contemporary juridical and conflict practices and therefore should be updated and upgraded on a regular basis in order to be weighed in the right context. Preferably, juridical experts should cooperate with others in a multidisciplinary setting to do this.

In contemporary U.S. and NATO usage, military necessity is phrased as a measure not forbidden by the laws of war that can rightfully be applied to achieve a successful conclusion of a military operation. From this perspective, military necessity is treated as a tool just as CPP can be a tool to reach the end state of a mission. In essence, military necessity is considered part of just war theory dealing with the conduct of warfare.[17] Since it is a concept used in IHL, it is part of the legal justification for attacks on legitimate military targets that may have adverse consequences for civilians and civilian objects. For some this holds the implication that military forces in planning military actions are permitted to take into account the practical requirements of a military situation and the imperatives (prerequisite) of winning at any given moment. Here opinions differ; therefore, some viewpoints need to be compared.[18]

---

14 Source: Greenwood, Christopher in: Singapore Journal of International and Comparative Law (1997) 1 pp. 441–467.

15 Source: ⟨http://www.diakonia.se/sa/node.asp?node=888⟩ revised: 18/03/2011. [17 July 2011].

16 Rogers. 1996. p. 4.

17 Just War Theory has 3 main components 1) *jus ad bellum*: the justice of going to war 2) *jus in bello*: the means by which war is conducted and 3) *jus post bellum*: the means by which the war is concluded and the peace restored.

18 Being no juridical expert I was supported enormously by the information and arguments given by Professor Charles Garraway during two interviews and exchange of email messages.

Military necessity acknowledges that even under the laws of war, winning the war or battle is a legitimate consideration, though it must be put alongside other considerations of IHL.[19]

This means that military necessity does not automatically give armed forces immunity for taking actions that would otherwise be impermissible, for it is always balanced against the humanitarian requirements of IHL. Three requirements or constraints upon exercising military necessity are important: First any attack must be intended with a goal leading to the military defeat of the enemy; attacks not so intended cannot be justified by military necessity because they would have no military purpose. Second: even an attack aimed at the military weakening of the enemy must not cause harm to civilians or civilian objects that is excessive in relation to the concrete and direct military advantage anticipated. Third: military necessity cannot justify violation of the other rules of IHL.

Garraway has a slightly different interpretation. He establishes military necessity to be now defined as "the principle whereby a belligerent has the right to apply any measures which are required to bring about the successful conclusion of a military operation and which are not forbidden by the laws of war." This is the current description in the UK LOAC Manual.[20] The manual refines this even more by explaining the legitimate purpose of a conflict: "a state engaged in an armed conflict may use that degree and kind of force, not otherwise prohibited by the law of armed conflict, that is required in order to achieve the legitimate purpose of the conflict, namely the complete or partial submission of the enemy at the earliest possible moment with the minimum expenditure of life and resources." The following remark seems in place here: in many other military planning documents "submission of the enemy" is replaced by "reaching the end state of a mission" to describe the legitimate purpose of the conflict. When CPP is at stake, we must first distinguish between two perspectives that are inextricably linked. In the strict military sense, the end state of the military mission in armed conflict is the complete or partial submission of the enemy at the earliest possible moment with the minimum expenditure of life and resources. However, in a more modern and general sense, that includes a political perspective and refers more to operations outside of

---

[19] Source: Crimes of War A–Z guide Military Necessity, Françoise Hampson, ⟨http://www.crimesofwar.org/a-z-guide/military-necessity/⟩ [17 July 2011].

[20] Professor Garraway is general editor of the current version of this manual.

armed conflict like peace support missions; often the desired end state is the establishment of a safe social environment in which civilian institutions can take over from the military. Nevertheless, Garraway makes the point that military necessity is not a "get out of jail free card!" On top of that, he identifies a noticeable change between the wording used in the Hague Regulations 1907 and that in Geneva Additional Protocol I in 1977. In 1977 the definition of a military objective is "those objects which by their nature, location, purpose or use make an effective contribution to military action and whose total or partial destruction, capture or neutralization, in the circumstances ruling at the time, offers a definite military advantage." Here the change is in the use of the word "advantage"—a much lower threshold or test as Garraway calls it. In 1999 in the Second Protocol to the Hague Convention of 1954, military necessity is further narrowed down in Article 6. For a start, cultural property cannot be attacked unless it is a military objective—but then that is the general rule for civilian objects and as we have seen is a low test depending on "military advantage." However, cultural property must become a military objective "by function." It can be a military objective by any other means and not lose protection. Thus if by its location it is an advantage to attack it, that is not sufficient. A civilian object becomes a military objective and therefore liable to attack (subject to proportionality etc.) if there is a "definite military advantage" to that attack. The attack does not need to be "necessary." In conclusion, Garraway disagrees with Eisenhower's statement as far as it would imply that today's law including the descriptions of military necessity is not adequate.

The above line of reasoning by Garraway illustrates even to the non-juridical-trained that the mix of legal, military, and civil considerations constitutes a complicated challenge. For that reason, multidisciplinary expert advice and the research of actual cases is needed to decide on matters of necessity and proportionality when it comes to handling CPP matters in theater. It goes without saying that this entire evolving mechanism causes constant tensions between civil and military interests that can be contradictory and on occasion multi-interpretable. Finally, military necessity is not a static phenomenon, nor are the conditions, perspectives, or rules under which it can be applied. In fact, today military necessity is sometimes treated as a tool just as CPP can be a tool to reach the end state of a mission. Patrick Boylan's arguments are more in line with Eisenhower when he states that "military commanders on the ground have already relied on this tool (military necessity) in the past for example when arguing that a certain high church tower might be used for military purposes such as observation or sniping by the defending forces."[21] However, it is also a fact that military necessity was used as a standard defense used by accused war criminals in trials following World Wars I and II.[22]

Having established the flexible nature of Military Necessity we can understand both Eisenhower's and Boylan's concerns about whether the military necessity concept is used as a response to a "necessity" or "military convenience"? To make things less convenient, Boylan did seek to restrict the military necessity exemption. At the same time, he anticipated on the changing methods and conditions of warfare and conflict and created the Second Protocol to the Hague Convention of 1954. Article 11-2 of the new protocol states that immunity as granted to cultural property according to Chapter II article 8 can be lifted in case of "exceptional cases of unavoidable military necessity." This level of necessity can only be established by a commander of a force the equivalent of a division in size or larger. It appears to be an indication of the high importance the treaty gives to the quality of military decision making on the subject and the quality of expert advice obviously needed for a commanders' considerations while making the decision. In practice the commander of a division equivalent will be at least a two-star general often heading a multinational mission. From a logical point of view advice concerning withdrawing immunity has to be given by military strategic experts, military lawyers, and subject matter experts, in this case cultural property experts. Results of assessments and research undertaken prior to the mission should normally play a role in this. The immunity waiver of the Convention's second Protocol still leaves matters open. Therefore juridical experts both civil as well as military should at least communicate and execute research together in order to fully understand its consequences. Subjects to be argued and studied are for instance if the described restriction on necessity should also reflect situations like events involving a commander of a force smaller than a division and a situation where this commander is unexpectedly forced to make an instant decision concerning cultural property. It is also questionable whether the treaty provides a directive for military decision-making in case of acclaimed cultural property that is not (yet) on any national or international list. Finally an ordinance urging a

[21] Military necessity is very much more than military convenience, presentation by Prof. Patrick J. Boylan (City University London, UK) during the conference Protecting Cultural Heritage in Times of Conflict Tallinn Estonia 2008. ⟨http://hague2008tallinn.kul.ee/eng/prog⟩ [17 July 2011].

[22] Merryman 2000. page 105.

Commander to seek expert advice as is the normal procedure with legal issues would add nicely to article 11-2 of the Second Protocol.

Apart from all this, the fact cannot be ignored that countries have different perspectives or references when interpreting military necessity. These can entail social, cultural, political, historical, and legal considerations. The military authorities in the United States, for instance, deal with cultural destruction within the framework of their more general Law of War (LOW) that offers a lot of room for the principle of military necessity.[23] This might change in the future since the United States ratified the 1954 Hague Convention (but not the protocols) in 2008.

Nevertheless, the United States has a long tradition in characterizing military necessity. The Lieber code dating from the U.S. civil war defines necessity as measures that are indispensable for securing the ends of a war that are lawful under modern law and usages of war. By doing so Francis Lieber for the first time defines military necessity in the context of *jus ad bellum*,[24] applying to the measures mentioned above as being indispensable and not simply convenient.[25] In strong contrast with such an interpretation is the not-accepted German approach as developed prior to World War I; namely, the principle of *Kriegsraison geht vor Kriegsmanier* that interprets military necessity more as a justification than a limitation.

Of influence to the changing status of military necessity are also continuous developing military conditions like the transformation of warfare from symmetrical into asymmetrical that started after World War II. This process lasted at least until the end of the Cold War marked by the falling of the Berlin Wall. Nevertheless, some matters remain the same such as snipers that take high positions in the terrain. However, instead of church bell towers, positions are taken in minarets e.g. Samarra Iraq.[26] Yet new lessons learned from recent field experiences will undoubtedly lead to more contemporary cases and examples to be discussed in relation to military necessity so we no longer have to work with the old practical cases that involve church towers and convoys with Blue Shield emblems. Typical examples

---

23 *Yale Human Rights & Development Law Journal*. Vol. 8. pp. 164–166, 2005.

24 Legal norms restricting the circumstances in which states can use force, source: Forrest 2007.

25 Forrest 2007.

26 The destruction of the Al-Askariyya Shrine in Samarra, Iraq better known as the golden mosque. The Askariya shrine's dome was destroyed on Feb. 22nd, 2006, in a bombing blamed on Sunni Muslim militants believed to be linked to al-Qaida that unleashed a wave of sectarian violence. Insurgents blew up the two minarets in Samarra, on, June 13, 2007.

of modern cases to be described and used for education are the detonation of obsolete ammunition inflicting damage to monuments through vibrations, and the building of military camps causing environmental and cultural damage, for example, FOB Wolverine and the destroyed ancient Karez water supply system. As for now, the trend is that in practical situations, field commanders place other values higher than cultural preservation labeling such "values" a military necessity.[27] However, some experts make a plea for a strict interpretation: only allow military necessity when expressly permitted by the particular rule itself. The mere plea of military necessity is not sufficient to evade compliance with the laws of war. Otherwise, the concept of military necessity would reduce the entire body of the laws of war to a code of military convenience, having no further sanction than the sense of honor of the individual commander.[28]

As discussed, the Hague Convention of 1954 and other conventions hold many exceptions for military necessity but in fact, this is also a means to make the conventions credible, i.e., to be aware that in certain extreme situations it can be impossible to apply the rules in a strict manner. This opens the door for making excuses. Already some historical cases are described where military necessity has been alleged as an excuse. The Pavle Strugar case concerning the shelling of Dubrovnik is one of them.[29] However while Strugar and others have run the alleged excuse of military necessity, it did not succeed! Still, it is a potential tool for the defense, even if it is hopeless!

We have to realize that there are in fact different levels of protection for cultural property. This is well-illustrated in the opinions and interpretations of juridical experts from both the military and civil spheres. As established when discussing juridical high or higher tests involving adjectives like "imperative," different levels in the intrinsic value (needed), when implementing or codifying prohibitions such as military necessity, do exist. Charles Garraway explains the value and application of military

---

[27] Merryman 2000b.

[28] Leslie C. Green, "The contemporary law of armed conflict," Manchester 2000, pp. 122–123.

[29] Strugar is a former Yugoslav People's Army (JNA) General charged with crimes in the Croatian city of Dubrovnik in 1991. On 31 January 2005, He was found guilty and sentenced to eight years by a Trial Chamber for attacks on civilians; destruction or willful damage done to institutions dedicated to religion, charity and education, the arts and sciences, historic monuments and works or art and science, all in relation to JNA's attack on Dubrovnik in 1991. According to the judgment, Strugar had both legal and effective control of the JNA forces who conducted the military action at Dubrovnik, including the shelling of the Old Town of Dubrovnik.

prohibitions very clearly: when the first codification of restrictions on the conduct of hostilities was taking place, there was a division between those prohibitions that were absolute (use of poison) and those that were not (destruction of property). In the latter, specific exemptions were built in using terms like "imperative military necessity." Unless that exemption is in the treaty law, military necessity is no justification.[30] This explanation shows that though military necessity is flexible and can have different applications as well as degrees of strength it is codified. In other words the rules have been made clearer since Eisenhower's argument. Nevertheless, Thomas Desch states in *Protection of Cultural Property in the Event of Armed Conflict* that the term imperative is not defined for use in connection with military necessity within the treaty text.[31] Therefore, it is up to each state's party to interpret the term causing ambiguity in state practices as well as the risk of misuse.

As can be seen in above statements and clarification there is still a risk of erosion, deflation and misuse of military necessity. If the concept was foolproof, additions such as imperative would not have been necessary. Like with many other juridical or technical instruments, much depends on the skills and intentions of the users or advisers. Besides, military necessity is not a static issue; for instance, its definition triggered intense discussions during the preparations in 1999 for the second protocol of the Hague Convention of 1954. Consequently it was determined that a waiver on the basis of imperative military necessity could only be invoked in case of an act of hostility against CP that was (temporarily) by its function made into a military objective. A requirement was the unavailability of alternatives to reach an equal military advantage. Other restrictions codified concerned the level of military command allowed to make the decision to invoke the waiver meaning the highest level possible (most likely at least a Brigadier-general) and a warning to be given before any attack while all precautions should be taken to minimize damage to the cultural property. As Patty Gerstenblith put it: the Military necessity waiver should only be granted when no feasible alternatives are available to obtain a similar military advantage and when it is not disproportional excessive in comparison with the obtainable military

---

[30] Interview of the author with Professor Colonel Charles Garraway reflections laid down in an email message to the author dated 1 April 2011.

[31] Desch 2002 in *Protection of Cultural property in the event of Armed Conflict—A challenge in Peace Support Operations*. Eds. Edwin R. Micewski and Gerhard Sladek, Vienna 2002, p. 13, "Problems in the Implementation of the Convention from the Perspective of International law."

advantage.[32] This brings in the principle of proportionality that prohibits military action in which negative effects such as collateral civilian causalities clearly outweigh the military gain. This balancing may be done on target-to-target basis but also may be weighed in over-all-terms against campaign objectives.[33] It is my opinion that both solutions are needed, simultaneously as well as a reconsideration of military necessity. When cultural property experts are actually involved in the planning process, this will automatically happen; still, such experts must get accurate advice on the legal implications or be aware of related juridical aspects themselves.

In any case, military necessity cannot be taken separately from the legal concept of proportionality. According to Fischer, the principle of proportionality is embedded in almost every national legal system and underlies the international legal order.[34] Proportionality's function in domestic law is to relate means to ends. In armed conflict, the principle is used to judge first, the lawfulness in *jus ad bellum* in other words the *ad bellum* test or the amount of force to be used and second, the lawfulness in *jus in bello* or the *in bello* test weighing the expected military advantage with the expected incidental loss and damage. The latter has nothing to do with the degree of force. It should be stressed again, especially for the juridical novice, that the proportionality tests are different between *ad bellum* and *in bello*.[35]

In the Gulf War, allied forces acted in individual and collective self-defense against Iraq under Article 51 of the UN Charter, but they disagreed whether the principle of proportionality permitted them to occupy Iraqi territory or oust Saddam Hussein.[36] Many States felt that only the liberation

---

[32] Gerstenblith 2008, p. 82.

[33] Green 2000, pp. 122–124.

[34] Fischer 2007.

[35] Do not mix here the different meanings of *in bello* and *ad bellum*. Proportionality in going to war in the first place looks at "campaign objectives." However, proportionality in its *in bello* meaning is much more restrictive. Additional Protocol I talks of "the concrete and direct military advantage anticipated." Many seek to add "from that specific attack" i.e., limited to the immediate action. However, that is too narrow as a feint attack may be designed to give advantage elsewhere on the battlefield. The UK statement on ratification says, "the military advantage anticipated from an attack is intended to refer to the advantage anticipated from the attack considered as a whole and not only from isolated or particular parts of the attack." This is generally accepted as an accurate statement of the law. Thus, one can go wider than the specific local attack and consider the operation as a whole but not the campaign itself. Source: email correspondence of the author with prof. Charles Garraway dated 28 April 2011.

[36] Charles Garraway argues that the issue in 1991 of whether to occupy Iraq was not one of proportionality since it was interpretation of the various Security Council Resolutions: source interview with Charles Garraway, March 2011.

of Kuwait was a permitted goal. In the same perspective it can be argued by (commanders of) forces on a mission if proportionality allows or urges them to protect CP when, for instance, humanitarian or military strategic goals ask for priority.

The laws of war, however, can be interpreted in various ways. Today's problem is that not all belligerents may comply with the same set of written or customary laws, and even written international law does not cover all situations. For example, the Geneva Conventions principally assumes the fighting parties are nation-states. In a modern military environment, this is no longer a matter of course. For example, if an insurgent force fighting an advanced opponent should follow the rule of wearing distinctive emblems noticeable at a distance (mandatory under the Geneva Conventions to get protection for e.g. the wounded), the other side could detect them and kill them at ranges beyond ranges of their own. With this issue, we also touch upon the notion of distinction that has both military and juridical aspects. Distinction not only plays a role in CPP as seen from philosophical and sociological perspectives (e.g. identity) but is also an international legal concept connected with military operations. It is a principle under international humanitarian law governing the legal use of force in an armed conflict. Belligerents for instance must distinguish between combatants and non-combatants (civilians).

Distinction and proportionality are important factors when assessing military necessity in the sense that damages caused to civilians or civilian property must be proportional and not excessive in relation to the direct military advantage anticipated by an attack on a military objective.[37] As noticed, distinction also plays a role when considering to have non-militarized CPP experts working together with military experts. Nevertheless, distinction applies too in case of selection or exclusion of monumental (cultural) objects. Monitoring cultural property during armed conflict according to IHL is not easy since both parties are responsible for distinction between civilian and military objectives of course at the same time.[38]

---

[37] See: Protocol Additional to the Geneva Conventions of 12 August 1949, and relating to the Protection of Victims of International Armed Conflicts (Protocol I), 8 June 1977.

[38] Chapter II: "Civilians and Civilian Population" of Protocol I Additional to the Geneva Conventions covers distinction. Article 50 defines who is a civilian and what a civilian population is. Article 51 describes the protection, which should be given to civilian populations. Chapter III regulates the targeting of civilian objects. Article 8(2)(b)(i) Rome Statute of the International Criminal Court also prohibits attack directed against civilians. Not all states have ratified Protocol I or the Rome Statute, but it is an accepted principle of international

Attacks should be limited to military objectives. If objects like museums or churches are used for military purposes by one or both sides, there is no proper application of distinction and sanctions that can apply.[39] In order to impose sanctions and for that matter to note actions and behaviors that are not in line with regulations, certain instruments and systems are vital.

Control Mechanisms and Sanctions

All legal concepts discussed here can only function properly with the help of control mechanisms and penal sanctions. First, a concrete example is given and then the line of thinking behind certain legal instruments, especially those restricting the use of military necessity, will be explained. Article 8(2) (b) (iv) of the Rome Statute of the International Criminal Court[40] criminalizes: Intentionally launching an attack in the knowledge that such attack will cause incidental loss of life or injury to civilians or damage to civilian objects or widespread, long-term and severe damage to the natural environment which would be clearly excessive in relation to the concrete and direct overall military advantage anticipated;[41]

Article 8(2) (b) (iv) draws on the principles in Article 51(5) (b) of the 1977 Additional Protocol I to the 1949 Geneva Conventions, but restricts the criminal prohibition to cases that are "clearly" excessive. The application of Article 8(2) (b) (iv) requires, inter alia, an assessment of:

(a) the anticipated civilian damage or injury;
(b) the anticipated military advantage;
(c) and whether (a) was "clearly excessive" in relation to (b).[42]

---

humanitarian law that the direct targeting of civilians is a breach of the customary laws of war and is binding on all belligerents.

39 See for example Radio free Europe Iraq: Laws Of War Tested Amid Battle Near Al-Najaf Holy Sites August 12, 2004 by Robert McMahon.

40 The Rome Statute of the International Criminal Court is the treaty that established the International Criminal Court. It was adopted at a diplomatic conference in Rome on 17 July 1998 and it entered into force on 1 July 2002.

41 There is a juridical debate about if and how to distinguish and consider between civil as state responsible or individual criminal accountability. The words "clearly" and "overall" were inserted to differentiate between the civil and criminal tests. Where the anticipated damage is "excessive," there is a breach of IHL involving state responsibility i.e. civil responsibility decided on a balance of probabilities. However, for criminal responsibility of the individual, it must be "clearly excessive." Garraway, for instance, finds criminal courts not the place to second-guess decisions made by commanders in the heat of battle.

42 Statement from the Chief Prosecutor of the International Criminal Court The Hague

Currently there are different ways to control military necessity. One approach is described in the Second Protocol of the 1954 Hague Convention. There are however possibilities from a wider perspective. In his article "The Doctrine of Military Necessity and the Protection of Cultural Property during Armed Conflicts," Graig Forrest discusses the humanitarian law doctrine of military necessity and its manifestations in the 1954 Hague Convention that underlie both *jus ad bellum* as well as *jus in bello* and stresses that first the requirements for necessity to resort to armed conflict have to be met.[43] This entails that states are not free to wage unrestricted warfare. Any response must be proportionate to the legitimate aims of the use of force such as for instance the minimum required for self-defense. In this context, proportionality is considered an important restriction for the choice of methods and means to conduct war or armed conflict. Forrest distinguishes that necessity can legitimize the armed attack whereas proportionality determines the amount of force to be used. The classic motto is do not cause unnecessary suffering or damage. According to Forrest this limitation is not predominantly humanitarian in nature but is also based on: 1.economic 2. political and 3. military considerations. Taking this into account, I find these three considerations also technically applicable to the protection of cultural property in the event of conflict. To be more specific the three considerations can for instance easily be substituted (following the same order) by: 1.tourism, labor, and export revenues 2. status 3. force acceptance and force multipliers.

Following this the "modern" perspective should be considered that cultural heritage cannot be seen separately from natural heritage (see also the preface); in fact, the same three substitutions can be made. An important treaty aimed at controlling this is the 1972 UNESCO Convention concerning the Protection of the World Cultural and Natural Heritage also known as the World Heritage Convention (WHC). Part of this convention is the World Heritage List containing both cultural and natural heritage sometimes combined. The World Heritage List includes 936 properties forming part of the cultural and natural heritage, which the World Heritage Committee considers as having outstanding universal value. In fact the aim is to maintain a list of world heritage that could be in danger in times of conflict or

Luis Moreno-Ocampo, 9 February 2006 The Hague, 9 February 2006. ⟨http://www.icc-cpi.int/NR/rdonlyres/04D143C8--19FB-466C-AB77-4CDB2FDEBEF7/143682/OTP_letter_to_senders_re_Iraq_9_February_2006.pdf⟩ [17 July 2011].

[43] Forrest 2007.

natural disaster.[44] To be exact, properties described on the list are eligible for international assistance when threatened by specific dangers, among them "the outbreak or threat of an armed conflict."[45] Finally, it has to be stressed that expert advice to commanders for all areas mentioned or aimed at a certain situation is needed before deciding on applying military necessity. The main legal reference or legal driver for this study is the Hague Convention of 1954 and its two protocols. Of course, some treaty obligations are already provided for in the respective national legislations of states parties to the convention but these differ per country.

I hoped that I could follow and analyze the Hague Convention of 1954 to understand and describe how directives for protection were actually implemented by the various stakeholders. Still, instead of utilizing the convention as a framework and legal driver to create a guiding principle, it was found that most countries have no policy designed or special provisions made to enforce the legal obligations the convention requires concerning the military aspects. This gives room for half solutions that are not in accordance with the spirit of the treaty. Formally, there are of course some provisions in the respective national laws and signatories to the 1954 Hague Convention state parties are expected to integrate as far as possible what is stated in the convention into their national legislation. In practice, most state parties lag in creating national legislation. Nevertheless, in urgent cases there still is a possibility to negotiate a so-called SOFA or States of Forces Agreements between the military of two nations on a bilateral basis. Such an agreement was executed in 2008 between the governments of Iraq and the United States to make provisions for protecting existing and newly to be discovered cultural heritage. In this case, there is also a strong connection with environmental rules and considerations as is common in the United States. Notwithstanding this type of mostly bilateral solution, it is clear that a mechanism or stringent regime or ideally an international body to oversee compliance of the instrument can provide for a better result. UNESCO did not want to take this role partly to not discourage non-member states to become parties to the convention.[46] UNESCO did bring together a committee of experts to prepare a draft text that stressed the need for a stringent regime but at the same time considered it a costly and complicated undertaking. This says a lot about how the subject is

---

44 Sources ⟨http://whc.unesco.org/en/list⟩ and ⟨http://whc.unesco.org/en/comittee/⟩ [6 September 2011].

45 O'Keefe 2006.

46 Ibid, p. 165.

perceived in terms of priority and status. Today the control system under the convention is composed of three elements: namely, representatives of parties to the conflict, Commissioners General for Cultural Property, and protecting powers.

The committee initiated by UNESCO advised to use the already established system of protecting powers, meaning a third state chosen by a belligerent power to perform certain functions on its behalf. In fact, it is a solution to create communication channels between hostile powers. In the case of CPP, a protecting power would take care of the interest of cultural property in accordance with article 22 (1&2) of the Hague Convention of 1954. Until now, no party in any conflict has entrusted a protecting power with safeguarding its cultural heritage. However, the system was expanded with control possibilities by a Commissioner General for Cultural Property.

The system of Commissioners General interlinked with the system of the protecting powers worked only once as I described in the paragraph about UNESCO. It should be revived and redesigned since it creates a possibility to deal with urgent problems that need to be handled in an intensive manner (e.g. Afghanistan, Iraq, and recently Libya and Egypt, though it can be disputed whether the latter is an armed conflict and therefore if IHL applies). Additionally, the review of the 1954 Hague Convention, which resulted in the elaboration and adoption of the Second Protocol, provided for the establishment of a new supervisory body—the twelve-member Committee for the Protection of Cultural Property in the Event of Armed Conflict. The committee members were elected for the first time at the meeting of the parties to the Second Protocol in October 2005. The committee had its first session on 26 October 2006, during the UNESCO General Conference.

Common Denominators as Part of Solutions

Before going deeper into common denominators I want to stress that they are not representing universal laws but can differ under the influence of space and time. While acquiring new data and insights within the context of this research, common denominators were identified. As far as they are linked to the military sphere, such denominators can be used to demonstrate to the military that parties hold some things in common. For example, militaries too are interested in cultural heritage. Military museums, collections, and war monuments and their preservation and conservation are excellent examples. The same goes for historical battlefields, fortifications, shelters, bunkers, and the like. However, the denominator can be linked to civil society too; in the United States, for instance, attention for the terrains of military installations is interlinked with preservation of on-site Native American ritual places and burial grounds. In many countries, e.g. Norway, the Ministry of Defense is one of the biggest real estate owners; often this ownership includes cultural properties. Not all stakeholders addressed in this study are conscious of the fact that CPP can bring intangible incentives as well. It appears that many military commanders, for instance, do not realize that the whole exercise of educating and reflecting about CPP issues improves intellectual skills of the people involved. As illustrated in the description of CPP stakeholders, there are all kinds of connections and interests that are of equal interest for multiple parties within the playing field. In a positive sense, such common denominators, when regarded upon as shared interests, can contribute to overcome many of the perceived challenges and problems. As an example: costs can be shared to save money and at the same time improve quality and save overlaps. In addition, the media are interested in news stories that can at the same time draw attention to a problem and generate means to overcome such a problem for instance by triggering (extra) site protection or financial means. These are all good reasons to identify, examine, and analyze positive common denominators within the complex of stakeholders.

Common denominators with a more negative connotation can be distinguished too.

An example valid for all parties engaged in CPP is the perception that they seem to be in competition with each other. Another issue in common is that all parties involved have a tendency to sense potential danger and instability or at least irritation in cultural property, and each of them thinks they are best equipped to control these aspects. This situation creates turmoil triggered by questions as: who is allowed to act by whom? who will become known as the moral defender of a piece of global heritage? and who will get good PR and thus maintain their market share? In fact, parties behave as if they are in a contest instead of being satisfied with doing something to preserve civilization. Apart from this, rivalry focuses on the issue of by whom and how the importance or relevance of certain objects or sites will be determined. The same goes for who is in charge and in control. Consequently, behaviors triggered by these issues are often driven by a competition to obtain and sustain funding. Taking into account that stakeholders not only have different interests but also dissimilar levels of expertise and perception when CPP is at stake, it is obvious that communication about implementation is difficult. It goes without saying that these common attitudes can culminate in conflicts between stakeholders. Nevertheless, the objective has to be finding and examining aspects held in common that contribute to, or serve as a basis for, solutions and improvement.

Many of the identified dilemmas of this research contribute to the current state of affairs regarding the protection of cultural property in the context of conflict. To be specific, there is little or no movement or improvement in the present unsatisfactory situation. It has for instance been found, and this is also a common denominator, that the few successful initiatives and projects are for the large part personality driven. Examples are the training *in situ* projects in Egypt and Jordan and all playing cards projects. If not for a small group of individuals who sometimes even spend their personal resources, these ventures would not have taken place. This aspect does not make these activities unsustainable or less sustainable. Nonetheless, proactive conduct and visionary ideas are indispensable in this phase of developing sustainable CPP strategies, certainly those that involve the military. If military CPP could become part of the scientific discourse, its basis would become more solid and accepted. This is not easy since the current scholarly discourse on cultural heritage is quite elitist while a new input comprising the military aspects including the legal implications increases its complexity and makes the debate multidisciplinary.[47] Nevertheless, the time seems right; discussions are already becoming more intense since the cultural disasters in Baghdad and Afghanistan. As a result, new though not always enriching insights surface on preservation, memory, identity, stewardship and ethical considerations related to working with the military. Concluding, it can be said that on the one hand the general scientific heritage discourse is becoming more profound while on the other hand the debate on military cultural property protection is still in an embryonic phase, and it remains under attack by a civilian perspective sometimes driven by anti-military sentiments.[48]

Opportunities for Effective Implementation of Military Cultural Property Protection

As argued, proactive, creative, and anticipating strategies are needed to achieve an effective and sustainable implementation of military CPP. Such

---

[47] As can for instance be read in Grijzenhout 2009, van der Laarse, 2005, and Lowenthal 1996.

[48] See for example Lowenthal 1996, 2005 and Hamilakis 2009.

an opportunity for getting CPP embedded in the military systems is the connection that already exists on paper between environmental issues and the combination natural and cultural resources. Partnering, in this case with military environmental departments and often the corps of engineers, makes a position within military structures stronger, especially with parties that are already established and firmly anchored in the organization. Certainly at this stage of implementing cultural property protection, logical and effective partners are military environmental policy and protection departments as is already put in practice in the United States. From an international perspective, a potential umbrella to house capabilities could be NATO.

Cultural property obligations combined with environmental responsibilities are codified in NATO's STANAG 7141 EP doctrine. The document considers natural and cultural resources to be characteristics of the environment to be taken into account for NATO led military activities.[49] Mandatory is the identification of potential (environmental) impacts caused by military activities including possible effects on natural and cultural resources. Environmental impacts should be prevented where possible. A really important directive is the desire to implement feasible mitigation measures and to consider alternative locations or activities while still achieving the military objective of the training or operation. The phrase mitigation measures gives possibilities to start protection of cultural property in planning and assessment phases of operations. Of course there has to be a per case agreement with all parties involved on the nature of proposed mitigation methods. A very good example of mitigation that involves both environmental and cultural property issues took place in Afghanistan. In October 2010, General David Petraeus and Major General McHale, with the support of Ambassador Karl Eikenberry, tasked U.S. Army engineers to build a storage facility and conservation lab for archaeological finds exposed in preparation for the mining of a copper quarry at Mes Anyak, Logar Province. The facilities will function as a holding house during a three-year archaeological salvage project. This project demonstrates awareness among commanders and civil top officials about the value of diverse cultural heritage as a measure in reconciliation and public diplomacy.[50]

---

[49] See in the doctrine under 7 b. (5) see also (7), under c. see also e.

[50] Source: CENTCOM White Paper. A Cultural Heritage Strategy as a Force Multiplier for Operation Enduring Freedom. Prepared by Cheryl White, PhD. USCENTCOM/CCJ2–7115.

Another opportunity to engage CPP is NATO's Environmental Training Workgroup (ETWG). The workgroup aims to study and report on selected environmental training issues, including environmental training issues during NATO led operational deployments. Their mission is to consider environmental training issues either as part of routine training, special training prior to operational deployments, or training in theater after any period of conflict. This gives the chance for scientific research critical to get the military debate to a higher level. ETWG's mission statement lists a number of points that justify multi national cooperation training and research as also underpinned by the STANAG 7141 EP doctrine.[51] For instance identifying and recommending suitable environmental training projects to consolidate training within NATO through bilateral or multilateral co-operative training arrangements thus clearing the way for co-operative cultural property protection training *in situ*.

All opportunities mentioned can contribute to raising general awareness of environmental and cultural heritage issues especially areas subject to national and international statutory or legal responsibilities. In case of cultural property protection, these are at least the 1954 Hague Convention and the UNESCO treaty of 1970 (illicit traffic of artifacts).

Apparently, there is not only room but also a desire to strengthen international cooperation on environmental training through bilateral or multilateral training arrangements in which case the focus is on rationalization and specialization. Taken this into account, it seems fair to conclude that when combined with cultural resources training and research a win-win situation can be created. The potential partners mentioned have the right organizational infrastructure and networks to host or incorporate cultural property protection. The link with environmental issues gives a more sustainable basis for effective implementation in an international military setting while at the same time providing for deploying international military experts, e.g., cultural emergency assessment teams. Initial steps to make different countries and potential partners aware of possibilities were taken in October 2009 when the first cultural property protection briefing by the author of this book took place at the NATO School in Oberammergau during the Environmental Management for Military Forces Course. After a well-received presentation, appointments were made to proceed with more lectures. Regrettably, the subject was dropped due to interference of (again) the head of the Dutch MoD's cultural awareness department, who, after

---

[51] See: ⟨http://www.nato.int/structur/ntg/etwg/mission.html⟩ [17 July 2011].

hearing about the initiative, wanted his department to give these lessons although they were not equipped to do so.[52] A letter signed by a General was send to the NATO school in Oberammergau. The result of this Dutch approach is that the current situation is unclear and, as far as could be established, there are no CPP lectures offered anymore in Oberammergau. To engage the EWTG opportunity, the topic of CPP was presented on 9 December 2009 during the EWTG meeting at NATO's Head quarters in Brussels; at the time the workgroup was chaired by the Dutch. The outcome was that CPP would be considered after consulting a higher echelon in the NATO organization; however, by March 2012 still nothing has happened.

The last opportunities to explain here are military incentives or deliverables that can derive from heritage protection. These opportunities become manifest in the context of the new type of conflicts and post-conflict resolutions implemented by military missions. They are the so-called military force multipliers. These force multipliers first have to be identified and then utilized as opportunities for instance within the framework of the so-called comprehensive approach.

Because of changing methods in conflict management and the nature of conflicts, a new role for the military in the context of reconstruction and peacekeeping is becoming evident. The framework in which this takes place at present is known as the Comprehensive Approach or the 3D approach (Development, Defense, and Diplomacy).[53] The Dutch armed forces are using a second generation of this 3D concept, based on four areas of concern: security, politics, and social and economic well-being. CPP activities fit into this concept because internationally and nationally it can be positive for a country's public image. Not the least since by actively demonstrating a CPP policy and meeting treaties and obligations mandatory under IHL, support from a country's inhabitants for national and international military operations is strengthened. The Dutch MoD does not provide for a position of CPP within this 3D approach. This is in contrast with signals given by the ministry during the CPP seminar organized in 2009, where it was indicated that CPP was considered important.[54] In the spirit of the 3D strategy, Coalition forces in Afghanistan and Iraq have developed Provincial Reconstruction Teams (PRTs) designed to help improve stability by increasing the host nation's capacity to govern; enhancing economic viability; and

---

52 Source: internal correspondence Dutch MoD March 9th 2010 Nota 2010004413.

53 Kila 2010a.

54 Cultural Property Protection in Times of Conflict, 25 March 2009 Peace Palace The Hague.

strengthening local government's ability to deliver public services such as security and health care. Staffed by military, militarized and civilian experts CPP should be a part of this. As explained, the comprehensive approach that comprises the PRTs is the perfect design to incorporate the issue of cultural property protection. There is a logical connection between protecting cultural objects and safety, economy, and identity concerns. In other words, a relationship exists between respect for cultural property and successful accomplishing a military mission. Consequently, also the PRT model demands for an adaptation of the military frame of mind.

Research, Education, and Exercise

This section treats the case of Bright Star Egypt June 2009 and October 2009.[55] Before looking into this case it has to be emphasized that it is about training of *non*-Egyptian troops in the periphery of this big military exercise that under normal conditions takes place every two years; the Egyptian MoD did not want their troops to participate in this training. Given the discussions about the recent upheavals in Egypt that came with plunder, damage, and theft of artifacts and sites, already insinuations have been made regarding this specific training. Allegations were made suggesting that training of Egyptian troops about CPP was a cover for unknown American activities. This is not true, actually; U.S. Central Command (CENTCOM) completed the first ever on-site historical cultural training for U.S. military personnel in the Middle East. The opportunity was given for Egyptian military and other countries involved in Bright Star to participate in the cultural training. With the cooperation of the Egyptian Supreme Council of Antiquities, thirty-seven people representing all branches of the U.S. Armed Forces met 20 June 2009 at the ancient pyramid complex of Saqqara in order to experience first hand the importance of cultural preservation during global operations. The Supreme Council (then lead by Dr. Zahi Hawass) provided free access for a tour of the site, including the opening of two tombs that are usually off limits to visitors. Saqqara houses the Step Pyramid, the oldest standing stone structure in the world. Many tombs and temples surround the pyramid complex with some archaeological sites probably yet to be discovered. Relevant for the training was that the terrain shows empty spaces, at least for the untrained eye. Archaeologists and historians from the CENTCOM Historical Cultural Action Group (CHCAG) and the international military cultural resources working group (IMCuRWG) used the archaeological

[55] Sources: the author and Dr. Laurie Rush, U.S. Army Archaeologist.

Figure 39. Training in Saqqara; everybody is dressed as civilians so as not unnecessarily provoke the local population. Photo by U.S. Army.

setting as a background to discuss the strategic importance of recognizing ancient remains in host nation landscapes. Participants learned to identify artifacts and features in a desert landscape that indicate the presence of a site, not always obvious to a casual observer. Saqqara also offered a realistic example of how tourism to a cultural site contributes to the economy, offering income and stability to local inhabitants.

Different Perceptions of the Relevance and Need for Training between the Military and Parties Who Want to Follow Up on the Hague Convention of 1954's Article 25

As discussed, the military themselves seem not really interested in cultural property protection, which makes them an easy target for critique. Consequently the military do not give enough input for the debate on CPP and heritage in general; therefore, the military perspective remains underexposed and is never been examined seriously apart from research from the juridical angle. Reflective thinking, e.g. the parallel drawn by Mark Yanaway (see Chapter 3 the Egypt turmoil case) takes place on another level compared to the civil scientific debate. It seems fair to conclude that little empirical research has been done on the issue and theory is almost non-existing, so reflections are scarce. Accordingly, the military subject requires balance between theoretical reflection and empirical research. This omission that contributes to a general lack of understanding generates a negative effect on worldwide efforts to protect cultural property during conflicts. The situation is especially unsatisfactory as the military are directly confronted with cultural property issues in today's missions; they are a key player when it comes to protection. In the light of all matters explained it is obvious that education and training are vital instruments to improve matters.

Teaching and Training

For a civilian it is not easy to lecture about CPP aspects to the military, just as it can be hard to transfer knowledge on the military aspects to civilians when you are from the military. The main reasons are the cultural and jargon differences, though also ethical issues can play a role. For instance, some scholars feel that when they lecture to the military they give away knowledge that can be used for military purposes. The fact remains that the teacher is responsible for the interpretation of history, even his or her selection of topics and cases makes a presentation of history more subjective. It is difficult to give a method that is well-suited; especially since military are involved, one has to be careful not to unwittingly reinforce self-conceptions of certain identities related to groups like, in this case, regiments, services such as navy, army, etc. As Eric Foner put it: "there is nothing wrong with people developing from history either a sense of identity or taking pride in their nation's accomplishments. However, when history locates supposedly primordial characteristics shared only with members of one's own group it negates the interpenetration of cultures that is so much part of a nation's past."[56] Ideal are trainers and lecturers that have ties with military and academic institutions and preferably a military reserve or active rank because the military prefer to be trained by "colleagues." As established, there is a shortage of educational materials and tools. Especially case studies and handbooks are needed as well as tools that are more modern. Currently there is an initiative to develop a CPP computer game. The idea is that most young soldiers are familiar with these types of games. Recently a demo version of such a game was developed as a private initiative. The game can be

[56] Foner 2002. pp. xvi–xv.

played on different levels and can be adjusted according to rank, service, nationality of armed forces, and operational environment. Although there are many games to exercise and simulate battlefield situations, it will be difficult to find funds for the production of a CPP game. The project can probably only be realized with support from governments or international organizations.

More efforts are being made to establish adequate training and education, and various types of instruction are being tested and, as far as possible, implemented. All of these are in the embryonic phase, but it is possible to distinguish different approaches and examples of good practice. In the next paragraph, a number of examples will be discussed.

Training strategies for military must take into account the fact that instructing and teaching military differs from lecturing to university students. Backgrounds, language, and intellectual levels vary, so methods for transfer of knowledge have to be tailormade for the target group. First, awareness on the subject of culture and heritage must be raised to make the students more receptive and appreciative to cultural objects. When education is provided for the strategic level a basic introduction to art history is essential. Important tools for the teacher are the use of practical examples, anecdotes, discussion, working groups such as syndicates, training *in situ*, guest lecturers, visits to museums and libraries. There has to be a clear relation between the matters addressed during lectures and the positioning of CPP in the military planning and setting. The lecturer has to be aware of military customs, habits, and expressions before acting as a teacher; this is essential and a condition for success. Personnel in charge of training should take into account that ongoing research on the topic, including the scientific and theoretical aspects, is necessary. This can be done in cooperation with military academies or civil educational institutions. A good method for training is the use of replicas or mock-ups when on-site education is not possible. Advantages are that there is no risk of damage to cultural objects (especially in case of bigger groups) and no need for traveling. The Legacy Funded In Theater Heritage Training Project from the Cultural Resources Section of the U.S. Army is developing and implementing this type of training; however, it requires thorough research and preparation. Training with mock-ups supplements the avoidance target list provided to the U.S. Air Force by Middle East Archaeology subject matter specialists. An example of a potentially good activity based on inaccurate information is the following: the replica on the picture is from a stone cone mosaic tower from the ancient city of Uruk in Iraq. It is an avoidance target on Fort Drum's Adirondack Aerial Gunnery Range 48.

Figure 40. Mock up cone temple wall. Fort Drum, United States. Photo by Laurie Rush, U.S. Army.

Figure 41. The real cone temple wall in Uruk without a reference to put its size in perspective. Public domain. This file is licensed under the Creative Commons Attribution-Share Alike 2.5 Generic license.

Figure 42. The real cone wall *in situ*. Photo: Diane Siebrandt for Laurie Rush, U.S. Army.

Nevertheless, the mock-up is modeled after the picture of the original cone temple wall fragment that, as the picture shows is still *in situ* in Uruk. At the time the replica was made nobody checked, or was able to check, the real measurements *in situ* probably because of safety concerns due to the unrest in Iraq at the time. In April 2009, Laurie Rush Fort Drum's archaeologist was able to visit Uruk and found that the scale was completely wrong, as the pictures demonstrate. Anyhow, it is an excellent lesson learned emphasizing the argument that specialists, in this case academics, have to be consulted whenever possible.

In addition, three mock cemeteries and a number of architectural mock sites were completed at Fort Drum to train the ground troops for their Iraq deployment. According to the In Theater Heritage Training Project, construction of these assets was extremely cost effective.

In the UK, training focusing on Afghanistan takes place on the Defense Training Estate East at Thetford while archaeological activities are taking place in the Defense Training Estate Salisbury Plain.[57]

---

[57] Source: Estatement, issue 67 Summer 09 Defense Estates. UK.

Figure 43. Mock up Islam cemetery Fort Drum, United States. Photo by Ian Warden, U.S. Army.

Training in situ

On-site training is aimed at planners, higher officers, military attachés, policymakers, etc., and takes place in and on actual monuments or archaeological sites. Training courses are planned or took place in Jordan (Petra 2011) Egypt (Saqqara 2009) and Vienna. Besides the transfer of specific knowledge, it is a good possibility to raise awareness on CPP among military and other stakeholders. The ideal would be to have lectures first as an introduction, and then go to an archaeological site to continue lectures using the examples *in situ* as illustrations. Topics can include recognition of archaeological terrain, artifacts, and features; avoiding disturbance to the context of the site; guarding and protection of sites; and the use of simple documentation techniques. In addition, problems can be addressed such as dealing with situations where art is (mis)used as propaganda and identification of cultural objects including how to make a basic iconographic description and possible damage assessment. Solutions are of course intermingled with the perception of culture amongst the personnel involved but discussing this can generate synergy. The Saqqara training case from 2009 shows that political motives and manipulations can play a role or even interfere during training *in situ*. That these implications can have repercussions for the protection and safeguarding of cultural property during conflict is clearly established in the Egypt Emergency Mission casus from 2011. The Combat Command Historical Cultural Action Group (CCHAG) in cooperation with IMCuRWG plans to offer additional on-site trainings in the Middle East in association with planners of future exercises.[58] These intentions are based on the feedback of the military students engaged in the Saqqara training. Many students clearly expressed that there is no comparison for an *in situ* training. In fact, the instructors learned as much as the students did. The lessons learned included: the desirability of experienced military trainers used to communicate with military in the CPP educational process; wearing civilian clothes when teaching at host nation sites; and the importance of a multinational approach in order to depoliticize the training. International cooperation on CPP is essential. CPP is a very sensitive subject connected with identity and status issues of a host country; damage inflicted by foreigners counts much more heavy than that inflicted by its own population. It is also important to distinguish that training foreign military is not an attempt by foreigners to teach local nationals about their history and cultural heritage. Where possible, host nation experts should be utilized.

The Egypt training was funded by the U.S. Department of Defense Environmental International Cooperation funds and by the Office of the Secretary of Defense Legacy Resource Management Program with indirect support from Installation Management Command. In addition, the training was sponsored and coordinated by the Central Command Historical Cultural Working Group now called CCHAG with cooperation from the Bright Star Planners and IMCuRWG. It turned out that it was critical to use an international approach to achieve success. Saqqara can and should become the model for military CPP training of the future. During the training of military planners in June 2009, the Egyptian MoD suddenly did not allow their military to take part in CPP training, though due to the sensitiveness of foreign experts training host nation military, this was not even suggested by the Americans. Still a way was found to train the military planners

[58] The CCHWG first changed its name in to CCHAG (Central Command Historical Cultural Advisory Group) but is recently renamed again in now the Combat Command Historical/Cultural Action Group.

The reason is that the group now has global concerns beyond the CENTCOM area of responsibility.

without help of the Egyptian MoD and without going on military terrains, and the training was successful.[59] In October 2009 the proposed trainings ran into unforeseen problems due to travel restrictions in Egypt for U.S. personnel and subsequently was very limited.

There are a number of lessons learned from the Bright Star cultural property protection training project such as the need to be patient and to use opportunities. Nevertheless, it became clear again that due to cultural differences and sensitiveness communication problems might occur. Political motives can interfere with training too; an Egyptian General, for instance, thought that the United States would train Egyptians on culture. It was also said that the United States with their reputation as destroyers of CP in Babylon was not allowed to teach about culture in Egypt.

It was not possible to verify the exact sources of these impediments; they were probably partly the results of miscommunications and misunderstanding. However, the trainers were patient and looked for opportunities to use. In October, first a team of British military and a small number of U.S. officers and DoD employees were trained; later training of U.S. military was allowed and could be done in cooperation with the U.S. Moral, Welfare and Recreation team attached to the Bright Star exercise. At this time, the Egyptian revolts of January and February 2011 that included looting and theft of artifacts were of course not foreseen, but they prove that preparations in peacetime are necessary. A last tool to be used both for training and in theater is developed by Laurie Rush; namely, the Archaeology Check List for military in the field, see figure 44. This list is designed for use by personnel without any formal knowledge about cultural property and demonstrates the link cultural resources have with environmental issues.

Examples of Other Means for Training Military: the CPP Playing Cards

An initiative from the United States originally for Iraq and Afghanistan are the Defense Department CPP decks of playing cards, this time showing some of the countries' most precious archaeological sites instead of the most-wanted former regime officials. Some 100,000 new decks of playing cards were sent to troops in both Iraq and Afghanistan as part of an awareness program so troops could help preserve the heritage of those countries. It is aimed at making troops aware that they should not pick up and take

[59] This was also a missed opportunity since in Egypt many military terrains contain archaeological objects and monuments.

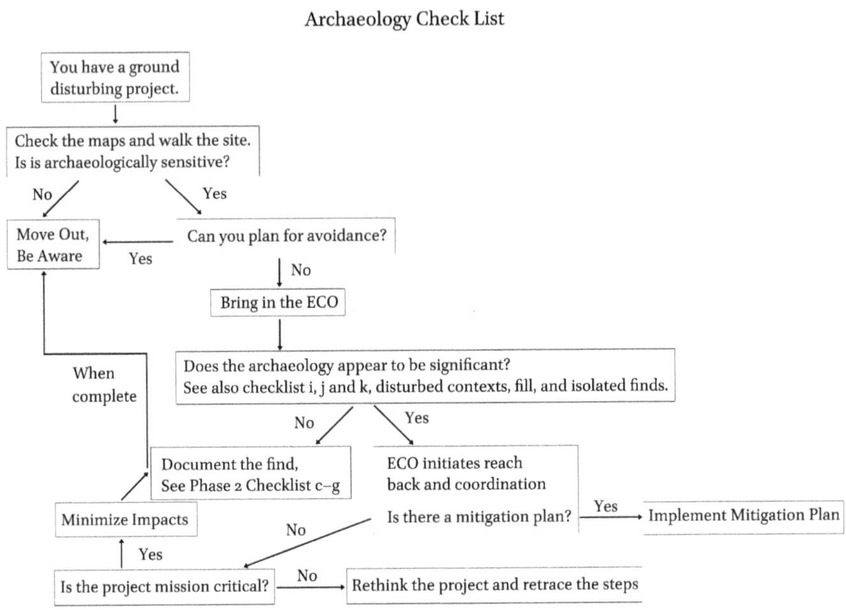

Figure 44. Archaeology checklist NB. ECO = Environmental Conservation Officer. © Laurie Rush U.S. Army.

home artifacts and that they should avoid causing damage to historic sites. Each card in the deck shows an artifact or site or gives a tip on how to help preserve antiquities. For the Bright Star exercise that takes place in Egypt every two years, a special deck focusing on Egyptian CP has been developed.

In collaboration with the Netherlands National Commission for UNESCO, the Netherlands Ministry of Education, Culture, and Science (Department of Cultural Heritage and the State Inspectorate for Cultural Heritage), the Netherlands MoD developed a deck of CPP playing cards. The cards are an educational and informational tool with the purpose to disseminate the principles of the 1954 Hague Convention and its protocols to Protect Cultural Property in the event of armed conflict, especially to military and policy makers.

Figure 45. The Dutch playing cards © Joris Kila.

Geographic Information Systems (GIS) and Satellite Remote Sensing

Within both the Combat Command Historical Cultural Action Group and IMCuRWG a subcommittee exists consisting of civil GIS experts and specialists from various sections within the U.S. and European Armed Forces. As addressed in the paragraph on looting and poverty, new techniques related to GIS such as Satellite Remote Sensing can play an important role in pre-deployment assessments since terrain can be studied from space looking for ancient features on the ground.[60] Furthermore, GIS can help archaeological sites preservation by detecting and documenting looting. Of course related ethical issues have to be discussed among stakeholders. Outcomes and data of these committees can be made available to support adjacent activities like mapping initiatives, web sites, and environmental aspects. As indicated earlier, a good source for getting acquainted with the subject is a book by Sarah Parcak. She gives a comprehensive oversight of satellite remote

60 Satellite Remote Sensing means collecting data about the earth's surface using satellites circling around the planet.

sensing for archaeology. Techniques and data sets described are fit to be used for assessments helping safeguarding cultural property in case of conflict. Furthermore if combined or at least in cooperation with military sources and experts a lot of information otherwise difficult to obtain will be available for CPP. If good cooperation with military experts can be established, it should be made possible to obtain aerial pictures from reconnaissance flights and even from unmanned aerial vehicles or drones to check for damages, looting patterns, and the like.

Current Examples of Military CPP Implementation, a Comparative Analysis

At present, there is some movement at the international front, in large part triggered by the United States. The U.S. Department of Defense recognized that destructions of cultural property as occurred in Iraq and Afghanistan affected the U.S. military mission in a negative way. Critical press coverage resulted in bad PR for the United States. It was time to show to the world a willingness to avoid intentional and, even more important, unintentional damage to cultural sites. In 2008, the United States ratified the Hague Convention of 1954.[61] The fact that the United States ratified a 1954 treaty in 2008 or in fact officially on March 13, 2009 when its instrument of ratification was deposited with UNESCO needs clarification. The United States helped to draft and signed (but did not ratify) the convention already in 1954.[62] The reason is that at this time the treaty was self-implementing. In other words, nothing had to change regarding national U.S. legislation. The first protocol was not ratified due to strong opposition from the antiquities market and museums.[63] The second protocol is also today out of the question since it is not at all self-implementing and requires the creation of a criminal offense, providing criminal responsibility, intent, and knowledge are proven. General U.S. opinion, however, states that even only ratifying the Convention and not the protocols still gives a positive signal to the rest of the world. A

61 Without the 1st and 2nd protocols.

62 At the time the U.S. Executive Branch decided not to transmit the treaty to the Senate for ratification due to military concerns about how it might affect policy at the height of the Cold War. Source website U.S. Blue Shield, ⟨http://www.uscbs.org/resources.htm⟩ [17 July 2011].

63 This had to do with regulations ordering to prevent export of cultural property from occupied territory and to seize cultural property imported into its territory from any occupied territory and to return seized property to the formerly occupied territory.

measurable positive effect is that the U.S. Department of Defense inspired by the Hague Convention of 1954 has started to implement training and is seeking international cooperation on the subject. In Europe many military appear not to be aware—or choose not to be aware—of obligations following the convention; exceptions are Austria, Italy, and Poland. When reminded, the absence of direct orders from the civilian government is used as a justification. A more practical reason seems to be the avoidance of extra work and financial costs.[64] In addition, possible projects and awareness raising on the subject are hindered because civil cultural scientists and policy makers are not familiar with military cultures and priorities. In countries like the Netherlands, the direct link that existed between civil society and the armed forces was lost when conscription was suspended.[65] On top of that, part of the civil society is inclined to associate the armed forces with violence and destruction of property resulting in a tendency to keep a distance from "the army." Of course perceptions differ; some consider an Israeli soldier more dangerous than let's say a Belgian warrior.

Because of the gradual shift in the type of armed conflicts from symmetric or interstate to asymmetric and today's interconnected role of the military with reconstruction related development issues, opinions are slowly beginning to change.[66] This is part of the continued process of adjusting military mindsets that at the same time brings opportunities for CPP.

The process of change in the nature of conflict particularly reveals deficiencies and weaknesses in the 1954 Hague Convention such as the multi-interpretability of military necessity, the degree of effectiveness of the concept of special protection, cultural property protection in non-international conflicts, the efficiency of sanctions for breaches of the Convention, and the control system of the Convention.[67] Shortcomings related to these aspects

---

64 A reaction I got on more occasions while teaching cultural property protection at Dutch military courses.

65 The Draft was effectively suspended in 1996. ⟨http://www.statengeneraaldigitaal.nl/thema_dienstplicht.html⟩ [12 January 2011].

66 Symmetric warfare is the clash of two conventional adversaries in battles. Symmetric operations involve the engagement of similar military forces in force-on-force warfare, Colin S. Gray, "The Nature of Land Warfare," ⟨www.defence.org.cn/aspnet/vip-usa/.../2008.../chapter1.pdf⟩ [17 July 2011]. The term "Asymmetrical warfare" appears to date from the early 1990s. In it, a relatively small and lightly equipped force attacks points of weakness in an otherwise stronger opponent by unorthodox means. All guerrilla activity, especially urban terrorism, falls within this definition. Source: World Wide Words © Michael Quinion, Oct 20 2001.

67 Source: Report on the implementation of the 1954 Hague Convention for the Protection of Cultural Property in the event of armed conflict and its two 1954 and 1999 protocols. Report

are addressed in this study. On the other hand it should be stressed that international agreements and shared legal concepts also become more important because new asymmetric conflicts and warfare often require the use of shifting coalitions. Military from respective coalition partners will have different rules, ideas, and cultures and consequently varying notions of proportionality and necessity including the effects on CPP.

In the meantime, discussions with peers and stakeholders and my own experience show that attempts to initiate training of military on CPP and realizing of Ministry of Defense dedicated cultural capabilities are still challenged.[68] The nature of these challenges is discussed in the paragraph about dilemmas or challenges that restrain CPP implementation, but it seems fair to say that many parties involved are currently not acting in compliance with international legal appointments that include military obligations as those stated in the Hague Convention for the Protection of Cultural Property of 1954.[69] Consequently, new insights touching directly on modern types of conflicts and their connections with cultural icons, identity, and political control are ignored by parties that could use them to benefit their operational planning, as will be demonstrated in the case of FOB Wolverine.[70] Even so there are countries and institutions that can serve as examples of good practice or are catching up rapidly after signing the 1954 Hague Convention.[71]

Before giving a limited account of today's international activities, a contextualization is needed. Internationally hardly any military doctrine has been developed for cultural property protection in times of armed conflict.[72] The United States has a chapter on historical and cultural preservation in an environmental regulation of Central Command.[73] NATO gives some provisions and procedures through its Joint Doctrine for Environmental Protec-

---

on the activities from 1995 to 2004 ⟨http://unesdoc.unesco.org/images/0014/001407/140792e.pdf⟩ [17 July 2011].

68 My experience: five years of lecturing and training military personnel about CPP and taking part in numerous conferences and seminars, meetings and witnessing different attempts to start CPP programs and create CPP capabilities.

69 For instance, the Hague Convention articles 25 and 30: Dissemination of the Convention.

70 The U.S. Military Expanded a Base (Wolverine) and Inadvertently Disrupted Ancient Afghan Canals. ⟨http://online.wsj.com/article/NA_WSJ_PUB:SB124224652409516525.html⟩ [17 July 2011].

71 Some examples of good practice are Austria, the Polish CIMIC organization, the Carabinieri, and new U.S. DoD Initiatives.

72 Doctrine gives a general frame of reference for all military. This helps standardizing operations and military tasks.

73 U.S. CENTCOM reg 200-2. See appendix A4.

tion during NATO-led Military Activities, but these are not embedded or codified in any domain or operational planning process. Even if the importance of CPP will be recognized by the international military community, implementation processes will take a long time.

The current international political situation that carries risks for multiple conflicts calls for immediate precautions to safeguard cultural heritage. To prevent unnecessary damage in the near future, international cooperation on the topic is necessary. Financial as well as personnel means are too scarce to be able to provide a total solution for any individual country. Joint cooperation can be more efficient and will cost less. Areas of common benefit are training and education, developing training tools, joint exercises and in theater assessments. In order to achieve this, it is necessary for military planners and experts to work together with civil experts in order to develop doctrines. Only this way cultural property protection can be incorporated in military planning and become recognized as a DoD or MoD dedicated (Navy, Army, Air force, Military Police) embedded capability.

As described in the paragraph on opportunities for effective implementation of Military CPP there is also an opportunity to link cultural resources management to environmental management doctrines like NATO's STANAG 7141 EP doctrine. This definitively opens alternative options for embedding Cultural Property Expertise within military organizations.

An example of good practice can be found within the U.S. DoD where possibilities are studied for expanding training activities and embedding capabilities in the DoD. Starting points include environmental programs with already employed archaeologists plus other experts. Within Civil Affairs (civil military cooperation units), training is also being given, focusing on museums and art. Cultural Resource managers and archaeologists can be found in all the services. In addition, the Army's Integrated Training Area Management Program includes an archaeological site protection component. The Combat Commands have an Historical/Cultural Action Group (CCHAG) and an input into the newly founded International Military Cultural Resources Working Group (IMCuRWG). There is a close cooperation with Colorado State University. In 2009, a cultural property protection *in situ* training took place in Egypt, in cooperation with a Dutch expert from the Netherlands. The CCHAG was instrumental in the creation of the historical and cultural preservation chapter in the CENTCOM Contingency Environmental Guidance R-200-2; this can be considered a breakthrough.

The United Kingdom has a goal of ratifying the 1954 Hague Convention and its Protocols within the near future. However, matters are repeatedly delayed apparently due to busy parliamentary meeting schedules, according to another source due to the MoD.[74] There are, however, archaeologists working within the British MoD to protect Defense Estates.[75] A civil cultural heritage expert gives advises to the Defense Committee of the British Parliament and will involve the outcomes of the seminar held in The Hague.[76] For the time being apparently not much more will be undertaken due to financial restraints.

In Austria, the subject of CPP is already firmly on the agenda. In 1999 a workshop on the Protection of Cultural Property was organized in Klagenfurt by the Austrian Federal Ministry of Defense and the Austrian Society for the Protection of Cultural Property. This initiative was aimed at harmonizing cooperation on CPP during theoretical and practical defensive operations between military professionals and reservists with CPP background.

Cultural Property Protection Officers (CPPO) are currently deployed in all branches of the Austrian Armed Forces. CPP is fully integrated in training and planning. The Institute for Human and Social Sciences that is part of the Defense Academy is doing research on the subject of CPP. A military CPP course aimed at officers from Eastern Europe took place in October 2010 at the Austrian Defense Academy (National Defense Academy in Vienna) in cooperation with UNESCO. The newly found Association of National Committees of the Blue Shield (ANCBS) has an Austrian president.[77] From 19 November to 2 December 2011 an important event took place at the Austrian National Defence Academy in Vienna.

The Austrian Ministry of Defence, in cooperation with NATO's Allied Command Transformation (ACT based in Virginia) and the International Military Cultural Resources Working Group (IMCuRWG) organized the first ever pilot course on cultural property protection in accordance with The 1954 Hague Convention for the Protection of Cultural Property in the event of armed conflict and protocols and NATO's STANAG 1741 EP. As mentioned, Austria organized multiple courses and seminars on CPP before, but this was the first time ever with NATO and with international "students," both military as well as civilian.

This initiative demonstrated that the Austrian MoD was and still is one of the few institutions that really implements The Hague Convention especially the directives on dissemination, training and education. Apart

---

[74] Source: information from Peter Stone, January 2011; Charles Garraway, March 2012.
[75] For instance for Defence Estates Operations North in Salisbury UK.
[76] Peter Stone the chairman of the military operational seminar in The Hague.
[77] Karl von Habsburg (Austria Blue Shield).

from that several components of this course were really useful in a practical sense. To mention some of them: a contribution was made to lift the subject of CPP and the military perspective on CPP in the international scientific discourse. Via an exercise, an inquiry was made into the practice of military planning and the conditions, restraints, and possibilities for CPP officers to function within the military planning process. Outcomes showed many problems but also opportunities to make this participation possible, not only based on the Austrian situation where it is already happening but also from an international perspective, for instance, with NATO-led operations. To actually experience the planning process, an exercise was presented and tested with the participants that took place in Wiener Neustadt.

New case studies were introduced by different speakers. These cases were based on recent asymmetric conflicts; a number of them are also presented in this book. Is there an explanation for the special attitude of Austria towards implementing the 1954 Hague Convention for the protection of cultural property? A possible reason dates from 1968 in the context of the so-called Prague Spring. At the time the Austrian government and military leadership thought that Soviet troops crossed Austrian soil on their way to Prague, thus violating Austria's sovereignty and neutrality.[78] It was clear the country could not stop the Soviets with military means. Following an initiative of the Federal Bureau for Monuments and Sites, hundreds of Blue Shield emblems (the emblem of the 1954 Hague Convention) were attached to historical and cultural monuments (for the purpose, a largely-exaggerated number of monuments) along the envisaged Soviet route through Austria. The idea was that the "enemy" would acknowledge that with every step through Austria they were in violation of international law. This was a form of resistance without force in the middle of the Cold War and at the same time started a sort of Blue Shield movement in Austria in 1980 resulting in the Society for the Protection of Cultural Property, in which organization many military participate as members and in board positions. However, seen from the perspective of this book and supporting the argument of CPP's value as a military deliverable, a significant conclusion can be drawn; namely that in fact the Austrian MoD for the first time (maybe without realizing this) used CPP as a Military Force Multiplier or as a means to solve a military problem.

---

[78] All information about the Austrian Prague motive is based on Rush 2010, chapter 14, pp. 145–146 and talks with Dr. Friedrich Schipper and Karl von Habsburg on 22 February 2012.

In Italy in the 1960s the Ministry of Education requested the establishment of a special unit of the Carabinieri. This unit, dealing with the defense of the national paleontological, archaeological, artistic, and historic heritage was the *Comando Carabinieri Ministero Pubblica Istruzione—Nucleo Tutela Patrimonio Artistica* (Ministry of Education Carabinieri Division—Unit for the Defence of Cultural Heritage) currently known as the *Comando Carabinieri Tutela Patrimonio Culturale*. Apart from fighting illicit traffic and tomb robbing (Etruscan vases are still stolen from archeological sites in Italy), the division has been very active in Iraq. The World Association for the Protection of Cultural Property in times of conflict (WATCH)[79] is located in Rome and maintains a big network with stakeholders in the Middle East and the Mediterranean countries.

A case of good practice is an event that took place in Estonia.[80] The Estonian Ministry of Culture and the MoD organized a conference called Protecting Cultural Heritage in Times of Armed Conflict in February 2008 in Tallinn. During this event, a Memorandum of Cooperation between the Estonian Ministry of Culture and the Estonian Ministry of Defense was presented. The document contained an agreement to work on implementing cultural property protection together. A publication following the conference was released in September 2009 and is available on the internet though only in the Estonian language.[81] So far, the initiative did not result in any follow up regarding special CPP training for the Estonian or Baltic Armed Forces.

Article 90 of the Dutch Constitution states explicitly that the Dutch government is bound to promote and strengthen international justice. One can assume that this important directive serves as a basis and an argument for the Dutch participation and undersigning of international treaties. Concerning the Hague Convention of 1954, the practical implementation is not sufficient especially when obligations regarding military implementation are involved. The following case examples substantiate this assumption: the Ministry of Defense organized a seminar on the subject in The Hague in March 2009. During the conference the MoD made a statement that was put into words by a high ranking officer who said: "the Netherlands MoD will work on CPP because we have to, we are able to and we want to do this since we acknowledge the relevance and big importance of CPP."[82] After

---

79 See www.eyeonculture.net.

80 Kila 2009.

81 See: ⟨www.muinsuskaitse.ee/failid/157_est_haagi_konvents.pdf⟩ [17 July 2011].

82 Opening speech at the Dutch MoD Seminar of 25 March 2009 in The Hague by Commodore E. Kopp.

the conference a report was prepared with recommendations for the way ahead including the creation of a relatively small MoD dedicated cultural property protection capability. The report was offered to the Dutch Chief of Defense, but it was not taken into consideration due to internal financial cutbacks and opposition from the cultural awareness department.[83] Playing cards to be used as training tools for military troops deployed abroad have been developed in cooperation with the author of this study; until now they have not been used to train the Dutch troops.

Due to the events in Libya, IMCuRWG attempted to get in touch again with the Dutch MoD and managed to hand over coordinates of important Libyan cultural heritage sites. The coordinates were meant to be used by the Dutch F16 pilots who under NATO command took part in imposing a no-fly zone in Libya under the UN 1973 resolution. It was hoped that the IMCuRWG initiative towards the Dutch MoD would create more contacts and possibilities in the future. Later, in August 2011, IMCuRWG also managed to give the coordinates directly to NATO's SHAPE in Belgium.[84]

In Poland, international law in relation to CPP is included in the Regulations of Tactical Actions of the Ground Forces issued by the Polish Army General Staff in 1994. The Defense Ministry has established a permanent cultural property protection department that coordinates actions in the field of the protection of cultural heritage in the armed forces, including the implementation of CPP activities following the 1954 Hague Convention. During research, I found that many activities are carried out through the Polish CIMIC organization. Apparently, the Polish have a distinct and more effective interpretation of NATO's CIMIC Doctrine AJP-9. A clear account of Polish military cultural activities in Iraq is given by Miroslav Olbrys in "Archaeologists on Duty in Iraq: Polish Approach to the Protection and Salvage of Archaeological Heritage in Central South Iraq."[85]

---

83 There is ongoing opposition from the Army's Cultural Awareness department. Many, actions are undertaken internally to keep new initiatives out. The dept. claims that CPP is completely covered by them. This is another clear example of tension between the two disciplines CPP and Cultural Awareness causing serious restraints as will be further addressed in the next paragraph.

84 Supreme Headquarters Allied Powers Europe (SHAPE) near Mons, Belgium is the Headquarters of Allied Command Operations (ACO), one of NATO's two strategic military commands. It performs the operational duties previously undertaken by Allied Command Europe and Allied Command Atlantic. ACO is commanded by the Supreme Allied Commander Europe (SACEUR) and is responsible for all Alliance military operations. ⟨http://www.aco.nato.int/page1544341.aspx⟩ [24 August 2011].

85 Olbrys 2007.

Concluding Remarks:
Proceeding From Violently Opposed to Being Accepted as Self-Evident

The changing military role in operations offers new possibilities for cultural intervention in theaters of conflict. In order to anticipate and prepare for this a more sophisticated understanding of the current situation including parties, playing fields, and their interactions as described in this study is useful. Possible grounds for the lack of interest or even neglect from both military leadership, civilian policy, and decision makers as discussed in this research should be continuously identified and analyzed. It can do no harm to investigate geographical influences too while asking why appreciation of CPP differs per country. The Italians, for instance, pay more attention to military cultural property protection during international missions than most other countries, but in spite of the fact that the term *Beni Culturali* is Italian, it has not been researched whether they pay the same attention to environmental implications connected with cultural resources. In the same spirit it seems worthwhile to investigate if there is a causal link between appreciating national cultural resources and military cultural property protection during international operations and if this is influenced by national identity. As established, the modern concept of identity has multiple characteristics. Identity issues are often part of conflict causes, but at the same time respective owners of identities, among them the military, can be influenced by their urge for distinction while making decisions about conflict resolution. Moreover, in the context of training and debate it has been identified as a major perception problem that cultural property protection is often mixed up or too closely linked with cultural awareness.[86] The confusion again demonstrates lack of information and training on cultural property issues, but also the necessity for cultural property experts to operate separate from cultural awareness specialists especially in a military setting.

A new issue, potentially fit for misunderstanding and wrong interpretations, is already emerging. It's the question of whether CPP should be fitted in the model of kinetic warfare and older styles of special forces warfare or if it should be part of intelligence-driven decision making, giving room for extra confusion about the term COIN.[87] As argued in the paragraph about the media, the answer is not in favor of military intelligence, but is still

---

86 Wunderle 2006, Baker 2003.

87 See also: J. Price, Whose side are you on boys? The problem for embedded anthropologists in the U.S. Human Terrain System teams, *Forum Archaeologiae* 55/VI/2010 (http://farch.net).

difficult to give since the majority of legislation is based on the old symmetric conflict situation. Most of the legal framework in which CPP is codified dates from the fifties, or even before. However, the kinds of potential cultural property damage or modern iconoclasm that take place in contemporary conflicts must be managed and solved using modern means and techniques. CPP also needs to be a component of peacekeeping operations and the military delivery of humanitarian aid. A first start would be to set up a serious dialogue between cultural, military, and legal experts aimed at upgrading the legalities. This investigation verifies that in general most civil and military parties are unaware of the military strategic, juridical, and tactical implications of cultural property protection. As a result, civil stakeholders are not only showing ignorance, but on occasions some express strong antimilitary sentiments thus compromising proper implementation of the 1954 Hague Convention.[88] The military from their perspective are for the larger part not aware of the relevance of cultural property nor are they aware about the current scholarly debate on cultural heritage. If the subject would have been considered relevant within military circles in the positive sense, meaning to save heritage according to international legislation and not merely as a military intelligence tool, scenarios would have been developed sooner for use in training and planning.

Until recently, and as established earlier, only a few materials using examples from World War II and the period of the Cold War were available. These materials were based on the symmetric type of warfare and therefore almost obsolete.[89] Experiences gained during conflicts in former Yugoslavia, Iraq and Afghanistan illustrated the role of "iconoclasm" in contemporary, often asymmetric, armed conflicts.[90] Over the last few years, a modest number of case studies deriving from these conflicts were published among others by the author of this book. As addressed in the training paragraph, new tools have been created or are in the process of development. Nevertheless, there is still an urgent need for up-to-date training materials. At the same time, cultural resources considerations sometimes combined with environmental obligations must be included in the military planning process. It is difficult to say if this will happen soon since there are not many legal instruments suitable for state parties to enforce compliance with the 1954 Hague Convention. Nevertheless, the Convention is clear about the obligation to

---

88 Hamilakis 2009.

89 New materials are now available such as playing cards through the U.S. DoD and a Dutch initiative.

90 Gamboni, 1997.

disseminate its contents and directives. Parties to the 1954 Convention and its Protocols must disseminate the treaty provisions as widely as possible, seeking to strengthen appreciation and respect for cultural property among the general population. Particular effort should be taken to disseminate information among the armed forces and personnel engaged in the protection of cultural property.[91] Investigations like this one demonstrate that dissemination is not happening in most state parties to the convention and, regrettably, this includes the Netherlands. The lack of possibilities or willingness to disseminate what is stated in the convention and subsequently the significance of CPP especially for the military contributes to the situation in which most military do not see nor understand the relevance of cultural heritage in the context of their profession and responsibilities. Even in the rare cases that commanders open the doors for experts to start education and implementation regarding CPP there is still an intellectual restraint. It is a challenge for cultural property protection professionals to prove and explain to the military the social values of CP as carriers of collective memory and identity. In addition, the fact remains that cultural property is hard to pin down and consequently difficult to control in situations connected to (potential) conflicts. From the practical military point of view, any relation between a certain cultural object or site and identity remains either unclear or difficult to understand. An interesting parallel is that this ambiguity can occur on the individual level when works of art are involved. Art has the potential to cause commotion through what it communicates or actually through what people think it communicates.[92] A historical example is the so-called *Entartete Kunst*. The Nazis destroyed much of it in 1937, and later they found that this type of art could be sold for hard currency.[93] It makes one wonder if military also should have access to some basic education about art.

There is however a simple solution for the dissemination problem. Governments, especially signatories to the 1954 Hague Convention, can order their MoDs to implement cultural property protection strategies including training and preparations in peacetime. This is not likely to happen mainly due to financial reasons though de facto the financial motive stands for lack

---

[91] Hague Convention Art. 25; Protocol 2, Art. 30. Source: International Committee of the Red Cross, ADVISORY SERVICE ON INTERNATIONAL HUMANITARIAN LAW, 09/2002. ⟨www.savingantiquities.org/pdf/Cultural_property.pdf⟩ [1September 2011].

[92] Leydesdorff 2010.

[93] Literarily: degenerate art. The Nazis organized the exhibition Entartete Kunst, in July 1937 in München. The exhibit was designed to ridicule and denigrate creative works not upholding the right National Socialist virtues.

of appreciation of CPP. The current situation where in the best case half-measures are taken is the result. Subsequently many MoDs and some civil parties do not comply with international legislation and do not sufficiently prevent destruction, looting, and iconoclasm of national and international cultural heritage.

As established and explained in this account there are military CPP deliverables, but many commanders are not aware or are not convinced of incentives brought by proper CPP implementation. On top of that, all parties involved are too busy with cultural differences and competence struggles. This too gets in the way of initiating sustainable implementation and cooperation. In practical terms, it seems fair to conclude that in today's situation the blind are leading the blind when cultural property protection is concerned. To put it in a different way: parties engaged in (preparing) safeguarding cultural property in the event of armed conflict have on a micro level the same problems that on a macro level lead to the conflicts in which heritage is attacked or misused. This phenomenon made investigations including observing in theater difficult. Therefore, a creative, knowledge-producing and initiating approach was needed.

This approach includes taking risks by provoking peers and decision makers. The same can be said for each individual of the small group of experts that are working internationally with the military on CPP, so it is evident that most current successful CPP initiatives and networks are personality driven. This does not guarantee sustainability. However, to refer again to Schopenhauer's statement as mentioned in the introduction, "All truth passes through three stages. First, it is ridiculed. Second, it is violently opposed. Third, it is accepted as being self-evident."[94]

Taking into account examining the present situation regarding implementation of CPP in military organizations, this translates into the following conclusions for the countries most mentioned here. In the Netherlands, appreciation is between the first and second stage. In the United States, triggered by the Baghdad and FOB Wolverine disasters, it is between the second and third stage. Apart from a few exceptions, Europe lags behind. Big countries such as France and Germany are not known to have implemented military CPP following the directives of the 1954 Hague Convention, while

[94] As cited in Mahlon Marr, *Truth: Resuming the Age of Reason* (2006); the earliest attribution of this to Schopenhauer yet found dates to around 1986; it is also sometimes misattributed to George Bernard Shaw, and a similar statement is often attributed to Mahatma Gandhi: "First they ignore you, then they laugh at you, then they fight you, then you win." ⟨http://en.wikiquote.org/wiki/Arthur_Schopenhauer⟩ [1 September 2011].

Asia and Africa, as far as can be established, did not start military implementation. Assessing the situation in these continents will be a good subject for more research. Through the international military working group, new contacts have been established with countries in the Caribbean and South America; it remains to be seen what these contacts will bring. New strategies are needed to open doors that give access to CPP implementation. Again, it should be said that an excellent method is to identify and present CPP-related military deliverables to military senior leadership and decision makers. In addition, current risks to cultural property related to social disorder, conflict and natural disaster should be explained better to military leadership and politicians. It will help if newly described situations where cultural property is at risk especially those involving military and civil -military partnerships were to be gathered, studied and processed into lessons learned to be finally incorporated in training and planning.

To test its receptiveness for new subjects, the ever-adapting military mindset was investigated from different angles. It became clear that under normal conditions transformations take place gradually. However, within the context of contemporary military operations, soldiers are forced to transform from destroyers to protectors several times a day. Apparently quick adjustments are possible in modern operations. Therefore, certain flexibility can be expected when CPP is concerned, providing there are clear orders and preparations. A less prominent but still ongoing issue is the opposition from a number of civil cultural experts, some of them self-acclaimed experts on the subject of military cultural involvement. Civil-cultural heritage scientists that fiercely oppose those working together with the military should realize that they are in a relatively luxurious position that enables them to debate and reflect about heritage on a sophisticated abstract level. Their "alleged opponents" are not in such a position but are still struggling to get the subject accepted among all parties. While doing so they are not afraid of taking risks. I never met any of the colleagues that criticize cooperation with the military on the ground during conflicts. However, if they really wanted to help, some of them could have come to conflict zones as civilians embedded within humanitarian NGOs. The scarce number of cultural property specialists that were actually present, for instance in Iraq, did their best to mitigate the physically destructive impacts of war on cultural property. The efforts of these individuals and others that more recently started to prepare for protecting cultural properties in the event of conflict are not yet reducing the number of challenges to be faced when trying to get CPP and its experts accepted by the military. Many of the CPP experts that are active today in Europe invest their own time and financial resources in building contacts with the European military that are not very appreciative to say the least. Bearing this in mind, it seems very overwrought to speak about a "military-archeology complex posing serious political and ethical challenges," as some opponents do.[95]

A debate with peers with different opinions is needed and relevant, but it seems besides the point to include questions of authenticity and uniquity, post-modern relativism, and assumed imperialistic perspectives at this stage.[96] The same goes for making connections with cultural power structures and attributed political values.[97] It would, however, be more useful to look from these perspectives in the direction of cultural awareness experts and their links to—or potential openings for—military intelligence. The reality is that cultural property protection experts are bound to the Hague Convention of 1954 and cultural awareness experts are not. Potential dangers are more likely to be found in the area of cultural anthropology and related social sciences. As established, CPP involving the military is a new scientific topic that needs time to be studied and reflected upon. In its current phase, it is on a less profound level when compared with the abstract heritage debates in academic circles. It will enter the civil cultural heritage discourse in due time, but for now CPP already demonstrated its use in the field as a primary tool for preventive and active conservation of cultural heritage. On the other hand, the cases like Egypt demonstrate that there is still inability or unwillingness to act in the spirit of The Hague by military as well as by organizations. As the quote in the introduction of this book exclaims, "Stuff Happens." At first glance, this seems to summarize today's valuation of failing cultural property protection strategies in the event of conflict. However, in itself the quote can be argued and adapted as a credo urging a better protection of cultural property. To paraphrase secretary Rumsfeld words, shit happens but stuff can be prevented or at least corrected.

Valorization of the Research Outcomes

At the end of this study, it seems appropriate to present some outcomes that are of direct use for all stakeholders. If agreed upon, these do not need much discussion or planning to be implemented or taken into account.

---

95 Hamilakis 2010.
96 For the alleged imperialistic angles see Perring and van der Linde 2009.
97 Hamilakis 2010.

Cultural property protection should be approached in a proactive fashion, not just in a re-active approach.

Cultural property protection expertise and capabilities developed during and immediately after the Second World War have been allowed to disappear, resulting in the fact that many State Parties to the 1954 Hague Convention and its Protocols are not meeting the obligations stated in these instruments.

Cultural property protection has been forced back onto political and military agendas because of damage to cultural property in addition to the catastrophic theft and looting in Iraq since 2003; this is no new development; see the many examples of such activity since World War II.

Cultural property protection is a military "force multiplier" and should never be regarded as an unnecessary burden legally imposed but militarily problematic and useless.

Military success can no longer be defined in terms of battlefield victory but has to take into account the post-conflict political, social, and economic stability of countries involved.

Cultural property protection touches upon the issue of general "cultural awareness" but is actually a separate issue with particular concerns that required specialized skills, different to those for general cultural awareness.

Cultural property protection is critical to any comprehensive approach and to the post-conflict long-term political, social, and economic (through tourism) stability of many countries.

International cooperation is not only needed but is a condition for a successful realization of cultural property protection that also should include joint training.

The ethical problems about working together with the military to protect cultural property addressed in this study have to be considered to ensure cooperation between militarized social scientists and academic reach back capabilities. However, the following must be taken into account: in order to protect and safeguard cultural heritage during conflict one has to be on the ground in time. Often this is only possible when military logistics and safety measures can provide access. In situations where heritage is at risk, the military are normally the first on the ground. Comparisons are made with the debate about military embedded or non-embedded journalists reporting about conflicts.[98] These comparisons are invalid since CPP experts work under the 1954 Hague Convention; just like military medical experts

---

98 Brand 2011, p. 168.

they are bound to regulations (in case of physician's ethical codes). For the same reason, it can be argued that experts that do not follow the directives of the 1954 Hague Convention, making it mandatory for the military to protect cultural property, behave unethically.

Cultural property protection capabilities should be embedded in the MoDs to be available for all services of the Armed Forces and must function both in "peace time" as well as during operations.

Specialized staff functions should be incorporated into military structures or assignment of specific CPP duties to the existing staff members should be introduced. Specific training for specialized military personnel in charge of this subject also has to be provided.

Cultural property can be considered as a significant economical asset. Its protection helps to secure income and tourism-related jobs for the future, thus supporting stabilization. In fact, cultural property can help a community rebuild its social fabric after a conflict or disaster.

Seen from the perspective of this investigation, for the protection of cultural property in conflict, UNESCO remains too passive. It is of vital importance that funding related to the 1954 Hague Convention and Protocols is spent on proactive cultural emergency initiatives and training. UNESCO should consider at least establishing active liaison with military organizations and supporting cultural military initiatives both financially and by providing expertise.

The Netherlands MoD is staying behind with the implementation of CPP as regulated in the 1954 Hague Convention and Protocols. There is proof of the fact that the MoD's department for cultural background information is blocking initiatives to implement CPP as stated in the 1954 Hague Convention. The recommendations and the Policy Note that were prepared following the Dutch CPP seminar that took place in the Peace Palace, The Hague in 2009 should be taken into account. So far, attempts to find solutions and requests to carry out what is mandatory concerning CPP, as stated in this Policy Note, were not followed up.[99]

A good thing is that the Dutch MoD accepted cultural heritage coordinates regarding important sites in Libya. These data were gathered through

99 The status of the Policy Note remains unclear; though the concept received a reference number, it was never officially taken into consideration or answered by the Chief of Staff. Several attempts made to get comments or react to issues concerning the Dutch MoD mentioned in this publication remained unanswered by the Dutch MoD. Since the comments and recommendations that involve Dutch governmental institutions are of vital importance to this research, the decision was made to make use of data such as this particular policy note, ref. S2009009624.

international cooperation of the USCBS, CCHAG, academia, and IMCuRWG and offered to the Dutch MoD by IMCuRWG.

NATO's STANAG 7141 EP doctrine is not, as far as CPP is concerned (in the STANAG referred to as cultural resources), followed by the Netherlands MoD.

NATO should act in accordance with their own NATO's STANAG 7141 EP doctrine and implement training, education, and research on CPP in its institutions. NATO should also consider very seriously creating military CPP capabilities and emergency units. The latest information shows that NATO via their Allied Command Transformation Department is taking matters seriously, which would be a great step forwards and in concurrence with the North Atlantic Treaty of Washington D.C.—4 April 1949, to be referred to as the Washington Treaty establishing NATO, which says, "[the parties are determined to safeguard the freedom, *common heritage* and civilization of their peoples."[100]

[100] Source: ⟨http://www.nato.int/cps/en/natolive/official_texts_17120.htm⟩ [9 September 2011].

SUMMARY

Heritage under Siege is the result of a multidisciplinary research carried out between 2004 and mid 2011. The project focused on military implementation procedures for protecting and safeguarding cultural heritage in the event of armed conflict. The study took into account what is feasible in a practical sense and the ideal perspective as described in international treaties that concern CPP and prohibit illicit traffic of cultural property.

The subject necessitated detailed consideration of legal obligations and implications. The main juridical framework in which Cultura property protection (CPP) activities take place is the Convention for the Protection of Cultural Property in the Event of Armed Conflict to be referred to as the Hague Convention of 1954.

This book is in large part based on qualitative research. Since too few recent cases and empirical sources were available, this seemed to be the best research method. A number of circumstances and conditions influenced the research process, for instance, the military aspect of CPP was relatively unknown. Therefore, not only an analysis but also an introduction to the subject seemed appropriate. Participant field research provided for new case studies. To execute this type of research, the author had to enlist with the Dutch Armed Forces. During the field research, it was possible to follow, analyze, and test various processes. The explorations did not exclusively focus on unique happenings, but aimed as far as possible at distinguishing and testing patterns and mechanisms. Processes that included international, interagency, and interdisciplinary cooperation during military operations in conflict areas were put to the test. In addition, preparations for CPP that should start in "peacetime" were investigated as far as they actually took place. The aim was to quantify qualitative data from a multidisciplinary perspective that included fields like archaeology, cultural policy studies, sociology, and law. Other sources comprised published and unpublished literature, documents, and interviews. Via the author's position in the armed forces, authentic materials could be gathered in theater, along with observation of military exercises, planning and operations, and behaviors of different CPP stakeholders when implementing CPP projects was possible. This *modus operandi* necessitated working in conflict areas where looting, illicit traffic, and iconoclasm take place. However, permission for research *in situ* did not come naturally. Although a modest capability of cultural experts was available at the time within the Dutch armed forces, they were, due to organizational and priority issues, not deployed. Consequently, the researcher had to initiate CPP activities including actual projects in a conflict area. This was the only way to test potential CPP strategies in practice. The challenge asked for a proactive attitude that paid off and provided for the author to go on different missions to war zones. Much information was obtained in theater although the work was restrained by the fact that the military tend to shield off matters for researchers especially in case of new and complicated subjects.

The book consists of three main parts. It starts with an introduction and a section about the research methods and sources used including a number of small case examples. Overall, the cases are not limited to situations in conflict areas but comprise examples of CPP training components in military exercises and the preparations for such activities in places like Egypt and the United States. A preliminary indication is given of challenges and impediments to be met while initiating and executing military CPP. Relevant expertise and capabilities that were build up in the past, for instance, by the allies in World War II, were not maintained and consequently lost. Today's relevance of military involvement in CPP is examined using and explaining cultural heritage's link with identity. To address the volatile character of cultural objects a practical example is used from the last Gulf War, namely, the case of the "Jewish Archives" from Iraq. In addition, the importance of the relation between looting archaeological sites and poverty is explained, thus stressing the relevance of prevention and protection of archaeological sites. From a military perspective it is argued that this use is not only apparent as a pure military aspect necessary to secure a safe civil environment, but that CPP also has value as a military incentive and so-called force multiplier.

After the introduction, the study continues with Chapter 2 presenting the playing field of cultural property protection (CPP) and its players. All relevant players are, where necessary with practical examples, introduced and discussed extra attention is given to the military as a new relatively unknown player. Tensions among stakeholders are recognized and explained while the multi-layered connection of cultural property with identity is emphasized. Cultural differences between military and civilian parties as well as cultural differences within the military are identified and discussed starting with the military then the media, governmental institutions, non-governmental organisations, international organisations, working groups and advisory groups, the fields of commerce, crime, law and order, religion, and, finally, science. From sociological and art-historical perspectives, attention is paid to the shifting status of cultural objects, their availability for manipulation and abuse and the development of national and individual identities. This section is followed by a historical background description of cultural property protection and destruction until 1954.

My research *in situ* resulted in a number of new case studies that are incorporated in Chapter 3 of this book in chronological order. Some of them are based on already published chapters of books and articles that represent a good image of the developments of the research during a time frame of approximately three years.

1. "The Role of Nato and Civil Military Affairs," in Lawrence Rothfield. (ed.) *Antiquities under Siege*, Part II, Chapter 16, New York (2008), pp. 175–192. This publication gives an accurate description of obligations for NATO concerning CPP during military operations in 2007 and 2008. Practical examples from Iraq are addressed such as the contributions of Polish military experts who implemented CPP projects in the Polish area of responsibility (AOR) in Iraq.

2. "Utilizing Military Cultural Experts in Times of War and Peace: an introduction," in Paul Meerts, (ed.), *Culture and International Law*, Chapter 12, The Hague (2008), pp. 183–229. A general introduction to military CPP including case studies about the archaeological important site of Uruk in Iraq and its protection against looting by Dutch military CPP specialists. In addition attention is paid to misuse of HESCOs (barriers used to build walls around military camps) in Babylon and the case of the Ethnographic Museum in Kabul in Afghanistan.

3. "Embedding cultural property protection within the Military in Planning for Protection of Cultural Heritage in Times of Conflict," in L. Lijnzaad and N. van Woudenberg, (eds.), *Protecting Cultural Property in Armed Conflict. An insight into the 1999 Second Protocol to the 1954 Hague Convention for the Protection of Cultural Property in the Event of Armed Conflict*, Leiden (2010), pp. 95–105. This publication addresses juridical implications that play a role in military CPP implementation in the event of conflict. Special attention is paid to ethical issues involving the so-called Human Terrain Teams.

4. "Can white men sing the blues? Cultural Property Protection in times of armed conflict deploying military experts," in Laurie Rush, (ed.), *Archaeology, Cultural Property and the Military*. Woodbridge 2010. pp. 41–59. This publication contains a extensive case study about damages inflicted to the Matejce Monastery in Macedonia (FYROM). The destruction took place

during the conflict between ethnic Albanians and the Macedonian armed forces while the paramilitary UCK (ethnic Albanian) occupied the monastery from 2000 to 2002. Dutch military CIMIC experts attempted in 2002 to restore the damage.

5. "*Überlegungen zum Status quo der Beteiligung des Militärs am Schutz von Kulturgut.*" Some thoughts on the current state of military involvement in Cultural Property Protection, following the 1954 Hague Convention and Protocols. Article in ÖMZ (Austrian Military Magazine) no. 5. This article is in the German language and is published in September–October 2011. The piece analyses the current state of affairs concerning European implementation of CPP by the military. Addressed are issues like education, ethical considerations, and the link between CPP and environmental matters as codified in the NATO doctrine STANAG 7141 EP; another topic is the confusion between the terms cultural awareness and CPP. Finally, an overview is presented of international implementation of CPP and the relationship with the so-called comprehensive approach method utilized in recent international military operations. The publication is in particular important because the German speaking countries can be informed about CPP.

6. *Cultural Property Protection in the Context of Military Operations: The Case of Uruk, Iraq*, Conservation and Management of Archaeological Sites (CMAS), Vol. 13 No. 4, November 2011, 311–333. The article contains an upgrade on the Uruk Case combined with recent conclusions deriving from the research. Originally this piece was meant for a publication on Cultural Emergency initiated by the Prince Claus Fund in the Netherlands, but they wanted to censor parts of the article that were considered critical towards subsidizers, so I withdraw the article.

7. Egypt February 12–16 2011. This article has not been published; the subject concerns a cultural emergency assessment mission carried out by the author and an Austrian colleague during the so-called Egyptian revolution of January and February 2011, in order to register what happened to the Egyptian cultural heritage. The mission had to be low profile because the situation on the ground was not safe. The article contains a detailed report of the mission team's findings and confirms a number of suppositions made in this book, e.g., UNESCO's attitude in relation to conflicts and risk avoiding behaviors of some stakeholders as well as the value of cultural property as an economic asset.

8. "Libya's heritage under siege in 2011." The casus contains an indication of military measures to spare the cultural heritage of Libya during air strikes that started as from March 2011 by coalition forces. The information was

for the larger part gathered through international cooperation between networks that are created by individual CPP specialists such as IMCuRWG and CHHAG.

Chapter 4 reflects on the way ahead by first exploring possibilities for balancing the interests of the various parties by explaining identified dilemmas. Conflicting interests vary tremendously. They occur, for instance, on the political level involving humanitarian aid—in cultural policy strategy as well as ministerial and defense issues—but also on the scientific level where ethical problems play a role. Many discussed disagreements and (armed) conflict cases incorporate references to laws and treaties. A separate section is used to shed light on legal aspects linked to CPP plus related control mechanisms and sanctions. Topics range from the principle of military necessity to the law of war and international treaties. Compared and analyzed are different opinions of leading juridical experts. Possible solutions for different identified challenges and dilemmas are discussed by focusing on opportunities that, for example, derive from new military tasks in the context of peace keeping and reconstruction missions. Strategies addressed take into account the identification of common denominators and deliverables for different parties. Special attention is given to education and practical training while different training strategies are introduced and compared.

Finally, a paragraph is dedicated to the outcomes and potential deliverables of the study by presenting a set of results that can be perceived and used as recommendations to be considered by all stakeholders in the field of cultural property protection. This section also serves as a valorization of the study. The book includes references, a glossary, and a section with appendixes. The appendixes include: the NATO CIMIC Doctrine AJP 9, The Hague Convention for the Protection of Cultural Propery in the event of Armed Conflict of 1954 and its two protocols and the Blue Shield and IMCuRWG report of the Civil-Military Assessment Mission for Egyptian Heritage from February, 2011.

REFERENCES

Akinsja and Koslov 1996 · Akinsja, K. and G. Kozlov, *Operatie Kunstroof. De lotgevallen van het goud van Troje, de Koenigscollectie en andere Russische oorlogsbuit*, Amsterdam 1996.

Albarella 2009 · Albarella, Umberto, "Archaeologists in Conflict: Empathizing with which Victims?," in *Heritage Management*, Volume 2, Issue 1, spring 2009, pp. 105–114.

Arndt 2005 · Arndt, Richard T., *Cultural Diplomacy: The First Resort of Kings, American Cultural Diplomacy in the Twentieth Century*, Dulles (VA) 2005.

Arnold 1990 · Arnold, B., "The past as propaganda: totalitarian archaeology in Nazi Germany" in *Antiquity*, 64(244) 1990, pp. 464–478.

Asgard 2010 · Asgard, Ramin, "A Historical Perspective Asia and Islamic Civilization Spring 2010" in *al Nakhlah The Fletcher School Online Journal for issues related to Southwest U.S. Iran Cultural Diplomacy.* ⟨http://fletcher.tufts.edu/al_nakhlah/archives/Spring2010/Asgard,%20US-Iran%20Cultural%20Diplomacy.pdf⟩ [19 July 2011].

Baker 2003 · Baker, Jason B., "Winning Hearts with Cultural Awareness," in *Soldiers* 58:29 July 2003.

Bauman 2002 · Bauman, Zygmunt, *Society under Siege*, Cambridge 2002.

Bevan 2006 · Bevan, Robert, *The Destruction of Memory, Architecture at War*, London 2006.

Bogdanos 2006 · Bogdanos, Matthew, *Thieves of Baghdad*, New York 2006.

Bourdieu 1984 · Bourdieu, Pierre, *Distinction, A Social Critique of the Judgment of Taste*, Cambridge 1984.

Bourdieu and Passeron 1990 · Bourdieu, Pierre and Jean-Claude Passeron, *Reproduction in Education, Society, and Culture*, London 1990.

Bourdieu 1992 · Bourdieu, Pierre and Loïc J.D. Wacquant, *An Invitation to Reflexive Sociology*, Chicago 1992.

Bourdieu 2000 · Bourdieu, Pierre, *Pascalian Meditations*, Oxford 2000.

Boylan 1993 · Boylan, Patrick J., *Review of the Convention for the Protection of Cultural Property in the Event of Armed Conflict* (The Hague Convention of 1954), UNESCO document CLT-93/WS/12. Paris 1993.

Boylan 2002 · Boylan, Patrick J., "The Concept of Cultural Property Protection in Times of Armed Conflict: from the Crusades to the new Millennium," in N. Brodie and K.B. Tubb (eds.), *Illicit Antiquities*, London 2002, pp. 43–108.

Boylan 2006 · Boylan, Patrick J., *Implementing the 1954 Hague Convention and its Protocols: legal and practical implications.* Conference document, Protecting Cultural Heritage: International Law after the War in Iraq organized by the Cultural Policy Center, in collaboration with The Oriental Institute and The University of Chicago Law School, Chicago February 2006.

Brand 2011 · Brand, M., "Strijd om de beeldvorming bij militaire operaties," in *Militaire Spectator*, vol. 4, 2011, pp. 163–174.

Brown 2005 · Brown, Michael F., "Heritage Trouble: Recent Work on the Protection of Intangible Cultural Property," in *International Journal of Cultural Property* 12: 2005, pp. 40–61.

Celik 2005 · Celik, Murat, *Comparison of the British and Canadian CIMIC and the U.S. CMO doctrines to the NATO CIMIC doctrine.* Thesis. Naval Postgraduate School, Monterey 2005.

Clausewitz 1968 · Clausewitz, Carl von, *On War* (Volume 1), (1832), London 1968.

Coward 2009 · Coward, M., *Urbicide: the politics of urban destruction*, London and New York 2009.

Curtis, 2009 · Curtis, John. Relations between Archaeologists and the Military in the Case of Iraq in PIA Vol. 19 London 2009.

Den Boer 2005 · Boer, Pim den, "Geschiedenis, herinnering en 'lieux de memoire'," in R. van der Laarse (ed.), *Bezeten van vroeger. Erfgoed, identiteit en musealisering*, Amsterdam 2005, pp. 40–58.

Desch 2002 · Desch, Thomas, "Problems in the Implementation of the Convention from the Perspective of International Law," in Micewski, Edwin R. and Gerhard Sladek (eds.), *Protection of Cultural Property in the Event of Armed Conflict, A Challenge in Peace Support Operations*, Vienna 2002, pp. 13–27.

Duffield 1998 · Duffield, Mark, "Post-modern conflict: Warlords, post-adjustment states and private protection," in Civil Wars, 1:1, pp. 65–102, London 1998. ⟨http://www.tandfonline.com/doi/pdf/10.1080/13698249808402367⟩ [29 July 2011].

Edsel 2009 · Edsel, Robert, *The Monuments Men: Allied Heroes, Nazi Thieves and the Greatest Treasure Hunt in History*, New York 2009.

Emberling, Hanson 2008 · Emberling, Geoff and Katharyn Hanson, (eds.), *Catastrophe! The Looting and Destruction of Iraq's Past*, Chicago 2008.

Fagan 2004 · Fagan, Brian, *The Rape of the Nile*, Oxford 2004.

Feliciano 1997 · Feliciano, Hector, *The Lost Museum*, Paris 1997.

Feil 2008 · Feil, Scott R. "Engaging interagency processes to protect cultural sites: communities, authorities, and capabilities," in Lawrence Rothfield (ed.), *Antiquities under Siege: Cultural Heritage Protection after the Iraq War*, Lanham 2008, pp. 219–234.

Fischer 2007 · Fischer, Horst. "Proportionality, Principle of." Crimes of War, a-z guide. ⟨http://www.crimesofwar.org/thebook/proportion-princple.html⟩ [19 July 2011].

Foner, 2002 · Foner, Eric. *Who owns history? Rethinking the Past in a Changing World.* New York: Hill and Lang, 2002.

Forrest 2007 · Forrest, Graig J.S., "The Doctrine of Military Necessity and the Protection of Cultural Property during Armed Conflicts," in *California Western International Law Journal* Vol. 37. Number 2, 2007.

Gamboni 2007 · Gamboni, Dario, *The Destruction of Art. Iconoclasm and Vandalism since the French Revolution*, London 2007.

Garlake 1973 · Garlake, Peter, *Great Zimbabwe: New Aspects of Archaeology*, London 1973.

Garraway 2010 · Garraway, Charles. "Illegal Combatants and Counter-Terrorism, A Middle Way," in Opinio Juris, ⟨http://opiniojuris.org/author/charles-garraway/⟩ [9 July 2010].

Gerstenblith 2008 · Gerstenblith, P, "The 1954 Hague Convention on the Protection of Cultural Property in the Event of Armed Conflict: Its Background and Prospects for Ratification in the United States," in Lawrence Rothfield (ed.), *Antiquities under Siege*, part II chapter 7. New York 2008, pp. 79–88.

Gerstenblith 2009 · Gerstenblith, P., "Archaeology in the Context of War: Legal Frameworks for Protecting Cultural Heritage during Armed Conflict," in *Archaeologies* 5 (1), April 2009, pp. 18–31.

Gillman 2010 · Gillman, D., *The Idea of Cultural Heritage* (Revised Edition), Cambridge 2010.

Green 2000 · Green, L.C., *The Contemporary Law of Armed Conflict*, Manchester 2000.

Greenwood 1997 · Greenwood, Christopher, "Current Issues in the Law of Armed Conflict: Weapons, Targets and International Criminal Liability," in: *Singapore Journal of International and Comparative Law* 1997, 1, pp. 441–467.

Grijzenhout 2007 · Grijzenhout, Frans (ed.), *Erfgoed, de geschiedenis van een begrip*, Amsterdam 2007.

Gunn 2006 · Gunn, Simon, *History and Cultural Theory*, Harlow 2006.

Hamilakis 2009 · Hamilakis, Yannis, "The 'War on Terror' and the Military-Archaeology Complex: Iraq, Ethics, and Neo-Colonialism," in *Archaeologies Journal of the World Archaeological Congress*, Volume 6 /2010 DOI 10.1007/s11759-009-9095-y.

Hofstede and Hofstede 2003 · Hofstede, Geert and Geert H. Hofstede, *Culture's Consequences*, London 2003.

Huntington 1993 · Huntington, Samuel, "The Clash of Civilizations?," in *Foreign Affairs* vol. 72, no. 3 (1993), pp. 22–49.

Huntington 1997 · Huntington, Samuel P., *The Clash of Civilizations and the Remaking of World Order*, New York 1997.

Jamail 2009 · Jamail, Dahr., "How Some Anthropologists Have Learned to Stop Worrying and Start Loving the Army". ⟨www.truthout.org/051609Z 16 May 2009⟩ [not accessible]. ⟨http://www.militaryphotos.net/forums/showthread.php?157387-Article-on-Liberals-against-Anthropologists-fighting-the-War-on-Terror&s=389c85cf2415e93f267a80adce5f2808⟩ [10 September 2011].

Johnson, 2006 · Johnson, Jeannie L. and Jeffrey A. Larsen. *Comparative Strategic Culture Syllabus*, Fort Belvoir, Virginia, 2006

Johnson 2009 · Johnson, Jeannie L., Carrie M. Kartchner and Jeffrey A. Larsen, (eds.), *Strategic Culture and Weapons of Mass Destruction. Culturally Based Insights into Comparative National Security Policymaking*, New York 2009.

Kila 2003 · CIMIC Group North, Civil Assessment. Team Iraq Al Muthanna October 2003 NL MOD (eds.), LTC R. Schuurman, LTC J. Kila, Hoofdstuk 4 Cultuur, Internal Report Dutch MOD, 2003.

Kila 2008a · Kila, Joris, "The Role of Nato and Civil Military Affairs," in Lawrence Rothfield (ed.), *Antiquities under Siege*, part II chapter 16, New York 2008, pp. 175–192.

Kila 2008b · Kila, Joris, "Utilizing Military Cultural Experts in Times of War and Peace: an introduction," in Paul Meerts (ed.), *Culture and International Law*, Chapter 12, The Hague 2008, pp. 183–229.

Kila 2009 · Kila, Joris, "The relevance of cultural heritage protection in times of armed conflict. Utilizing military cultural experts in war and peacetime: cases and examples from the field," in an e-book by The Estonian Heritage Soci-

ety, Marju Reismaa (ed.), language Estonian, KULTUURIVÄÄRTUSTE KAITSE RELVAKONFLIKTI KORRAL 2009. ⟨http://www.muinsuskaitse.ee/failid/157_est_haagi_konvents.pdf⟩ [19 July 2011].
Kila 2010a · Kila, Joris, "Dissemination of the 1954 Hague Convention and the 1999 Second Protocol: Embedding Cultural Property Protection within the Military," in L. Lijnzaad and N. van Woudenberg (eds.), *Protecting Cultural Property in Armed Conflict. An insight into the 1999 Second Protocol to the 1954 Hague Convention for the Protection of Cultural Property in the Event of Armed Conflict*, Leiden 2010, pp. 95–105.
Kila 2010b · Kila, Joris, "Can white men sing the blues? Cultural Property Protection in times of armed conflict deploying military experts," in Laurie Rush (ed.), *Archaeology, Cultural Property and the Military*, Woodbridge 2010, pp. 41–59.
Kila 2011a · Kila, Joris, "Überlegungen zum Status quo der Beteiligung des Militärs am Schutz von Kulturgut" (Some thoughts on the current state of military involvement in Cultural Property Protection, following the 1954 Hague Convention and Protocols) in *ÖMZ* (Austrian Military Journal), Volume 5, September 2011.
Kila 2011b · Kila, Joris, "Cultural Property Protection in the Context of Military Operations: The Case of Uruk, Iraq," in *Conservation and Management of Archaeological Sites (CMAS)*, Vol. 13 No. 4, November 2011, 311–333.
Kohl 1998 · Kohl, Philip L., "Nationalism and Archaeology: On the Constructions of Nations and the Reconstructions of the Remote past," in *Annual Review of Anthropology*, October 1998, Vol. 27, pp. 223–246.
Kristoffersen 2005 · Kristoffersen, Lene. "Civil Military Cooperation. Norwegian CIMIC in Afghanistan." Master Thesis University of Oslo. Oslo 2005.
Laarse, van der 2005 · Laarse, R. van der (ed.), *Bezeten van vroeger. Erfgoed, identiteit en musealisering*, Amsterdam 2005.
Lauterpacht 1952 · Lauterpacht, H, "The problem of the revision of the law of war," in *British Yearbook of International Law (B.Y.I.L.)*, 1952, pp. 360–382.
Leydesdorff 2010 · Leydesdorff, Loet, "Luhmann reconsidered: Towards an empirical research programme in the sociology of communication," in Colin B. Grant (ed.), *Beyond Universal Pragmatics: Studies in the Philosophy of Communication*, Oxford 2010.
Lowenthal 1996 · Lowenthal, R., *The Heritage Crusade and the Spoils of History*, New York 1996.
Lowenthal 2005 · Lowental, R., "Heritage and History: Rivals and Partners in Europe," in R. van der Laarse (ed.), *Bezeten van vroeger. Erfgoed, identiteit en musealisering*, Amsterdam 2005, pp. 29–39.
Luengo 2009 · Luengo, M., "Landscape and Culture," Irish National Landscape Conference 2009. ⟨www.heritagecouncil.ie/fileadmin/user_upload/Events/Landscape_Events/conferencepapers/Landscape_and_Culture.pdf⟩ [19 July 2011].
Lijnzaad and van Woudenberg 2010 · Lijnzaad, L. and N. van Woudenberg, (eds.), *Protecting Cultural Property in Armed Conflict. An insight into the 1999 Second Protocol to the 1954 Hague Convention for the Protection of Cultural Property in the Event of Armed Conflict*. Leiden 2010.
Mac Ginty 2004 · Mac Ginty, Roger, "Looting in the context of violent conflict," in *Third World Quarterly*, Vol. 25, No. 5, 2004, pp. 857–870.

Merryman 2000a · Merryman, John Henry, Albert Edward Elsen, Stephen K. Urice, *Law, Ethics and the Visual Arts*. Alphen aan den Rijn 2007.

Merryman 2000b · Merryman, John Henry, *Thinking about the Eligin Marbles*, London 2000.

Merryman, 2005 · Merryman, John Henry. "Cultural Property Internationalism," *International Journal of Cultural Property*, 12:1. Cambridge 2005, 11–39.

Micewski and Sladek 2002 · Micewski, Edwin R. and Gerhard Sladek (eds.), *Protection of Cultural Property in the Event of Armed Conflict, A Challenge in Peace Support Operations*, Vienna 2002.

Mitchell 2006 · Mitchell, Stephen. *Gilgamesh: A New English Version*. New Jersey. 2004.

NATO · CIMIC Doctrine NATO AJP-9 non classified CIMIC Policy doc. June 2003

Nelson and Olin 2003 · Nelson, Robert S. and Margaret Olin (eds.), *Monuments and Memory, Made and Unmade*, Chicago 2003.

Nemeth 2010 · Nemeth, E. "The Art of Cultural Intelligence: intelligence for countering threats to cultural property in conflict," in *Forum Archaeologiae* 55/VI/2010. ⟨http://farch.net⟩ [19 July 2011].

Nicholas 1994 · Nicholas, Lynn H., *The Rape of Europa*, New York 1994.

Nicolet 1980 · Nicolet, Claude, *The World of the Citizen in Republican Rome*, Princeton 1980.

Olbrys 2007 · Olbrys, M., "Archaeologists on Duty in Iraq: Polish Approach to the Protection and Salvage of Archaeological Heritage in Central South Iraq (November 2003–April 2005)," in *Conservation and Management of Archaeological Sites (CMAS)* vol. 8, 2007, pp. 88–108.

O'Keefe 1997 · O'Keefe, Patrick J. *Trade in Antiquities*, UNESCO, Paris 1997.

O'Keefe 2006 · O'Keefe, Roger, *The Protection of Cultural Property in Armed Conflict*, Cambridge 2006.

Parcak 2009 · Parcak, Sarah, H., *Satellite Remote Sensing for Archaeology*, New York 2009.

Pesendorfer and Speckner 2006 · Pesendorfer, Michael and Hubert Speckner, *Operation Pallas Athena, Protection of Cultural Property in Peace Support Operations*. Vienna 2006.

Perring and Van der Linde 2009 · Perring, Dominic and Sjoerd van der Linde, "The Politics and Practice of Archaeology in Conflict," in *Conservation and Management of Archaeological Sites (CMAS)*, Vol. 11 Nos. 3–4, 2009, London 2010, pp. 197–213.

Polybius 1960 · Polybius. The Histories. Translated by Paton, W.R. London 1960.

Price 2008 · Price, David, "The Leaky Ship of Human Terrain Systems," in *Counterpunch Weekend Edition* December 12/14, 2008.

Price 2010 · Price, David, "Human Terrain Systems Dissenter Resigns, Tells Inside Story of Training's Heart of Darkness," in *Counterpunch* 15, February 2010. ⟨http://www.counterpunch.org/price02152010.html⟩ [17 July 2011].

Price 2010a · Price, Jon "Whose side are you on boys?" The problem for embedded anthropologists in the US Human Terrain System teams, in *Forum Archaeologiae* 55/VI/2010 ⟨http://farch.net⟩ [8 September 2011].

Prott 2006 · Prott, Lyndell V., "The Protection of Cultural Movables from Afghanistan: developments in international management," in Juliette van Krieken-

Pieters (ed.), *Art and Archaeology of Afghanistan: Its Fall and Survival. A Multi-Disciplinary Approach*, Leiden 2006, pp. 189–200.
Riedlmayer 1995 · Riedlmayer, Andras, "Erasing the Past: The Destruction of Libraries and Archives in Bosnia-Herzegovina," in *Middle East Studies Association Bulletin*, vol. 29 no. 1, July 1995, pp. 7–11.
Rogers 1996 · Rogers, A.P.V., *Law on the Battlefield*, Manchester and New York 1996.
Rothfield 2008 · Rothfield, Lawrence (ed.), *Antiquities under Siege*, Lanham 2008.
Rothfield 2009 · Rothfield, Lawrence, *The Rape of Mesopotamia*, Chicago 2009.
Rush 2010 · Rush, Laurie (ed.), *Archaeology, Cultural Property and the Military*, Woodbridge 2010.
Sandes 2010 · Sandes, Caroline, A., *Archaeology, conservation and the city: post-conflict redevelopment in London, Berlin and Beirut*. Oxford 2010.
Schindler and Toman 1988 · Schindler, D. and J. Toman, *The Laws of Armed Conflicts*, (third revised and completed edition), Henry Dunant Institute Geneva, Dordrecht 1988.
Simpson 1997 · Simpson, Elizabeth, (ed.), *The Spoils of War. The Loss, Reappearance, and Recovery of Cultural Property*. Proceedings of the Symposium held in January 1995 New York Bard Graduate Center. New York 1997.
Snow 2001 · Snow, David. "Collective Identity and Expressive Forms". University of California at Irvine: Center for the Study of Democracy. 2001. ⟨http://escholarship.org/uc/item/2zn1t7bj⟩ [17 July 2011].
Sorabella 2000 · Sorabella, Jean, "The Grand Tour," in *Heilbrunn Timeline of Art History*, New York: The Metropolitan Museum of Art, 2000—http://www.metmuseum.org/toah/hd/grtr/hd_grtr.htm (October 2003) [27 July 2011].
Stone 2008 · Stone, Elizabeth C, "Archaeological Site Looting: the Destruction of Cultural Heritage in Southern Iraq," in Geoff Emberling and Katharyn Hanson (eds.), *Catastrophe! The Looting and Destruction of Iraq's Past*, Chicago 2008, pp. 65–80.
Stone and Farchakh 2008 · Stone, P.G. and Bajjaly J. Farkhach (eds.), *The Destruction of Cultural Heritage in Iraq*. Woodbridge 2008.
Swartz 1997 · Swartz, David, *Culture & Power, The Sociology of Pierre Bourdieu*. Chicago, London 1997.
Thomassen 2010 · Thomassen, B., "Archeology as Memory Practice and the Archeologization of Politics," in *Forum Archaeologiae* 55/VI/2010. ⟨http://farch.net⟩ [17 July 2011].
Thurlow 2005 · Thurlow, Matthew D., "Protecting cultural property in Iraq: how American military policy comports with international law," in *Yale Human Rights and Development Law* Vol. III, January 1st 2005. ⟨www.law.yale.edu/documents/pdf/LawJournals/thurlow.pdf⟩ [30 August 2011].
Tilmans, van Vree and Winter 2010 · Tilmans, Karin, Frank van Vree and Jay Winter (eds.), *Performing the Past: Memory, History, and Identity in Modern Europe*, Amsterdam 2010.
Toman 2009 · Toman, Jiri, *Cultural Property in War: Improvement in Protection: commentary on the 1999 Second Protocol to the Hague Convention of 1954 for the Protection of Cultural Property in the Event of Armed Conflict*, UNESCO, Paris 2009.
Van Vree 2010 · Vree, Frank van, "Indigestible images. On the ethics and limits of representation" in Karin Tilmans, Frank van Vree and Jay Winter (eds.),

Performing the Past: Memory, History, and Identity in Modern Europe, Amsterdam 2010.

Verhaert 2006 · Verhaert, Isabelle, *URBICIDE Beirut 1975–2006*. Master Thesis, Leuven 2006.

Watson 2006 · Watson, Peter, *The Medici Conspiracy*, New York 2006.

Weizman 2006 · Weizman, Eyal, "The Art of War," in *Frieze* Issue 99, May 2006, p. 146. ⟨http://www.frieze.com/issue/article/the_art_of_war/⟩ [17 July 2011].

Weizman 2007 · Weizman, Eyal, *Hollow Land: Israel's Architecture of Occupation*, London 2007.

Wilkie 2008 · Wilkie, Nancy C., "Governmental Agencies and the Protection of Cultural Property in Times of War," in Lawrence Rothfield (ed.), *Antiquities under Siege*, Lanham 2008, pp. 237–249.

Wilson 1989 · Wilson, James, Q., *Bureaucracy. What Government Agencies Do and Why They Do It*, New York 1989.

Wunderle 2006 · Wunderle, William D., *Through the Lens of Cultural Awareness: A Primer for US Armed Forces Deploying to Arab and Middle Eastern Countries*, Fort Leavenworth 2006.

GLOSSARY

ACT	Allied Command Transformation.
AIA	Archaeological Institute of America.
AJP-9	Allied Joint Publication number 9
ANCBS	The Association of National Committees of the Blue Shield.
AOR	Area of Responsibility or mission area.
ARCA	Association for Research into Crimes against Art
CA	Cultural Awareness.
CA	Civil Affairs.
CCHAG	COCOM Cultural Heritage Action Group
CEMML	The Center for Environmental Management of Military Lands.
CENTCOM	US Central Command.
CHAMP	Cultural Heritage by AIA-Military Panel.
CHCAG	CENTCOM Historical/Cultural Advisory Group. Recently renamed Combatant Command Historical/Cultural Action Group.
CIMIC	Civil Military Cooperation.
CMAS	Conservation and Management of Archaeological Sites
COIN	Counter Insurgency.
COM	Commander.
CPP	Cultural Property Protection.
CSU	Colorado State University.
DAI	Deutsches Archäologisches Institut
DRTF	Disaster Relief Task Force
ECOSOC	Economic and Social Council (UN).
ETWG	NATO Environmental Training Workgroup.
EU	European Union
FOB	Forward Operating Base
FYROM	Former Yugoslave Republic of Macedonia
GCI	Getty Conservation Institute
GIS	Geographic Information Systems.
HTS	Human Terrain Systems.
IARC	Illicit Antiquities Research Centre
ICA	International Council on Archives.
ICBS	The International Committee of the Blue Shield.
ICCROM	International Centre for the Study of the Conservation and Restoration of Cultural Heritage.
ICOM	International Council of Museums.
ICOMOS	International Council on Monuments and Sites.
ICRC	International Committee of the Red Cross.
IFLA	International Federation of Library Associations and Institutions.
IHL	International Humanitarian Law.

IMCuRWG	International Military Cultural Resources Working Group.
IO	International Organization.
IRD	International Relief and Development
JNA	Yugoslav People's Army.
LOAC	Law of Armed Conflict.
LOW	Law of War.
MFAA	Monuments, Fine Arts, and Archives program, also Monuments Men WW II.
MN	Military Necessity.
NARA	National Archives and Records Administration (Maryland US.)
NATO	North Atlantic Treaty Organisation
NGO	Non Governmental Organization.
ÖMZ	Österreichische Militärische Zeitschrift
Oplan	Operation Plan.
PMC	Private Military Company.
ROE	Rules of Engagement.
SAFE	Saving Antiquities for Everyone.
SBAH	State Board of Antiquities and Heritage
SCA	Supreme Council of Antiquities.
SFIR	Stabilization Force Iraq.
SOFA	Status of Forces Agreement
STANAG	NATO abbreviation for Standardization Agreement.
TRADOC	U.S. Army Training and Doctrine Command
UNESCO	United Nations Educational, Scientific and Cultural Organization.
UNIDROIT	International Institute for the Unification of Private Law
USCBS	United States Committee of the Blue Shield.
WAC	World Archaeological Congress.
WATCH	World Association for the protection of Tangible and Intangible Cultural Heritage in times of armed conflicts.
WHC	World Heritage Convention.
WMF	World Monuments Fund

INTERVIEWS

Professor Larry Rothfield, University of Chicago, July 2007 January 2008.
Cori Wegener, president of the American Blue Shield Committee. September 2005 and November 2007.
Dr. John Curtis, Keeper of the Middle East collections of the British Museum, August 2006, January 2007.
W. Hays Parks special assistant for law of war matters for the Army's Judge Advocate General November 2007 and May 2011.
Colonel Matthew Bogdanos US Marines, February 2006 and July 2007.
Colonel Harrie Knoop now retired, former CIMIC commander of the MND CS, January 2008
Professor Peter Stone, January 2008
Bgen. Wolfgang Peischel, November 2009.
Karl von Habsburg, August 2009, January 2011.
Dr. Laurie Rush, August 2009, July 2010.
Professor Charles Garraway, December 2010, March 2011.
Dr. Donny George, former director National Museum Baghdad, January 2008, January 2011.
(Dr. George died unexpectedly in March 2011).

APPENDIXES

APPENDIX ONE

THE HAGUE CONVENTION FOR THE PROTECTION OF CULTURAL PROPERTY IN THE EVENT OF ARMED CONFLICT OF 1954 AND THE FIRST AND SECOND PROTOCOLS

Convention for the Protection of Cultural Property in the Event of Armed Conflict with Regulations for the Execution of the Convention 1954

The High Contracting Parties,

Recognizing that cultural property has suffered grave damage during recent armed conflicts and that, by reason of the developments in the technique of warfare, it is in increasing danger of destruction;

Being convinced that damage to cultural property belonging to any people whatsoever means damage to the cultural heritage of all mankind, since each people makes its contribution to the culture of the world;

Considering that the preservation of the cultural heritage is of great importance for all peoples of the world and that it is important that this heritage should receive international protection;

Guided by the principles concerning the protection of cultural property during armed conflict, as established in the Conventions of The Hague of 1899 and of 1907 and in the Washington Pact of 15 April, 1935;

Being of the opinion that such protection cannot be effective unless both national and international measures have been taken to organize it in time of peace;

Being determined to take all possible steps to protect cultural property;

Have agreed upon the following provisions:

Chapter I. *General provisions regarding protection*

Article 1. *Definition of cultural property*
For the purposes of the present Convention, the term 'cultural property' shall cover, irrespective of origin or ownership:

(a) movable or immovable property of great importance to the cultural heritage of every people, such as monuments of architecture, art or history, whether religious or secular; archaeological sites; groups of buildings which, as a whole, are of historical or artistic interest; works of art; manuscripts, books and other objects of artistic, historical or archaeological interest; as well as scientific collections and important collections of books or archives or of reproductions of the property defined above;
(b) buildings whose main and effective purpose is to preserve or exhibit the movable cultural property defined in sub-paragraph (a) such as museums, large libraries and depositories of archives, and refuges intended to shelter, in the event of armed conflict, the movable cultural property defined in sub-paragraph (a);
(c) centers containing a large amount of cultural property as defined in sub-paragraphs (a) and (b), to be known as 'centers containing monuments'.

Article 2. *Protection of cultural property*
For the purposes of the present Convention, the protection of cultural property shall comprise the safeguarding of and respect for such property.

Article 3. *Safeguarding of cultural property*
The High Contracting Parties undertake to prepare in time of peace for the safeguarding of cultural property situated within their own territory against the foreseeable effects of an armed conflict, by taking such measures as they consider appropriate.

Article 4. *Respect for cultural property*

1. The High Contracting Parties undertake to respect cultural property situated within their own territory as well as within the territory of other High Contracting Parties by refraining from any use of the property and its immediate surroundings or of the appliances in use for its protection for purposes which are likely to expose it to destruction or damage in the event of armed conflict; and by refraining from any act of hostility, directed against such property.

2. The obligations mentioned in paragraph 1 of the present Article may be waived only in cases where military necessity imperatively requires such a waiver.
3. The High Contracting Parties further undertake to prohibit, prevent and, if necessary, put a stop to any form of theft, pillage or misappropriation of, and any acts of vandalism directed against, cultural property. They shall refrain from requisitioning movable cultural property situated in the territory of another High Contracting Party.
4. They shall refrain from any act directed by way of reprisals against cultural property.
5. No High Contracting Party may evade the obligations incumbent upon it under the present Article, in respect of another High Contracting Party, by reason of the fact that the latter has not applied the measures of safeguard referred to in Article 3.

Article 5. *Occupation*

1. Any High Contracting Party in occupation of the whole or part of the territory of another High Contracting Party shall as far as possible support the competent national authorities of the occupied country in safeguarding and preserving its cultural property.
2. Should it prove necessary to take measures to preserve cultural property situated in occupied territory and damaged by military operations, and should the competent national authorities be unable to take such measures, the Occupying Power shall, as far as possible, and in close co-operation with such authorities, take the most necessary measures of preservation.
3. Any High Contracting Party whose government is considered their legitimate government by members of a resistance movement, shall, if possible, draw their attention to the obligation to comply with those provisions of the Convention dealing with respect for cultural property.

Article 6. *Distinctive marking of cultural property*

In accordance with the provisions of Article 16, cultural property may bear a distinctive emblem so as to facilitate its recognition.

Article 7. *Military measures*

1. The High Contracting Parties undertake to introduce in time of peace into their military regulations or instructions such provisions as may ensure observance of the present Convention, and to foster in the

members of their armed forces a spirit of respect for the culture and cultural property of all peoples.

2. The High Contracting Parties undertake to plan or establish in peacetime, within their armed forces, services or specialist personnel whose purpose will be to secure respect for cultural property and to cooperate with the civilian authorities responsible for safeguarding it.

Chapter II. *Special protection*

Article 8. *Granting of special protection*

1. There may be placed under special protection a limited number of refuges intended to shelter movable cultural property in the event of armed conflict, of centers containing monuments and other immovable cultural property of very great importance, provided that they:
   (a) are situated at an adequate distance from any large industrial center or from any important military objective constituting a vulnerable point, such as, for example, an aerodrome, broadcasting station, establishment engaged upon work of national defense, a port or railway station of relative importance or a main line of communication;
   (b) are not used for military purposes.
2. A refuge for movable cultural property may also be placed under special protection, whatever its location, if it is so constructed that, in all probability, it will not be damaged by bombs.
3. A center containing monuments shall be deemed to be used for military purposes whenever it is used for the movement of military personnel or material, even in transit. The same shall apply whenever activities directly connected with military operations, the stationing of military personnel, or the production of war material are carried on within the center.
4. The guarding of cultural property mentioned in paragraph I above by armed custodians specially empowered to do so, or the presence, in the vicinity of such cultural property, of police forces normally responsible for the maintenance of public order shall not be deemed to be used for military purposes.
5. If any cultural property mentioned in paragraph 1 of the present Article is situated near an important military objective as defined in the said paragraph, it may nevertheless be placed under special protection if the High Contracting Party asking for that protection undertakes,

in the event of armed conflict, to make no use of the objective and particularly, in the case of a port, railway station or aerodrome, to divert all traffic there from. In that event, such diversion shall be prepared in time of peace.

6. Special protection is granted to cultural property by its entry in the 'Inter-national Register of Cultural Property under Special Protection'. This entry shall only be made, in accordance with the provisions of the present Convention and under the conditions provided for in the Regulations for the execution of the Convention.

Article 9. *Immunity of cultural property under special protection*
The High Contracting Parties undertake to ensure the immunity of cultural property under special protection by refraining, from the time of entry in the International Register, from any act of hostility directed against such property and, except for the cases provided for in paragraph 5 of Article 8, from any use of such property or its surroundings for military purposes.

Article 10. *Identification and control*
During an armed conflict, cultural property under special protection shall be marked with the distinctive emblem described in Article 16, and shall be open to international control as provided for in the Regulations for the execution of the Convention.

Article 11. *Withdrawal of immunity*

1. If one of the High Contracting Parties commits, in respect of any item of cultural property under special protection, a violation of the obligations under Article 9, the opposing Party shall, so long as this violation persists, be released from the obligation to ensure the immunity of the property concerned. Nevertheless, whenever possible, the latter Party shall first request the cessation of such violation within a reasonable time.
2. Apart from the case provided for in paragraph 1 of the present Article, immunity shall be withdrawn from cultural property under special protection only in exceptional cases of unavoidable military necessity, and only for such time as that necessity continues. Such necessity can be established only by the officer commanding a force the equivalent of a division in size or larger. Whenever circumstances permit, the opposing Party shall be notified, a reasonable time in advance, of the decision to withdraw immunity.

3. The Party withdrawing immunity shall, as soon as possible, so inform the Commissioner-General for cultural property provided for in the Regulations for the execution of the Convention, in writing, stating the reasons.

Chapter III. *Transport of cultural property*

Article 12. *Transport under special protection*

1. Transport exclusively engaged in the transfer of cultural property, whether within a territory or to another territory, may, at the request of the High Contracting Party concerned, take place under special protection in accordance with the conditions specified in the Regulations for the execution of the Convention.
2. Transport under special protection shall take place under the international supervision provided for in the aforesaid Regulations and shall display the distinctive emblem described in Article 16.
3. The High Contracting Parties shall refrain from any act of hostility directed against transport under special protection.

Article 13. *Transport in urgent cases*

1. If a High Contracting Party considers that the safety of certain cultural property requires its transfer and that the matter is of such urgency that the procedure laid down in Article 12 cannot be followed, especially at the beginning of an armed conflict, the transport may display the distinctive emblem described in Articlc 16, provided that an application for immunity referred to in Article 12 has not already been made and refused. As far as possible, notification of transfer should be made to the opposing' Parties. Nevertheless, transport conveying cultural property to the territory of another country may not display the distinctive emblem unless immunity has been expressly granted to it.
2. The High Contracting Parties shall take, so far as possible, the necessary precautions to avoid acts of hostility directed against the transport described in paragraph 1 of the present Article and displaying the distinctive emblem.

Article 14. *Immunity from seizure, capture and prize*

1. Immunity from seizure, placing in prize, or capture shall be granted to:
   (a) cultural property enjoying the protection provided for in Article 12 or that provided for in Article 13;

(b) the means of transport exclusively engaged in the transfer of such cultural property.

2. Nothing in the present Article shall limit the right of visit and search.

Chapter IV. *Personnel*

Article 15. *Personnel*

As far as is consistent with the interests of security, personnel engaged in the protection of cultural property shall, in the interests of such property, be respected and, if they fall into the hands of the opposing Party, shall be allowed to continue to carry out their duties whenever the cultural property for which they are responsible has also fallen into the hands of the opposing Party.

Chapter V. *The distinctive emblem*

Article 16. *Emblem of the convention*

1. The distinctive emblem of the Convention shall take the form of a shield, pointed below, persaltire blue and white (a shield consisting of a royal-blue square, one of the angles of which forms the point of the shield, and of a royal-blue triangle above the square, the space on either side being taken up by a white triangle).
2. The emblem shall be used alone, or repeated three times in a triangular formation (one shield below), under the conditions provided for in Article 17.

Article 17. *Use of the emblem*

1. The distinctive emblem repeated three times may be used only as a means of identification of:
   (a) immovable cultural property under special protection;
   (b) the transport of cultural property under the conditions provided for in Articles 12 and 13;
   (c) improvised refuges, under the conditions provided for in the Regulations for the execution of the Convention.
2. The distinctive emblem may be used alone only as a means of identification of:
   (a) cultural property not under special protection;
   (b) the persons responsible for the duties of control in accordance with the Regulations for the execution of the Convention;
   (c) the personnel engaged in the protection of cultural property;
   (d) the identity cards mentioned in the Regulations for the execution of the Convention.

3. During an armed conflict, the use of the distinctive emblem in any other cases than those mentioned in the preceding paragraphs of the present Article, and the use for any purpose whatever of a sign resembling the distinctive emblem, shall be forbidden.
4. The distinctive emblem may not be placed on any immovable cultural property unless at the same time there is displayed an authorization duly dated and signed by the competent authority of the High Contracting Party.

Chapter VI. *Scope of application of the Convention*

Article 18. *Application of the Convention*

1. Apart from the provisions which shall take effect in time of peace, the present Convention shall apply in the event of declared war or of any other armed conflict which may arise between two or more of the High Contracting Parties, even if the state of war is not recognized by, one or more of them.
2. The Convention shall also apply to all cases of partial or total occupation of the territory of a High Contracting Party, even if the said occupation meets with no armed resistance.
3. If one of the Powers in conflict is not a Party to the present Convention, the Powers which are Parties thereto shall nevertheless remain bound by it in their mutual relations. They shall furthermore be bound by the Convention, in relation to the said Power, if the latter has declared, that it accepts the provisions thereof and so long as it applies them.

Article 19. *Conflicts not of an international character*

1. In the event of an armed conflict not of an international character occurring within the territory of one of the High Contracting Parties, each party to the conflict shall be bound to apply, as, a minimum, the provisions of the present Convention which relate to respect for cultural property.
2. The parties to the conflict shall endeavour to bring into force, by means of special agreements, all or part of the other provisions of the present Convention.
3. The United Nations Educational, Scientific and Cultural Organization may offer its services to the parties to the conflict.
4. The application of the preceding provisions shall not affect the legal status of the parties to the conflict.

Chapter VII. *Execution of the Convention*

Article 20. *Regulations for the execution of the Convention*
The procedure by which the present Convention is to be applied is defined in the Regulations for its execution, which constitute an integral part thereof.

Article 21. *Protecting powers*
The present Convention and the Regulations for its execution shall be applied with the co-operation of the Protecting Powers responsible for safeguarding the interests of the Parties to the conflict.

Article 22. *Conciliation procedure*

1. The Protecting Powers shall lend their good offices in all cases where they may deem it useful in the interests of cultural property, particularly if there is disagreement between the Parties to the conflict as to the application or interpretation of the provisions of the present Convention or the Regulations for its execution.
2. For this purpose, each of the Protecting Powers may, either at the invitation of one Party, of the Director-General of the United Nations Educational, Scientific and Cultural Organization, or on its own initiative, propose to the Parties to the conflict a meeting of their representatives, and in particular of the authorities responsible for the protection of cultural property, if considered appropriate on suitably chosen neutral territory. The Parties to the conflict shall be bound to give effect to the proposals for meeting made to them.

The Protecting Powers shall propose for approval by the Parties to the conflict a person belonging to a neutral Power or a person presented by the Director General of the United Nations Educational, Scientific and Cultural Organization, which person shall be invited to take part in such a meeting in the capacity of Chairman.

Article 23. *Assistance of UNESCO*

1. The High Contracting Parties may call upon the United Nations Educational, Scientific and Cultural Organization for technical assistance in organizing the protection of their cultural property, or in connexion with any other problem arising out of the application of the present Convention or the Regulations for its execution. The Organization shall accord such assistance within the limits fixed by its programme and by its resources.

2. The Organization is authorized to make, on its own initiative, proposals on this matter to the High Contracting Parties.

Article 24. *Special agreements*

1. The High Contracting Parties may conclude special agreements for all matters concerning which they deem it suitable to make separate provision.
2. No special agreement may be concluded which would diminish the protection afforded by the present Convention to cultural property and to the personnel engaged in its protection.

Article 25. *Dissemination of the Convention*

The High Contracting Parties undertake, in time of peace as in time of armed conflict, to disseminate the text of the present Convention and the Regulations for its execution as widely as possible in their respective countries. They undertake, in particular, to include the study thereof in their programmes of military and, if possible, civilian training, so that its principles are made known to the whole population, especially the armed forces and personnel engaged in the protection of cultural property.

Article 26. *Translations reports*

1. The High Contracting Parties shall communicate to one another, through the Director-General of the United Nations Educational, Scientific and Cultural Organization, the official translations of the present Convention and of the Regulations for its execution.
2. Furthermore, at least once every four years, they shall forward to the Director-General a report giving whatever information they think suitable concerning any measures being taken, prepared or contemplated by their respective administrations in fulfillment of the present Convention and of the Regulations for its execution.

Article 27. *Meetings*

1. The Director-General of the United Nations Educational, Scientific and Cultural Organization may, with the approval of the Executive Board, convene meetings of representatives of the High Contracting Parties. He must convene such a meeting if at least one-fifth of the High Contracting Parties so request.
2. Without prejudice to any other functions which have been conferred on it by the present Convention or the Regulations for its execution,

the purpose of the meeting will be to study problems concerning the application of the Convention and of the Regulations for its execution, and to formulate recommendations in respect thereof.

3. The meeting may further undertake a revision of the Convention or the Regulations for its execution if the majority of the High Contracting Parties are represented, and in accordance with the provisions of Article 39.

Article 28. *Sanctions*

The High Contracting Parties undertake to take, within the framework of their ordinary criminal jurisdiction, all necessary steps to prosecute and impose penal or disciplinary sanctions upon those persons, of whatever nationality, who commit or order to be committed a breach of the present Convention.

Final provisions

Article 29. *Languages*

1. The present Convention is drawn up in English, French, Russian and Spanish, the four texts being equally authoritative.
2. The United Nations Educational, Scientific and Cultural Organization shall arrange for translations of the Convention into the other official languages of its General Conference.

Article 30. *Signature*

The present Convention shall bear the date of 14 May, 1954 and, until the date of 31 December, 1954, shall remain open for signature by all States invited to the Conference which met at The Hague from 21 April, 1954 to 14 May, 1954.

Article 31. *Ratification*

1. The present Convention shall be subject to ratification by signatory States in accordance with their respective constitutional procedures.
2. The instruments of ratification shall be deposited with the Director-General of the United Nations Educational, Scientific and Cultural Organization.

Article 32. *Accession*

From the date of its entry into force, the present Convention shall be open for accession by all States mentioned in Article 30 which have not signed it, as well as any other State invited to accede by the Executive Board of the United Nations Educational, Scientific and Cultural Organization. Accession shall be effected by the deposit of an instrument of accession with the Director-General of the United Nations Educational, Scientific and Cultural Organization.

Article 33. *Entry into force*

1. The present Convention shall enter into force three months after five instruments of ratification have been deposited.
2. Thereafter, it shall enter into force, for each High Contracting Party, three months after the deposit of its instrument of ratification or accession.
3. The situations referred to in Articles 18 and 19 shall give immediate effect to ratifications or accessions deposited by the Parties to the conflict either before or after the beginning of hostilities or occupation. In such cases the Director-General of the United Nations Educational, Scientific and Cultural Organization shall transmit the communications referred to in Article 38 by the speediest method.

Article 34. *Effective application*

1. Each State Party to the Convention on the date of its entry into force shall take all necessary measures to ensure its effective application within a period of six months after such entry into force.
2. This period shall be six months from the date of deposit of the instruments of ratification or accession for any State which deposits its instrument of ratification or accession after the date of the entry into force of the Convention.

Article 35. *Territorial extension of the Convention*

Any High Contracting Party may, at the time of ratification or accession, or at any time thereafter, declare by notification addressed to the Director-General of the United Nations Educational, Scientific and Cultural Organization, that the present Convention shall extend to all or any of the territories for whose international relations it is responsible. The said notification shall take effect three months after the date of its receipt.

Article 36. *Relation to previous conventions*

1. In the relations between Powers which are bound by the Conventions of The Hague concerning the Laws and Customs of War on Land (IV) and concerning Naval Bombardment in Time of War (IX), whether

those of 29 July, 1899 or those of 18 October, 1907, and which are Parties to the present Convention, this last Convention shall be supplementary to the aforementioned Convention (IX) and to the Regulations annexed to the aforementioned Convention (IV) and shall substitute for the emblem described in Article 5 of the aforementioned Convention (IX) the emblem described in Article 16 of the present Convention, in cases in which the present Convention and the Regulations for its execution provide for the use of this distinctive emblem.

2. In the relations between Powers which are bound by the Washington Pact of 15 April, 1935 for the Protection of Artistic and Scientific Institutions and of Historic Monuments (Roerich Pact) and which are Parties to the present Convention, the latter Convention shall be supplementary to the Roerich Pact and shall substitute for the distinguishing flag described in Article III of the Pact the emblem defined in Article 16 of the present Convention, in cases in which the present Convention and the Regulations for its execution provide for the use of this distinctive emblem.

Article 37. *Denunciation*

1. Each High Contracting Party may denounce the present Convention, on its own behalf, or on behalf of any territory for whose international relations it is responsible.
2. The denunciation shall be notified by an instrument in writing, deposited with the Director-General of the United Nations Educational, Scientific and Cultural Organization.
3. The denunciation shall take effect one year after the receipt of the instrument of denunciation. However, if, on the expiry of this period, the denouncing Party is involved in an armed conflict, the denunciation shall not take effect until the end of hostilities, or until the operations of repatriating cultural property are completed, whichever is the later.

Article 38. *Notifications*

The Director-General of the United Nations Educational, Scientific and Cultural Organization shall inform the States referred to in Articles 30 and 32, as well as the United Nations, of the deposit of all the instruments of ratification, accession or acceptance provided for in Articles 31, 32 and 39 and of the notifications and denunciations provided for respectively in Articles 35, 37 and 39.

Article 39. *Revision of the Convention and of the Regulations for its execution*

1. Any High Contracting Party may propose amendments to the present Convention or the Regulations for its execution. The text of any proposed amendment shall be communicated to the Director-General of the United Nations Educational, Scientific and Cultural Organization who shall transmit it to each High Contracting Party with the request that such Party reply within four months stating whether it:
   (a) desires that a Conference be convened to consider the proposed amendment;
   (b) favours the acceptance of the proposed amendment without a Conference; or
   (c) favours the rejection of the proposed amendment without a Conference.
2. The Director-General shall transmit the replies, received under paragraph 1 of the present Article, to all High Contracting Parties.
3. If all the High Contracting Parties which have, within the prescribed time-limit, stated their views to the Director-General of the United Nations Educational, Scientific and Cultural Organization, pursuant to paragraph 1(b) of this Article, inform him that they favour acceptance of the amendment without a Conference, notification of their decision shall be made by the Director-General in accordance with Article 38. The amendment shall become effective for all the High Contracting Parties on the expiry of ninety days from the date of such notification.
4. The Director-General shall convene a Conference of the High Contracting Parties to consider the proposed amendment if requested to do so by more than one-third of the High Contracting Parties.
5. Amendments to the Convention or to the Regulations for its execution, dealt with under the provisions of the preceding paragraph, shall enter into force only after they have been unanimously adopted by the High Contracting Parties represented at the Conference and accepted by each of the High Contracting Parties.
6. Acceptance by the High Contracting Parties of amendments to, the Convention or to the Regulations for its execution, which have been adopted by the Conference mentioned in paragraphs 4 and 5, shall be effected by the deposit of a formal instrument with the Director-General of the United Nations Educational, Scientific and Cultural Organization.
7. After the entry into force of amendments to the present Convention or to the Regulations for its execution, only the text of the Convention or of the Regulations for its execution thus amended shall remain open for ratification or accession.

Article 40. *Registration*
In accordance with Article 102 of the Charter of the United Nations, the present Convention shall be registered with the Secretariat of the United Nations at the request of the Director-General of the United Nations Educational, Scientific and Cultural Organization.

IN FAITH WHEREOF the undersigned, duly authorized, have signed the present Convention.

Done at The Hague, this fourteenth day of May, 1954, in a single copy which shall be deposited in the archives of the United Nations Educational, Scientific and Cultural Organization, and certified true copies of which shall be delivered to all the States referred to in Articles 30 and 32 as well as to the United Nations.

Regulations for the Execution of the Convention for the Protection of Cultural Property in the Event of Armed Conflict

Chapter I. *Control*

Article 1. *International list of persons*
On the entry into force of the Convention, the Director-General of the United Nations Educational, Scientific and Cultural Organization shall compile an international list consisting of all persons nominated by the High Contracting Parties as qualified to carry out the functions of Commissioner-General for Cultural Property. On the initiative of the Director-General of the United Nations Educational, Scientific and Cultural Organization, this list shall be periodically revised on the basis of requests formulated by the High Contracting Parties.

Article 2. *Organization of control*
As soon as any High Contracting Party is engaged in an armed conflict to which Article 18 of the Convention applies:

(a) It shall appoint a representative for cultural property situated in its territory; if it is in occupation of another territory, it shall appoint a special representative for cultural property situated in that territory;
(b) The Protecting Power acting for each of the Parties in conflict with such High Contracting Party shall appoint delegates accredited to the latter in conformity with Article 3 below;
(c) A Commissioner-General for Cultural Property shall be appointed to such High Contracting Party in accordance with Article 4.

Article 3. *Appointment of delegates of Protecting Powers*
The Protecting Power shall appoint its delegates from among the members of its diplomatic or consular staff or, with the approval of the Party to which they will be accredited, from among other persons.

Article 4. *Appointment of 'Commissioner-General*

1. The Commissioner-General for Cultural Property shall be chosen from the international list of persons by joint agreement between the Party to which he will be accredited and the Protecting Powers acting on behalf of the opposing Parties.
2. Should the Parties fail to reach agreement within three weeks from the beginning of their discussions on this point, they shall request

the President of the International Court of Justice to appoint the Commissioner-General, who shall not take up his duties until the Party to which he is accredited has approved his appointment.

Article 5. *Functions of delegates*
The delegates of the Protecting Powers shall take note of violations of the Convention, investigate, with the approval of the Party to which they are accredited, the circumstances in which they have occurred, make representations locally to secure their cessation and, if necessary, notify the Commissioner-General of such violations. They shall keep him informed of their activities.

Article 6. *Functions of the Commissioner-General*

1. The Commissioner-General for Cultural Property shall deal with all matters referred to him in connexion with the application of the Convention, in conjunction with the representative of the Party to which he is accredited and with the delegates concerned.
2. He shall have powers of decision and appointment in the cases specified in the present Regulations.
3. With the agreement of the Party to which he is accredited, he shall have the right to order an investigation or to, conduct it himself.
4. He shall make any representations to the Parties to the conflict or to their Protecting Powers which he deems useful for the application of the Convention.
5. He shall draw up such reports as may be necessary on the application of the Convention and communicate them to the Parties concerned and to their Protecting Powers. He shall send copies to the Director-General of the United Nations Educational, Scientific and Cultural Organization, who may make use only of their technical contents.
6. If there is no Protecting Power, the Commissioner-General shall exercise the functions of the Protecting Power as laid down in Articles 21 and 22 of the Convention.

Article 7. *Inspectors and experts*

1. Whenever the Commissioner-General for Cultural Property considers it necessary, either at the request of the delegates concerned or after consultation with them, he shall propose, for the approval of the Party to which he is accredited, an inspector of cultural property to be charged with a specific mission. An inspector shall be responsible only to the Commissioner-General.

2. The Commissioner-General, delegates and inspectors may have recourse to the services of experts, who will also be proposed for the approval of the Party mentioned in the preceding paragraph.

Article 8. *Discharge of the mission of control*
The Commissioners-General for Cultural Property, delegates of the Protecting Powers, inspectors and experts shall in no case exceed their mandates. In particular, they shall take account of the security needs of the High Contracting Party to which they are accredited and shall in all circumstances act in accordance with the requirements of the military situation as communicated to them by that High Contracting Party.

Article 9. *Substitutes for Protecting Powers*
If a Party to the conflict does not benefit or ceases to benefit from the activities of a Protecting Power, a neutral State may be asked to undertake those functions of a Protecting Power which concern the appointment of a Commissioner-General for Cultural Property in accordance with the procedure laid down in Article 4 above. The Commissioner-General thus appointed shall, if need be, entrust to inspectors the functions of delegates of Protecting Powers as specified in the present Regulations.

Article 10. *Expenses*
The remuneration and expenses of the Commissioner-General for Cultural Property, inspectors and experts shall be met by the Party to which they are accredited. Remuneration and expenses of delegates of the Protecting Powers shall be subject to agreement between those Powers and the States whose interests they are safeguarding.

Chapter II. *Special protection*

Article 11. *Improvised refuges*

1. If, during an armed conflict, any High Contracting Party is induced by unforeseen circumstances to set up an improvised refuge and desires that it should be placed under special protection, it shall communicate this fact forthwith to the Commissioner-General accredited to that Party.
2. If the Commissioner-General considers that such a measure is justified by the circumstances and by the importance of the cultural property sheltered in' this improvised refuge, he may authorize the High Contracting Party to display on such refuge the distinctive emblem defined

in Article 16 of the Convention. He shall communicate his decision without delay to the delegates of the Protecting Powers who are concerned, each of whom may, within a time limit of 30 days, order the immediate withdrawal of the emblem.

3. As soon as such delegates have signified their agreement or if the time limit of 30 days has passed without any of the delegates concerned having made an objection, and if, in the view of the Commissioner-General, the refuge fulfils the conditions laid down in Article 8 of the Convention, the Commissioner-General shall request the Director-General of the United Nations Educational, Scientific and Cultural Organization to enter the refuge in the Register of Cultural Property under Special Protection.

Article 12. *International Register of Cultural Property under Special Protection*

1. An 'International Register of Cultural Property under Special Protection' shall be prepared.
2. The Director-General of the United Nations Educational, Scientific and Cultural Organization shall maintain this Register. He shall furnish copies to the Secretary-General of the United Nations and to the High Contracting Parties.
3. The Register shall be divided into sections, each in the name of a High Contracting Party. Each section shall be subdivided into three paragraphs, headed: Refuges, Centers containing Monuments, Other Immovable Cultural Property. The Director-General shall determine what details each section shall contain.

Article 13. *Requests for registration*

1. Any High Contracting Party may submit to the Director-General of the United Nations Educational, Scientific and Cultural Organization an application for the entry in the Register of certain refuges, centers containing monuments or other immovable cultural property situated within its territory. Such application shall contain a description of the location of such property and shall certify that the property complies with the provisions of Article 8 of the Convention.
2. In the event of occupation, the Occupying Power shall be competent to make such application.
3. The Director-General of the United Nations Educational, Scientific and Cultural Organization shall, without delay, send copies of applications for registration to each of the High Contracting Parties.

Article 14. *Objections*

1. Any High Contracting Party may, by letter addressed to the Director-General of the United Nations Educational, Scientific and Cultural Organization, lodge an objection to the registration of cultural property. This letter must be received by him within four months of the day on which he sent a copy of the application for registration.
2. Such objection shall state the reasons giving rise to it, the only, valid grounds being that:
   (a) the property is not cultural property;
   (b) the property does not comply with the conditions mentioned in Article 8 of the Convention.
3. The Director-General shall send a copy of the letter of objection to the High Contracting Parties without delay. He shall, if necessary, seek the advice of the International Committee on Monuments, Artistic and Historical Sites and Archaeological Excavations and also, if he thinks fit, of any other competent organization or person.
4. The Director-General, or the High Contracting Party requesting registration, may make whatever representations they deem necessary to the High Contracting Parties which lodged the objection, with a view to causing the objection to be withdrawn.
5. If a High Contracting Party which has made an application for registration in time of peace becomes involved in an armed conflict before the entry has been made, the cultural property concerned shall at once be provisionally entered in the Register, by the Director-General, pending the confirmation, withdrawal or cancellation of any objection that may be, or may have been, made.
6. If, within a period of six months from the date of receipt of the letter of objection, the Director-General has not received from the High Contracting Party lodging the objection a communication stating that it has been withdrawn, the High Contracting Party applying for registration may request arbitration in accordance with the procedure in the following paragraph.
7. The request for arbitration shall not be made more than one year after the date of receipt by the Director-General of the letter of objection. Each of the two Parties to the dispute shall appoint an arbitrator. When more than one objection has been lodged against an application for registration, the High Contracting Parties which have lodged the 'objections shall, by common consent, appoint a single arbitrator. These two arbitrators shall select a chief arbitrator from the international list mentioned in Article 1 of the present Regulations. If such

arbitrators cannot agree upon their choice, they shall ask the President of the International Court of Justice to appoint a chief arbitrator who need not necessarily be chosen from the international list. The arbitral tribunal thus constituted shall fix its own procedure. There shall be no appeal from its decisions.

8. Each of the High Contracting Parties may declare, whenever a dispute to which it is a Party arises, that it does not wish to apply the arbitration procedure provided for in the preceding paragraph. In such cases, the objection to an application for registration shall be submitted by the Director-General to the High Contracting Parties. The objection will be confirmed only if the High Contracting Parties so decide by a two-third majority of the High Contracting Parties voting. The vote shall be taken by correspondence, unless the Directory-General of the United Nations Educational, Scientific and Cultural Organization deems it essential to convene a meeting under the powers conferred upon him by Article 27 of the Convention. If the Director-General decides to proceed with the vote by correspondence, he shall invite the High Contracting Parties to transmit their votes by sealed letter within six months from the day on which they were invited to do so.

Article 15. *Registration*

1. The Director-General of the United Nations Educational, Scientific and Cultural Organization shall cause to be entered in the Register, under a serial number, each item of property for which application for registration is made, provided that he has not received an objection within the time-limit prescribed in paragraph 1 of Article 14.
2. If an objection has been lodged, and without prejudice to the provision of paragraph 5 of Article 14, the Director-General shall enter property in the Register only if the objection has been withdrawn or has failed to be confirmed following the procedures laid down in either paragraph 7 or paragraph 8 of Article 14.
3. Whenever paragraph 3 of Article 11 applies, the Director-General shall enter property in the Register if so requested by the Commissioner-General for Cultural Property.
4. The Director-General shall send without delay to the Secretary-General of the United Nations, to the High Contracting Parties, and, at the request of the Party applying for registration, to all other States referred to in Articles 30 and 32 of the Convention, a certified copy of each entry in the Register. Entries shall become effective thirty days after dispatch of such copies.

Article 16. *Cancellation*

1. The Director-General of the United Nations Educational, Scientific and Cultural Organization shall cause the registration of any property to be cancelled:
   (a) at the request of the High Contracting Party within whose territory the cultural property is situated;
   (b) if the High Contracting Party which requested registration has denounced the Convention, and when that denunciation has taken effect;
   (c) in the special case provided for in Article 14, paragraph 5, when an objection has been confirmed following the procedures mentioned either in paragraph 7 or in paragraph 8 or Article 14.
2. The Director-General shall send without delay, to the Secretary-General of the United Nations and to all States which received a copy of the entry in the Register, a certified copy of its cancellation. Cancellation shall take effect thirty days after the dispatch of such copies.

Chapter III. *Transport of cultural property*

Article 17. *Procedure to obtain immunity*

1. The request mentioned in paragraph I of Article 12 of the Convention shall be addressed to the Commissioner-General for Cultural Property. It shall mention the reasons on which it is based and specify the approximate number and the importance of the objects to be transferred, their present location, the location now envisaged, the means of transport to be used, the route to be followed, the date proposed for the transfer, and any other relevant information.
2. If the Commissioner-General, after taking such opinions as he deems fit, considers that such transfer is justified, he shall consult those delegates of the Protecting Powers who are concerned, on the measures proposed for carrying it out. Following such consultation, he shall notify the Parties to the conflict concerned of the transfer, including in such notification all useful information.
3. The Commissioner-General shall appoint one or more inspectors, who shall satisfy themselves that only the property stated in the request is to be transferred and that the transport is to be by the approved methods and bears the distinctive emblem. The inspector or inspectors shall accompany the property to its destination.

Article 18. *Transport abroad*
Where the transfer under special protection is to the territory of another country, it shall be governed not only by Article 12 of the Convention and by Article 17 of the present Regulations, but by the following further provisions:

(a) while the cultural property remains on the territory of another State, that State shall be its depositary and shall extend to it as great a measure of care as that which it bestows upon its own cultural property of comparable importance;
(b) the depositary State shall return the property only on the cessation of the conflict; such return shall be effected within six months from the date on which it was requested;
(c) during the various transfer operations, and while it remains on the territory of another State, the cultural property shall be exempt from confiscation and may not be disposed of either by the depositor or by the depositary. Nevertheless, when the safety of the property requires it, the depositary may, with the assent of the depositor, have the property transported to the territory of a third country, under the conditions laid down in the present article;
(d) the request for special protection shall indicate that the State to whose territory the property is to be transferred accepts the provisions of the present Article.

Article 19. *Occupied territory*
Whenever a High Contracting Party occupying territory of another High Contracting Party transfers cultural property to a refuge situated elsewhere in that territory, without being able to follow the procedure provided for in Article 17 of the Regulations, the transfer in question shall not be regarded as misappropriation within the meaning of Article 4 of the Convention, provided that the Commissioner-General for Cultural Property certifies in writing, after having consulted the usual custodians, that such transfer was rendered necessary by circumstances.

Chapter IV. *The distinctive emblem*

Article 20. *Affixing of the emblem*

1. The placing of the distinctive emblem and its degree of visibility shall be left to the discretion of the competent authorities of each High Contracting Party. It may be displayed on flags or armlets; it may be painted on an object or represented in any other appropriate form.

2. However, without prejudice to any possible fuller markings, the emblem shall, in the event of armed conflict and in the cases mentioned in Articles 12 and 13 of the Convention, be placed on the vehicles of transport so as to be clearly visible in daylight from the air as well as from the ground. The emblem shall be visible from the ground:
   (a) at regular intervals sufficient to indicate clearly the perimeter of a centre containing monuments under special protection;
   (b) at the entrance to other immovable cultural property under special protection.

Article 21. *Identification of persons*

1. The persons mentioned in Article 17, paragraph 2(b) and (c) of the Convention may wear an armlet bearing the distinctive emblem, issued and stamped by the competent authorities.
2. Such persons shall carry a special identity card bearing the distinctive emblem. This card shall mention at least the surname and first names, the date of birth, the title or rank, and the function of the holder. The card shall bear the photograph of the holder as well as his signature or his fingerprints, or both. It shall bear the embossed stamp of the competent authorities.
3. Each High Contracting Party shall make out its own type of identity card, guided by the model annexed, by way of example, to the present Regulations. The' High Contracting Parties shall transmit to each other a specimen of the model they are using. Identity cards shall be made out, if possible, at least in duplicate, one copy being kept by the issuing Power.
4. The said persons may not, without legitimate reason, be deprived of their identity card or of the right to wear the armlet.

First Protocol to the Convention for the Protection of Cultural Property in the Event of Armed conflict 1954

The High Contracting Parties are agreed as follows:

I.

1. Each High Contracting Party undertakes to prevent the exportation, from a territory occupied by it during an armed conflict, of cultural property as defined in Article I of the Convention for the Protection of Cultural Property in the Event of Armed Conflict, signed at The Hague on 14 May, 1954.
2. Each High Contracting Party undertakes to take into its custody cultural property imported into its territory either directly or indirectly from any occupied territory. This shall either be effected automatically upon the importation of the property or, failing this, at the request of the authorities of that territory.
3. Each High Contracting Party undertakes to return, at the close of hostilities, to the competent authorities of the territory previously occupied, cultural property which is in its territory, if such property has been exported in contravention of the principle laid down in the first paragraph. Such property shall never be retained as war reparations.
4. The High Contracting Party whose obligation it was to prevent the exportation of cultural property from the territory occupied by it, shall pay an indemnity to the holders in good faith of any cultural property which has to be returned in accordance with the preceding paragraph.

II.

5. Cultural property coming from the territory of a High Contracting Party and deposited by it in the territory of another High Contracting Party for the purpose of protecting such property against the dangers of an armed conflict, shall be returned by the latter, at the end of hostilities, to the competent authorities of the territory from which it came.

III.

6. The present Protocol shall bear the date of 14 May, 1954 and, until the date of 31 December, 1954, shall remain open for signature by all States invited to the Conference which met at The Hague from 21 April, 1954 to 14 May, 1954.

7. (a) The present Protocol shall be subject to ratification by signatory States in accordance with their respective constitutional procedures.
   (b) The instruments of ratification shall be deposited with the Director General of the United Nations Educational, Scientific and Cultural Organization.
8. From the date of its entry into force, the present Protocol shall be open for accession by all States mentioned in paragraph 6 which have not signed it as well as any other State invited to accede by the Executive Board of the United Nations Educational, Scientific and Cultural Organization. Accession shall be effected by the deposit of an instrument of accession with the Director-General of the United Nations Educational, Scientific and Cultural Organization.
9. The States referred to in paragraphs 6 and 8 may declare, at the time of signature, ratification or accession, that they will not be bound by the provisions of Section I or by those of Section II of the present Protocol.
10. (a) The present Protocol shall enter into force three months after five instruments of ratification have been deposited.
   (b) Thereafter, it shall enter into force, for each High Contracting Party, three months after the deposit of its instrument of ratification or accession.
   (c) The situations referred to in Articles 18 and 19 of the Convention for the Protection of Cultural Property in the Event of Armed Conflict, signed at The Hague on 14 May, 1954, shall give immediate effect to ratifications and accessions deposited by the Parties to the conflict either before or after the beginning of hostilities or occupation. In such cases, the Director-General of the United Nations Educational, Scientific and Cultural Organization shall transmit the communications' referred to in paragraph 14 by the speediest method.
11. (a) Each State Party to the Protocol on the date of its entry into force shall take all necessary measures to ensure its effective application within a period of six months after such entry into force.
   (b) This period shall be six months from the date of deposit of the instruments of ratification or accession for any State which deposits its instrument of ratification or accession after the date of the entry into force of the Protocol.
12. Any High Contracting Party may, at the time of ratification or accession, or at any time thereafter, declare by notification addressed to the Director General of the United Nations Educational, Scientific and

Cultural Organization, that the present Protocol shall extend to all or any of the territories for whose international relations it is responsible. The said notification shall take effect three months after the date of its receipt.

13. (a) Each High Contracting Party may denounce the present Protocol, on its own behalf, or on behalf of any territory for whose international relations it is responsible.
    (b) The denunciation shall be notified by an instrument in writing, deposited with the Director-General of the United Nations Educational, Scientific and Cultural Organization.
    (c) The denunciation shall take effect one year after receipt of the instrument of denunciation. However, if, on the expiry of this period, the denouncing Party is involved in an armed conflict, the denunciation shall not take effect until the end of hostilities, or until the operations of repatriating cultural property are completed, whichever is the later.
14. The Director-General of the United Nations Educational, Scientific and Cultural Organization shall inform the States referred to in paragraphs 6 and 8, as well as the United Nations, of the deposit of all the instruments of ratification, accession or acceptance provided for in paragraphs 7, 8 and 15 and the notifications and denunciations provided for respectively in paragraphs 12 and 13.
15. (a) The present Protocol may be revised if revision is requested by more than one-third of the High Contracting Parties.
    (b) The Director-General of the United Nations Educational, Scientific and Cultural Organization shall convene a Conference for this purpose.
    (c) Amendments to the present Protocol shall enter into force only after they have been unanimously adopted by the High Contracting Parties represented at the Conference and accepted by each of the High Contracting Parties.
    (d) Acceptance by the High Contracting Parties of amendments to the present Protocol, which have been adopted by the Conference mentioned in sub-paragraphs (b) and (c), shall be effected by the deposit of a formal instrument with the Director-General of the United Nations Educational, Scientific and Cultural Organization.
    (e) After the entry into force of amendments to the present Protocol, only the text of the said Protocol thus amended shall remain open for ratification or accession.

In accordance with Article 102 of the Charter of the United Nations, the present Protocol shall be registered with the Secretariat of the United Nations at the request of the Director-General of the United Nations Educational, Scientific and Cultural Organization.

IN FAITH WHEREOF the undersigned, duly authorized, have signed the present Protocol.

Done at The Hague, this fourteenth day of May, 1954, in English, French, Russian and Spanish, the four texts being equally authoritative, in a single copy which shall be deposited in the archives of the United Nations Educational, Scientific and Cultural Organization, and certified true copies of which shall be delivered to all the States referred to in paragraphs 6 and 8 as well as to the United Nations.

Second Protocol to the Hague Convention of 1954 for the Protection of Cultural Property in the Event of Armed Conflict

The Parties,

Conscious of the need to improve the protection of cultural property in the event of armed conflict and to establish an enhanced system of protection for specifically designated cultural property;

Reaffirming the importance of the provisions of the Convention for the Protection of Cultural Property in the Event of Armed Conflict, done at the Hague on 14 May 1954, and emphasizing the necessity to supplement these provisions through measures to reinforce their implementation;

Desiring to provide the High Contracting Parties to the Convention with a means of being more closely involved in the protection of cultural property in the event of armed conflict by establishing appropriate procedures therefor;

Considering that the rules governing the protection of cultural property in the event of armed conflict should reflect developments in international law;

Affirming that the rules of customary international law will continue to govern questions not regulated by the provisions of this Protocol;

Have agreed as follows:

Chapter 1. *Introduction*

Article 1. *Definitions*
For the purposes of this Protocol:

a. "Party" means a State Party to this Protocol;
b. "cultural property" means cultural property as defined in Article 1 of the Convention;
c. "Convention" means the Convention for the Protection of Cultural Property in the Event of Armed Conflict, done at The Hague on 14 May 1954;
d. "High Contracting Party" means a State Party to the Convention;

e. "enhanced protection" means the system of enhanced protection established by Articles 10 and 11;
f. "military objective" means an object which by its nature, location, purpose, or use makes an effective contribution to military action and whose total or partial destruction, capture or neutralisation, in the circumstances ruling at the time, offers a definite military advantage;
g. "illicit" means under compulsion or otherwise in violation of the applicable rules of the domestic law of the occupied territory or of international law.
h. "List" means the International List of Cultural Property under Enhanced Protection established in accordance with Article 27, sub-paragraph 1(b);
i. "Director-General" means the Director-General of UNESCO;
j. "UNESCO" means the United Nations Educational, Scientific and Cultural Organization;
k. "First Protocol" means the Protocol for the Protection of Cultural Property in the Event of Armed Conflict done at The Hague on 14 May 1954;

Article 2. *Relation to the Convention*
This Protocol supplements the Convention in relations between the Parties.

Article 3. *Scope of application*
1. In addition to the provisions which shall apply in time of peace, this Protocol shall apply in situations referred to in Article 18 paragraphs 1 and 2 of the Convention and in Article 22 paragraph 1.
2. When one of the parties to an armed conflict is not bound by this Protocol, the Parties to this Protocol shall remain bound by it in their mutual relations. They shall furthermore be bound by this Protocol in relation to a State party to the conflict which is not bound by it, if the latter accepts the provisions of this Protocol and so long as it applies them.

Article 4. *Relationship between Chapter 3 and other provisions of the Convention and this Protocol*
The application of the provisions of Chapter 3 of this Protocol is without prejudice to:

a. the application of the provisions of Chapter I of the Convention and of Chapter 2 of this Protocol;

b. the application of the provisions of Chapter II of the Convention save that, as between Parties to this Protocol or as between a Party and a State which accepts and applies this Protocol in accordance with Article 3 paragraph 2, where cultural property has been granted both special protection and enhanced protection, only the provisions of enhanced protection shall apply.

Chapter 2. *General provisions regarding protection*

Article 5. *Safeguarding of cultural property*
Preparatory measures taken in time of peace for the safeguarding of cultural property against the foreseeable effects of an armed conflict pursuant to Article 3 of the Convention shall include, as appropriate, the preparation of inventories, the planning of emergency measures for protection against fire or structural collapse, the preparation for the removal of movable cultural property or the provision for adequate in situ protection of such property, and the designation of competent authorities responsible for the safeguarding of cultural property.

Article 6. *Respect for cultural property*
With the goal of ensuring respect for cultural property in accordance with Article 4 of the Convention:

a. a waiver on the basis of imperative military necessity pursuant to Article 4 paragraph 2 of the Convention may only be invoked to direct an act of hostility against cultural property when and for as long as:
   i. that cultural property has, by its function, been made into a military objective; and
   ii. there is no feasible alternative available to obtain a similar military advantage to that offered by directing an act of hostility against that objective;
b. a waiver on the basis of imperative military necessity pursuant to Article 4 paragraph 2 of the Convention may only be invoked to use cultural property for purposes which are likely to expose it to destruction or damage when and for as long as no choice is possible between such use of the cultural property and another feasible method for obtaining a similar military advantage;
c. the decision to invoke imperative military necessity shall only be taken by an officer commanding a force the equivalent of a battalion in size or larger, or a force smaller in size where circumstances do not permit otherwise;

d. in case of an attack based on a decision taken in accordance with sub-paragraph (a), an effective advance warning shall be given whenever circumstances permit.

Article 7. *Precautions in attack*
Without prejudice to other precautions required by international humanitarian law in the conduct of military operations, each Party to the conflict shall:

a. do everything feasible to verify that the objectives to be attacked are not cultural property protected under Article 4 of the Convention;
b. take all feasible precautions in the choice of means and methods of attack with a view to avoiding, and in any event to minimizing, incidental damage to cultural property protected under Article 4 of the Convention;
c. refrain from deciding to launch any attack which may be expected to cause incidental damage to cultural property protected under Article 4 of the Convention which would be excessive in relation to the concrete and direct military advantage anticipated; and
d. cancel or suspend an attack if it becomes apparent:
    i. that the objective is cultural property protected under Article 4 of the Convention;
    ii. that the attack may be expected to cause incidental damage to cultural property protected under Article 4 of the Convention which would be excessive in relation to the concrete and direct military advantage anticipated.

Article 8. *Precautions against the effects of hostilities*
The Parties to the conflict shall, to the maximum extent feasible:

a. remove movable cultural property from the vicinity of military objectives or provide for adequate in situ protection;
b. avoid locating military objectives near cultural property.

Article 9. *Protection of cultural property in occupied territory*
1. Without prejudice to the provisions of Articles 4 and 5 of the Convention, a Party in occupation of the whole or part of the territory of another Party shall prohibit and prevent in relation to the occupied territory:
    a. any illicit export, other removal or transfer of ownership of cultural property;

b. any archaeological excavation, save where this is strictly required to safeguard, record or preserve cultural property;
c. any alteration to, or change of use of, cultural property which is intended to conceal or destroy cultural, historical or scientific evidence.

2. Any archaeological excavation of, alteration to, or change of use of, cultural property in occupied territory shall, unless circumstances do not permit, be carried out in close co-operation with the competent national authorities of the occupied territory.

Chapter 3. *Enhanced Protection*

Article 10. *Enhanced protection*

Cultural property may be placed under enhanced protection provided that it meets the following three conditions:

a. it is cultural heritage of the greatest importance for humanity;
b. it is protected by adequate domestic legal and administrative measures recognising its exceptional cultural and historic value and ensuring the highest level of protection;
c. it is not used for military purposes or to shield military sites and a declaration has been made by the Party which has control over the cultural property, confirming that it will not be so used.

Article 11. *The granting of enhanced protection*

1. Each Party should submit to the Committee a list of cultural property for which it intends to request the granting of enhanced protection.
2. The Party which has jurisdiction or control over the cultural property may request that it be included in the List to be established in accordance with Article 27 sub-paragraph 1(b). This request shall include all necessary information related to the criteria mentioned in Article 10. The Committee may invite a Party to request that cultural property be included in the List.
3. Other Parties, the International Committee of the Blue Shield and other non-governmental organisations with relevant expertise may recommend specific cultural property to the Committee. In such cases, the Committee may decide to invite a Party to request inclusion of that cultural property in the List.
4. Neither the request for inclusion of cultural property situated in a territory, sovereignty or jurisdiction over which is claimed by more than one State, nor its inclusion, shall in any way prejudice the rights of the parties to the dispute.

5. Upon receipt of a request for inclusion in the List, the Committee shall inform all Parties of the request. Parties may submit representations regarding such a request to the Committee within sixty days. These representations shall be made only on the basis of the criteria mentioned in Article 10. They shall be specific and related to facts. The Committee shall consider the representations, providing the Party requesting inclusion with a reasonable opportunity to respond before taking the decision. When such representations are before the Committee, decisions for inclusion in the List shall be taken, notwithstanding Article 26, by a majority of four-fifths of its members present and voting.
6. In deciding upon a request, the Committee should ask the advice of governmental and non-governmental organisations, as well as of individual experts.
7. A decision to grant or deny enhanced protection may only be made on the basis of the criteria mentioned in Article 10.
8. In exceptional cases, when the Committee has concluded that the Party requesting inclusion of cultural property in the List cannot fulfil the criteria of Article 10 sub-paragraph (b), the Committee may decide to grant enhanced protection, provided that the requesting Party submits a request for international assistance under Article 32.
9. Upon the outbreak of hostilities, a Party to the conflict may request, on an emergency basis, enhanced protection of cultural property under its jurisdiction or control by communicating this request to the Committee. The Committee shall transmit this request immediately to all Parties to the conflict. In such cases the Committee will consider representations from the Parties concerned on an expedited basis. The decision to grant provisional enhanced protection shall be taken as soon as possible and, notwithstanding Article 26, by a majority of four-fifths of its members present and voting. Provisional enhanced protection may be granted by the Committee pending the outcome of the regular procedure for the granting of enhanced protection, provided that the provisions of Article 10 sub-paragraphs (a) and (c) are met.
10. Enhanced protection shall be granted to cultural property by the Committee from the moment of its entry in the List.
11. The Director-General shall, without delay, send to the Secretary-General of the United Nations and to all Parties notification of any decision of the Committee to include cultural property on the List.

Article 12. *Immunity of cultural property under enhanced protection*
The Parties to a conflict shall ensure the immunity of cultural property under enhanced protection by refraining from making such property the object of attack or from any use of the property or its immediate surroundings in support of military action.

Article 13. *Loss of enhanced protection*

1. Cultural property under enhanced protection shall only lose such protection:
   a. if such protection is suspended or cancelled in accordance with Article 14; or
   b. if, and for as long as, the property has, by its use, become a military objective.
2. In the circumstances of sub-paragraph 1(b), such property may only be the object of attack if:
   a. the attack is the only feasible means of terminating the use of the property referred to in sub-paragraph 1(b);
   b. all feasible precautions are taken in the choice of means and methods of attack, with a view to terminating such use and avoiding, or in any event minimising, damage to the cultural property;
   c. unless circumstances do not permit, due to requirements of immediate self-defence:
      i. the attack is ordered at the highest operational level of command;
      ii. effective advance warning is issued to the opposing forces requiring the termination of the use referred to in sub-paragraph 1(b); and
      iii. Reasonable time is given to the opposing forces to redress the situation.

Article 14. *Suspension and cancellation of enhanced protection*

1. Where cultural property no longer meets any one of the criteria in Article 10 of this Protocol, the Committee may suspend its enhanced protection status or cancel that status by removing that cultural property from the List.
2. In the case of a serious violation of Article 12 in relation to cultural property under enhanced protection arising from its use in support of military action, the Committee may suspend its enhanced protection status. Where such violations are continuous, the Committee may exceptionally cancel the enhanced protection status by removing the cultural property from the List.

3. The Director-General shall, without delay, send to the Secretary-General of the United Nations and to all Parties to this Protocol notification of any decision of the Committee to suspend or cancel the enhanced protection of cultural property.
4. Before taking such a decision, the Committee shall afford an opportunity to the Parties to make their views known.

Chapter 4. *Criminal responsibility and jurisdiction*

Article 15. *Serious violations of this Protocol*

1. Any person commits an offence within the meaning of this Protocol if that person intentionally and in violation of the Convention or this Protocol commits any of the following acts:
   a. making cultural property under enhanced protection the object of attack;
   b. using cultural property under enhanced protection or its immediate surroundings in support of military action;
   c. extensive destruction or appropriation of cultural property protected under the Convention and this Protocol;
   d. making cultural property protected under the Convention and this Protocol the object of attack;
   e. theft, pillage or misappropriation of, or acts of vandalism directed against cultural property protected under the Convention.
2. Each Party shall adopt such measures as may be necessary to establish as criminal offences under its domestic law the offences set forth in this Article and to make such offences punishable by appropriate penalties. When doing so, Parties shall comply with general principles of law and international law, including the rules extending individual criminal responsibility to persons other than those who directly commit the act.

Article 16. *Jurisdiction*

1. Without prejudice to paragraph 2, each Party shall take the necessary legislative measures to establish its jurisdiction over offences set forth in Article 15 in the following cases:
   a. when such an offence is committed in the territory of that State;
   b. when the alleged offender is a national of that State;
   c. in the case of offences set forth in Article 15 sub-paragraphs (a) to (c), when the alleged offender is present in its territory.

2. With respect to the exercise of jurisdiction and without prejudice to Article 28 of the Convention:
   a. this Protocol does not preclude the incurring of individual criminal responsibility or the exercise of jurisdiction under national and international law that may be applicable, or affect the exercise of jurisdiction under customary international law;
   b. except in so far as a State which is not Party to this Protocol may accept and apply its provisions in accordance with Article 3 paragraph 2, members of the armed forces and nationals of a State which is not Party to this Protocol, except for those nationals serving in the armed forces of a State which is a Party to this Protocol, do not incur individual criminal responsibility by virtue of this Protocol, nor does this Protocol impose an obligation to establish jurisdiction over such persons or to extradite them.

Article 17. *Prosecution*

1. The Party in whose territory the alleged offender of an offence set forth in Article 15 sub-paragraphs 1 (a) to (c) is found to be present shall, if it does not extradite that person, submit, without exception whatsoever and without undue delay, the case to its competent authorities, for the purpose of prosecution, through proceedings in accordance with its domestic law or with, if applicable, the relevant rules of international law.
2. Without prejudice to, if applicable, the relevant rules of international law, any person regarding whom proceedings are being carried out in connection with the Convention or this Protocol shall be guaranteed fair treatment and a fair trial in accordance with domestic law and international law at all stages of the proceedings, and in no cases shall be provided guarantees less favorable to such person than those provided by international law.

Article 18. *Extradition*

1. The offences set forth in Article 15 sub-paragraphs 1 (a) to (c) shall be deemed to be included as extraditable offences in any extradition treaty existing between any of the Parties before the entry into force of this Protocol. Parties undertake to include such offences in every extradition treaty to be subsequently concluded between them.
2. When a Party which makes extradition conditional on the existence of a treaty receives a request for extradition from another Party with which it has no extradition treaty, the requested Party may, at its

option, consider the present Protocol as the legal basis for extradition in respect of offences as set forth in Article 15 sub-paragraphs 1 (a) to (c).

3. Parties which do not make extradition conditional on the existence of a treaty shall recognise the offences set forth in Article 15 sub-paragraphs 1 (a) to (c) as extraditable offences between them, subject to the conditions provided by the law of the requested Party.
4. If necessary, offences set forth in Article 15 sub-paragraphs 1 (a) to (c) shall be treated, for the purposes of extradition between Parties, as if they had been committed not only in the place in which they occurred but also in the territory of the Parties that have established jurisdiction in accordance with Article 16 paragraph 1.

Article 19. *Mutual legal assistance*

1. Parties shall afford one another the greatest measure of assistance in connection with investigations or criminal or extradition proceedings brought in respect of the offences set forth in Article 15, including assistance in obtaining evidence at their disposal necessary for the proceedings.
2. Parties shall carry out their obligations under paragraph 1 in conformity with any treaties or other arrangements on mutual legal assistance that may exist between them. In the absence of such treaties or arrangements, Parties shall afford one another assistance in accordance with their domestic law.

Article 20. *Grounds for refusal*

1. For the purpose of extradition, offences set forth in Article 15 sub-paragraphs 1 (a) to (c), and for the purpose of mutual legal assistance, offences set forth in Article 15 shall not be regarded as political offences nor as offences connected with political offences nor as offences inspired by political motives. Accordingly, a request for extradition or for mutual legal assistance based on such offences may not be refused on the sole ground that it concerns a political offence or an offence connected with a political offence or an offence inspired by political motives.
2. Nothing in this Protocol shall be interpreted as imposing an obligation to extradite or to afford mutual legal assistance if the requested Party has substantial grounds for believing that the request for extradition for offences set forth in Article 15 sub-paragraphs 1 (a) to (c) or for mutual legal assistance with respect to offences set forth in Article 15

has been made for the purpose of prosecuting or punishing a person on account of that person's race, religion, nationality, ethnic origin or political opinion or that compliance with the request would cause prejudice to that person's position for any of these reasons.

Article 21. *Measures regarding other violations*
Without prejudice to Article 28 of the Convention, each Party shall adopt such legislative, administrative or disciplinary measures as may be necessary to suppress the following acts when committed intentionally:

a. any use of cultural property in violation of the Convention or this Protocol;
b. any illicit export, other removal or transfer of ownership of cultural property from occupied territory in violation of the Convention or this Protocol.

Chapter 5. *The protection of cultural property in armed conflicts not of an international character*

Article 22. *Armed conflicts not of an international character*

1. This Protocol shall apply in the event of an armed conflict not of an international character, occurring within the territory of one of the Parties.
2. This Protocol shall not apply to situations of internal disturbances and tensions, such as riots, isolated and sporadic acts of violence and other acts of a similar nature.
3. Nothing in this Protocol shall be invoked for the purpose of affecting the sovereignty of a State or the responsibility of the government, by all legitimate means, to maintain or re-establish law and order in the State or to defend the national unity and territorial integrity of the State.
4. Nothing in this Protocol shall prejudice the primary jurisdiction of a Party in whose territory an armed conflict not of an international character occurs over the violations set forth in Article 15.
5. Nothing in this Protocol shall be invoked as a justification for intervening, directly or indirectly, for any reason whatever, in the armed conflict or in the internal or external affairs of the Party in the territory of which that conflict occurs.
6. The application of this Protocol to the situation referred to in paragraph 1 shall not affect the legal status of the parties to the conflict.
7. UNESCO may offer its services to the parties to the conflict.

Chapter 6. *Institutional Issues*

Article 23. *Meeting of the Parties*

1. The Meeting of the Parties shall be convened at the same time as the General Conference of UNESCO, and in co-ordination with the Meeting of the High Contracting Parties, if such a meeting has been called by the Director-General.
2. The Meeting of the Parties shall adopt its Rules of Procedure.
3. The Meeting of the Parties shall have the following functions:
   (a) to elect the Members of the Committee, in accordance with Article 24 paragraph 1;
   (b) to endorse the Guidelines developed by the Committee in accordance with Article 27 sub-paragraph 1(a);
   (c) to provide guidelines for, and to supervise the use of the Fund by the Committee;
   (d) to consider the report submitted by the Committee in accordance with Article 27 sub-paragraph 1(d);
   (e) to discuss any problem related to the application of this Protocol, and to make recommendations, as appropriate.
4. At the request of at least one-fifth of the Parties, the Director-General shall convene an Extraordinary Meeting of the Parties.

Article 24. *Committee for the Protection of Cultural Property in the Event of Armed Conflict*

1. The Committee for the Protection of Cultural Property in the Event of Armed Conflict is hereby established. It shall be composed of twelve Parties which shall be elected by the Meeting of the Parties.
2. The Committee shall meet once a year in ordinary session and in extraordinary sessions whenever it deems necessary.
3. In determining membership of the Committee, Parties shall seek to ensure an equitable representation of the different regions and cultures of the world.
4. Parties members of the Committee shall choose as their representatives persons qualified in the fields of cultural heritage, defence or international law, and they shall endeavour, in consultation with one another, to ensure that the Committee as a whole contains adequate expertise in all these fields.

Article 25. *Term of office*

1. A Party shall be elected to the Committee for four years and shall be eligible for immediate re-election only once.

2. Notwithstanding the provisions of paragraph 1, the term of office of half of the members chosen at the time of the first election shall cease at the end of the first ordinary session of the Meeting of the Parties following that at which they were elected. These members shall be chosen by lot by the President of this Meeting after the first election.

Article 26. *Rules of procedure*

1. The Committee shall adopt its Rules of Procedure.
2. A majority of the members shall constitute a quorum. Decisions of the Committee shall be taken by a majority of two-thirds of its members voting.
3. Members shall not participate in the voting on any decisions relating to cultural property affected by an armed conflict to which they are parties.

Article 27. *Functions*

1. The Committee shall have the following functions:
   a. to develop Guidelines for the implementation of this Protocol;
   b. to grant, suspend or cancel enhanced protection for cultural property and to establish, maintain and promote the List of Cultural Property under Enhanced Protection;
   c. to monitor and supervise the implementation of this Protocol and promote the identification of cultural property under enhanced protection;
   d. to consider and comment on reports of the Parties, to seek clarifications as required, and prepare its own report on the implementation of this Protocol for the Meeting of the Parties;
   e. to receive and consider requests for international assistance under Article 32;
   f. to determine the use of the Fund;
   g. to perform any other function which may be assigned to it by the Meeting of the Parties.
2. The functions of the Committee shall be performed in co-operation with the Director-General.
3. The Committee shall co-operate with international and national governmental and non-governmental organizations having objectives similar to those of the Convention, its First Protocol and this Protocol. To assist in the implementation of its functions, the Committee may invite to its meetings, in an advisory capacity, eminent

professional organizations such as those which have formal relations with UNESCO, including the International Committee of the Blue Shield (ICBS) and its constituent bodies. Representatives of the International Centre for the Study of the Preservation and Restoration of Cultural Property (Rome Centre) (ICCROM) and of the International Committee of the Red Cross (ICRC) may also be invited to attend in an advisory capacity.

Article 28. *Secretariat*
The Committee shall be assisted by the Secretariat of UNESCO which shall prepare the Committee's documentation and the agenda for its meetings and shall have the responsibility for the implementation of its decisions.

Article 29. *The Fund for the Protection of Cultural Property in the Event of Armed Conflict*

1. A Fund is hereby established for the following purposes:
   a. to provide financial or other assistance in support of preparatory or other measures to be taken in peacetime in accordance with, inter alia, Article 5, Article 10 sub-paragraph (b) and Article 30; and
   b. to provide financial or other assistance in relation to emergency, provisional or other measures to be taken in order to protect cultural property during periods of armed conflict or of immediate recovery after the end of hostilities in accordance with, inter alia, Article 8 sub-paragraph (a).
2. The Fund shall constitute a trust fund, in conformity with the provisions of the financial regulations of UNESCO.
3. Disbursements from the Fund shall be used only for such purposes as the Committee shall decide in accordance with the guidelines as defined in Article 23 sub-paragraph 3(c). The Committee may accept contributions to be used only for a certain programme or project, provided that the Committee shall have decided on the implementation of such programme or project.
4. The resources of the Fund shall consist of:
   (a) voluntary contributions made by the Parties;
   (b) contributions, gifts or bequests made by:
      (i) other States;
      (ii) UNESCO or other organizations of the United Nations system;

(iii) other intergovernmental or non-governmental organizations; and
(iv) public or private bodies or individuals;

(c) any interest accruing on the Fund;
(d) funds raised by collections and receipts from events organized for the benefit of the Fund; and
(e) all other resources authorized by the guidelines applicable to the Fund.

Chapter 7. *Dissemination of Information and International Assistance*

Article 30. *Dissemination*

1. The Parties shall endeavour by appropriate means, and in particular by educational and information programmes, to strengthen appreciation and respect for cultural property by their entire population.
2. The Parties shall disseminate this Protocol as widely as possible, both in time of peace and in time of armed conflict.
3. Any military or civilian authorities who, in time of armed conflict, assume responsibilities with respect to the application of this Protocol, shall be fully acquainted with the text thereof. To this end the Parties shall, as appropriate:
   (a) incorporate guidelines and instructions on the protection of cultural property in their military regulations;
   (b) develop and implement, in cooperation with UNESCO and relevant governmental and non-governmental organizations, peacetime training and educational programmes;
   (c) communicate to one another, through the Director-General, information on the laws, administrative provisions and measures taken under sub-paragraphs (a) and (b);
   (d) communicate to one another, as soon as possible, through the Director-General, the laws and administrative provisions which they may adopt to ensure the application of this Protocol.

Article 31. *International cooperation*

In situations of serious violations of this Protocol, the Parties undertake to act, jointly through the Committee, or individually, in cooperation with UNESCO and the United Nations and in conformity with the Charter of the United Nations.

Article 32. *International assistance*

1. A Party may request from the Committee international assistance for cultural property under enhanced protection as well as assistance with respect to the preparation, development or implementation of the laws, administrative provisions and measures referred to in Article 10.
2. A party to the conflict, which is not a Party to this Protocol but which accepts and applies provisions in accordance with Article 3, paragraph 2, may request appropriate international assistance from the Committee.
3. The Committee shall adopt rules for the submission of requests for international assistance and shall define the forms the international assistance may take.
4. Parties are encouraged to give technical assistance of all kinds, through the Committee, to those Parties or parties to the conflict who request it.

Article 33. *Assistance of UNESCO*

1. A Party may call upon UNESCO for technical assistance in organizing the protection of its cultural property, such as preparatory action to safeguard cultural property, preventive and organizational measures for emergency situations and compilation of national inventories of cultural property, or in connection with any other problem arising out of the application of this Protocol. UNESCO shall accord such assistance within the limits fixed by its programme and by its resources.
2. Parties are encouraged to provide technical assistance at bilateral or multilateral level.
3. UNESCO is authorized to make, on its own initiative, proposals on these matters to the Parties.

Chapter 8. *Execution of this Protocol*

Article 34. *Protecting Powers*

This Protocol shall be applied with the co-operation of the Protecting Powers responsible for safeguarding the interests of the Parties to the conflict.

Article 35. *Conciliation procedure*

1. The Protecting Powers shall lend their good offices in all cases where they may deem it useful in the interests of cultural property, particularly if there is disagreement between the Parties to the conflict as to the application or interpretation of the provisions of this Protocol.

2. For this purpose, each of the Protecting Powers may, either at the invitation of one Party, of the Director-General, or on its own initiative, propose to the Parties to the conflict a meeting of their representatives, and in particular of the authorities responsible for the protection of cultural property, if considered appropriate, on the territory of a State not party to the conflict. The Parties to the conflict shall be bound to give effect to the proposals for meeting made to them. The Protecting Powers shall propose for approval by the Parties to the conflict a person belonging to a State not party to the conflict or a person presented by the Director-General, which person shall be invited to take part in such a meeting in the capacity of Chairman.

Article 36. *Conciliation in absence of Protecting Powers*

1. In a conflict where no Protecting Powers are appointed the Director-General may lend good offices or act by any other form of conciliation or mediation, with a view to settling the disagreement.
2. At the invitation of one Party or of the Director-General, the Chairman of the Committee may propose to the Parties to the conflict a meeting of their representatives, and in particular of the authorities responsible for the protection of cultural property, if considered appropriate, on the territory of a State not party to the conflict.

Article 37. *Translations and reports*

1. The Parties shall translate this Protocol into their official languages and shall communicate these official translations to the Director-General.
2. The Parties shall submit to the Committee, every four years, a report on the implementation of this Protocol.

Article 38. *State responsibility*

No provision in this Protocol relating to individual criminal responsibility shall affect the responsibility of States under international law, including the duty to provide reparation.

Chapter 9. *Final Clauses*

Article 39. *Languages*

This Protocol is drawn up in Arabic, Chinese, English, French, Russian and Spanish, the six texts being equally authentic.

Article 40. *Signature*
This Protocol shall bear the date of 26 March 1999. It shall be opened for signature by all High Contracting Parties at The Hague from 17 May 1999 until 31 December 1999.

Article 41. *Ratification, acceptance or approval*
1. This Protocol shall be subject to ratification, acceptance or approval by High Contracting Parties which have signed this Protocol, in accordance with their respective constitutional procedures.
2. The instruments of ratification, acceptance or approval shall be deposited with the Director-General.

Article 42. *Accession*
1. This Protocol shall be open for accession by other High Contracting Parties from 1 January 2000.
2. Accession shall be effected by the deposit of an instrument of accession with the Director-General.

Article 43. *Entry into force*
1. This Protocol shall enter into force three months after twenty instruments of ratification, acceptance, approval or accession have been deposited.
2. Thereafter, it shall enter into force, for each Party, three months after the deposit of its instrument of ratification, acceptance, approval or accession.

Article 44. *Entry into force in situations of armed conflict*
The situations referred to in Articles 18 and 19 of the Convention shall give immediate effect to ratifications, acceptances or approvals of or accessions to this Protocol deposited by the parties to the conflict either before or after the beginning of hostilities or occupation. In such cases the Director-General shall transmit the communications referred to in Article 46 by the speediest method.

Article 45. *Denunciation*
1. Each Party may denounce this Protocol.
2. The denunciation shall be notified by an instrument in writing, deposited with the Director-General.
3. The denunciation shall take effect one year after the receipt of the instrument of denunciation. However, if, on the expiry of this period,

the denouncing Party is involved in an armed conflict, the denunciation shall not take effect until the end of hostilities, or until the operations of repatriating cultural property are completed, whichever is the later.

Article 46. *Notifications*
The Director-General shall inform all High Contracting Parties as well as the United Nations, of the deposit of all the instruments of ratification, acceptance, approval or accession provided for in Articles 41 and 42 and of denunciations provided for Article 45.

Article 47. *Registration with the United Nations*
In conformity with Article 102 of the Charter of the United Nations, this Protocol shall be registered with the Secretariat of the United Nations at the request of the Director-General.

IN FAITH WHEREOF the undersigned, duly authorized, have signed the present Protocol.

DONE at The Hague, this twenty-sixth day of March 1999, in a single copy which shall be deposited in the archives of the UNESCO, and certified true copies of which shall be delivered to all the High Contracting Parties.

APPENDIX TWO

EXAMPLES OF CPP FIELD POCKET CARDS IN GERMAN AND DUTCH PREPARED IN COOPERATION WITH THE U.S. DOD LEGACY PROGRAM

Behoud van cultureel erfgoed

Aandachtspunten voor militairen

Hoe herkent men een archeologisch terrein/site?
- Antieke gebouwen of ruïnes.
- Oude of archeologische voorwerpen verspreid over het oppervlak.
- Sporen van vroegere bewoning zoals overblijfselen of fundamenten van huizen en andere gebouwen, afvalputten, vuurhaarden en kampementen.

Wat zijn artefacten?
- Door mensen gemaakte voorwerpen en delen van voorwerpen die zijn achtergelaten door bewoners uit het verleden.

Mark Altaweel

Wat zijn in een landschap de meest waarschijnlijke plekken om archeologische vondsten of sites aan te treffen?
- Verhogingen in het landschap; daar kunnen ruïnes of andere overblijfselen onder zitten.
- In de nabijheid van waterbronnen.
- Natuurlijke verdedigingslinies of restanten van door mensen gemaakte verdedigingswerken.

Wat te doen na de ontdekking van een archeologische site?
- Rapporteer de vondst aan uw hogere niveau.
- Baken het terrein af, markeer het een lint en zorg dat het terrein niet kan worden betreden.
- Raadpleeg de lokale autoriteiten.
- Leg de locatie vast en maak zo mogelijk foto's.
- Rapporteer en registreer bewijzen van plundering van de site.
- Beperk graafwerkzaamheden en andere grondwerkzaamheden zoveel als mogelijk.
- Zorg dat het vullen van Hesco's en zandzakken elders plaatsvindt.

Department of Defense

Indien u oudheidkundige voorwerpen en/of ruïnes tegenkomt:
- STOP MET GRAAFWERKZAAMHEDEN
- ZET GEEN ZWAAR MATERIEEL IN
- RIJ NIET OVER ANTIEKE BESTRATINGEN OF FUNDAMENTEN

PAS OP!!

- De vijand kan cultureel erfgoed zoals ruïnes, oude begraafplaatsen en religieuze gebouwen gebruiken als positie voor sluipschutters of geschut. Handel volgens de RoE.

Alexey Sergeev *© Victoria H. Hess 2007*

- Koop en verkoop van illegaal verkregen oudheidkundige voorwerpen kan meehelpen aan de financiering van opposing forces. Dit stimuleert verdere plundering en diefstal van objecten als munten, potten en vazen, stenen werktuigen, houtsnijwerk, decoratieve onderdelen van bouwwerken, sculpturen, schilderingen en sieraden.

Oriental Institute Museum *Oriental Institute Museum*

- Het bezoeken van bezienswaardigheden mag alleen met toestemming van uw hogere commandant.

NEEM NIETS MEE
BRENG GEEN GRAFFITI AAN
GEEN VANDALISME

Steun de missie
Toon respect
Win Hearts and Minds

APPENDIX THREE

NATO CIVIL-MILITARY CO-OPERATION (CIMIC) DOCTRINE AJP 9[1]

102. *Definition and Application*

1. Definition. CIMIC is defined as:

> "The co-ordination and co-operation, in support of the mission, between the NATO Commander and civil actors, including national population and local authorities, as well as international, national and non-governmental organisations and agencies."

2. Application. Four further factors condition the application of CIMIC:

   a. CIMIC activities form an integral part of the Joint Force Commander's (JFC) plan, are conducted in support of his mission and are related to implementing the overall strategy and achieving a stable and sustainable end-state.
   b. The Commander's CIMIC staffs are fully integrated into his Headquarters (HQ) and have full vision of and are authorised to co-ordinate CIMIC activities in the Joint Operations Area (JOA), theatre or region.
   c. In co-operating with a potentially wide range of civilian bodies, NATO forces will, as far as possible and within military means and capabilities, accommodate and support the activities of these bodies, providing this does not compromise the mission.
   d. CIMIC activities are carried out with a view to timely transition of those functions to the appropriate civilian organisations or authorities.

---

[1] Source: http://publicintelligence.net/nato-civil-military-co-operation-cimic-doctrine/

APPENDIX FOUR

REGULATION NUMBER 200-2
ENVIRONMENTAL QUALITY, CENTCOM CONTINGENCY ENVIRONMENTAL GUIDANCE

HEADQUARTERS UNITED STATES CENTRAL COMMAND
7115 SOUTH BOUNDARY BOULEVARD
MACDILL AIR FORCE BASE, FLORIDA 33621–5101
REGULATION
Number 200-2
Environmental Quality
CENTCOM CONTINGENCY ENVIRONMENTAL GUIDANCE

R 200-2

h. Conservation: USCENTCOM forces will conserve, protect and restore (if damaged) all HN natural and historical/cultural resources, using all practical means consistent with the USCENTCOM mission. See Chapter 6: Historical/Cultural.

Chapter 6
HISTORICAL AND CULTURAL PRESERVATION
6–1. SCOPE. This chapter establishes criteria to ensure the proper protection of historic and/or cultural resources within
USCENTCOM AOR countries engaged in contingency operations.
6–2. BACKGROUND. Historical/cultural protection is becoming more important around the world. In 2008, the USG ratified the 1954 Hague Convention (Protection of Cultural Property in the Event of Armed Conflict). Accordingly, USCENTCOM personnel should expect future misconduct and poor decisions involving HN natural and cultural resources to have more severe consequences.
6–3. ENVIRONMENTAL RESPONSIBILITIES. The LEC will have the following procedures in place for the management of HN historical/cultural properties:

a. A process to ensure each base camp Commander take into account the effect of any proposed military action on property listed on the World Heritage List (WHL) and/or on the HN equivalent of the U.S. National Register of Historic Places.
   (1) Proposed military actions should attempt to avoid and/or mitigate any adverse effects to such historic or cultural resources.
   (2) Proposed military actions include, but are not limited to, the following actions:
      (a) Construction
      (b) Demolition
      (c) Combat operations
      (d) Training
      (e) Land-use
b. World Heritage List (WHL): Ensure base camps have access to the WHL and/or the HN equivalent of the National Register of Historic Places to assist in historical/cultural planning and decision making.
c. Inventories: Base camps are required to do an archaeological inventory to record and report all historic and/or culturally significant locations at and near the base camp. The LEC will keep a master inventory.
d. Archaeological Maps: Each base camp is required to keep an updated map of all known or suspected archaeological and other historical/cultural resources at and near their base.
e. Interim Measures: Establish interim measures sufficient to protect archaeological or other historical/cultural resources until appropriate mitigation or preservation can be completed (e.g. signage, declaring the area off limits, or removal).
f. Infrastructure Improvements: Each base camp will take into consideration the possible harm to HN relationships and the potential damage to HN historic/cultural properties during base camp infrastructure improvements, new construction, demolition and/or mitigation projects. See Appendix K: Historical/Cultural Flowchart
g. Historical/Cultural Discoveries made on a Base Camp: Items of potential historical/cultural importance that are discovered during the course of construction and/or demolition work on a base camp will be preserved and protected. The base commander will consult with the LEC and then make a decision on final disposition.

If possible, include coordination with the HN authorities and do the following:

(1) Temporarily suspend work within a 5 meter radius of the find.
(2) Do not search for additional cultural material by digging or exploring within a 5 meter radius.
(3) Contact local or reach back historical/cultural experts to determine the significance of find.
(4) Document the date, location, and nature of the find with GPS, photography, and notes.
(5) Leave the find in place if possible and protect it from damage and/or additional damage.
(6) Place historical/cultural materials in a protective container (bag or box) and label the container with the location, date of encounter, name of contents, and name of recorder if they must be removed.
(7) Report the encounter and site location through the proper chain of command. All photographs, notes, and objects must remain together. Turn them into the nearest local museum as soon as possible if they are significant.

h. Historical/Cultural Discoveries off Base Camp: Items of potential historical/cultural importance discovered off base camp will be reported to the LEC. Record the location, description, and if possible pictures of the discovered items. This information will be transferred to the appropriate HN authorities if it is significant.

i. Proper Conduct: USCENTCOM personnel (military, civilians, contractors) must not pick up or disturb artifacts found on or below ground surface without proper authorization.
(1) Do not alter any standing monument or building suspected to be protected cultural property.
(2) Do not make military use of any protected cultural property, monument, archaeological site, historic or religious building unless there exists a genuine and imperative military necessity with no feasible or logical alternative.
(3) Do not purchase artifacts, antiquities, or cultural heritage items without proper authorization.
(4) Do not dig without first determining whether the location is a protected archaeological or historical/cultural site.

j. Training: Units involved in construction and/or ground disturbing activities will designate a historical/cultural resources manager. This individual will complete a basic archaeology awareness training course.

APPENDIX FIVE

STANAG 7141 EP JOINT NATO DOCTRINE FOR ENVIRONMENTAL PROTECTION DURING NATO LED MILITARY ACTIVITIES

A few excerpts that relate to Cultural Property Protection:

b. Identify the characteristics of the environment that may be impacted by or have an impact on NATO led military activities, i.e.:

(1) general environmental condition of the area;
(2) climate;
(3) water quality;
(4) air quality;
(5) natural and cultural resources;
(6) presence of endangered species and critical habitats;
(7) presence of birds or bird migration routes.

c. Identify potential (environmental) impacts caused by military activities, including the impacts of alternatives and contingencies, e.g.:

(1) **Water Pollution.** This pollution may include emissions from human wastes (black water), wash and rinse waters (grey water), erosion and

c. Identify potential (environmental) impacts caused by military activities, including the impacts of alternatives and contingencies, e.g.:

(7) **Endangerment of Natural and Cultural Resources.** Impacts on natural and cultural (historic and archaeological) resources should be prevented where possible.

b. Environmental planning. An environmental plan should be developed using this guidance, and should be part of the OPLAN or exercise directive as a separate annex. The plan should include provisions for environmental contingencies, a list of the identified risks and prescribed mitigation measures.

Evaluation of the plan should be conducted to incorporate any lesson learned in future planning.

c. Implementation. The commander should ensure all personnel are trained and aware of environmental issues. There must be clear assignment of responsibilities and resources where applicable for environmental protection.

Units must work with local authorities and the community to identify and resolve problems.

APPENDIX SIX

MISSION REPORT CIVIL-MILITARY ASSESSMENT MISSION FOR EGYPTIAN HERITAGE. BY BLUE SHIELD AND IMCURWG FEBRUARY 12 TO 16, 2011

Objective

The objective of the mission was to assess possible damages and looting attempts to Egyptian Heritage sites and museums after the recent unrests.

Many contradicting messages were reported regarding looting and vandalism, without the possibility of properly checking the real situation. Therefore there was an urgent need to send a mission especially to those sites that were supposedly affected by criminal acts, in order to document the situation, to state damages incurred and to encourage the parties involved to further efforts in protecting the invaluable Cultural Heritage of Egypt.

Composition of the Mission

The mission had 3 main persons involved.

Karl von Habsburg is President of the 'Association of National Committees of the Blue Shield' (ANCBS) since 2008. He is a former member of the European Parliament for Austria and has specialized in International Humanitarian Law and Intangible Cultural Heritage Protection. A former air force pilot, he is still serving in the reserve of the Austrian armed forces as Cultural Property Protection Officer. He is vice president of the Austrian Society for the Protection of Cultural Heritage and a founder member of Blue Shield Austria. Karl von Habsburg is frequent lecturer and author of several publications on the subject of Intangible Cultural Heritage Protection and Military Cultural Property Protection.

Dr. Joris Kila is chairman of the 'International Military Cultural Resources Work Group' (IMCuRWG). He is a researcher at the Institute of Culture and History of the University of Amsterdam. He has been acting chairman of the cultural affairs department at the Civil-Military Cooperation (CIMIC) Group North in the Netherlands, and in that capacity he undertook several cultural rescue missions in Iraq and FYROM (Macedonia). He is author and co-author of several publications on the subject of Cultural Property Protection in times of armed conflict utilizing militarized experts. He is a reserve Lieutenant Colonel and is regularly asked to advise the Dutch MoD on Cultural Property Protection issues. In 2008, he co-authored a study on "Vernacular Mudbrick Architecture in the Dakhla Oasis, Egypt".

Dr. Thomas Schuler is chairman of the Disaster Relief Task Force (DRTF) of ICOM (since 2005). He was director of the Stadtmuseum Tübingen (1985–1992) and of the Schlossbergmuseum Chemnitz (1992–2004). He has specialized in Museum Management and Disaster Preparedness and Management. He was lecturer at the Museology Department of HTWK Leipzig and is regularly offering training courses for museum staff.

Karl von Habsburg and Drs. Joris Kila went to Egypt, Dr. Thomas Schuler coordinated the mission from Germany and did background research.

Political Situation (*The Main Players*)

The political environment in Egypt was still very complicated and confusing. After Hosni Mubarak stepped down as President, the Parliament was dissolved and the Constitution declared invalid. This is problematic since only the Parliament can change or amend the Constitution. The process by which the President stepped down was also not according to the Constitution, which was then still valid. This put the whole legality of the State in question.

The de facto power lays currently with the military, so making the head of the Armed Forces Supreme Council, Field Marshal Tantawi, the actual ruler of the country.

The security system in Egypt was still not really in place. The police in Cairo had literally vanished after the beginning of the demonstrations, since they were identified with the repressive measures of the old regime. They were now slowly coming back. The police functions were taken over by the

military and by spontaneously created neighborhood watch groups. There were many roadblocks around Cairo and Alexandria manned by thugs, but this was now dissipating.

The demonstrations were overall peaceful and conducted with astonishing restraint. The Tahrir Square demonstrations were dealing with the democratization process and Hosni Mubarak. Currently most demonstrations are dealing with employment, wages, bad economy and other matters.

It is foreseen that elections will take place in September; the current government staying in place though changes would be announced by the military. If elections are held earlier, it is likely that the two organizations who have currently nationwide structures, Mubaraks old National Democratic Party NDP and the Muslim Brotherhood might gain the best result.

Joris Kila on Tahrir Square.

Preparatory Work

After it became clear by end of January that the Egyptian Cultural Heritage was really in danger through looting and vandalism, Karl von Habsburg and Joris Kila consulted with Thomas Schuler who had been following and analyzing the situation closely, regarding a mission to find out the truth between all conflicting messages and documenting the situation. All were aware of the very insecure situation: Travel warnings had been issued by almost all embassies in Cairo and foreigners evacuated in great numbers. Therefore it was decided that the mission should be small, flexible and conducted by Cultural Heritage Experts with military expertise. On February 5th the date was set for the mission to take place a week later.

While Thomas Schuler was conducting media research and liaising with academics, Karl von Habsburg and Joris Kila were activating their contacts in the political and diplomatic world, but also their personal contacts in Egypt. The staff of the Austrian Embassy in Cairo was also very helpful with information and organization.

Short Description of the Mission

Karl von Habsburg and Joris Kila arrived in Cairo on February 12 coming from Vienna. It was decided to take only small digital tourist cameras since until the day before often camera equipment was confiscated upon arrival. In the evening the mission decided to visit the area of the Egyptian Museum and Tahrir Square to get an impression of the situation. Getting around Cairo was very complicated, the fastest way usually by foot. Although the mood was generally jubilant, Mubarak had just stepped down and the situation was far from secure. The area of the museum was teeming with military and tanks. That evening the mission tried to make contact with their personal contacts in order to get an objective impression of the situation. A night curfew still existed.

On February 13 the mission visited the Dutch Institute. From there it was possible to reach an official of the Supreme Council of Antiquities (SCA) in Saqqara, who confirmed attempts of looting but denied anything had been stolen. A big problem was the constant stream of contradictive information as well as the large number of complot theories and fantasy or propaganda driven stories. It was also decided to focus on the archaeological sites around Cairo who had mostly not been visited by independent experts since the beginning of unrest in Egypt. The Egyptian Museum had already been visited several times at least by journalists, but the experience gained in Iraq showed that it is dangerous to focus only on one important museum and at the same time neglect the important archaeological sites. That day the mission received multiple background briefings on the situation in Egypt and Cultural Heritage. In the morning of February 14th the mission went to the area of Saqqara accompanied by the director of the Austrian Institute of Archaeology in Cairo, but was turned away by armed guards. In Memphis they managed to get access to the open air museum. To the great relief of the mission the museum was, in spite of many contrarian reports, seemingly untouched. At noon the mission had a meeting with the Minister of Antiquities Dr. Zahi Hawass. Dr. Hawass is personally known to the mission members since many years and promised his support for the mission to visit Saqqara, Abu Sir and Dahshur. The situation at the ministry, the former SCA building, was very tense. There were vast demonstrations outside the building and the mission members had to enter and leave the building through a besieged backdoor. In the afternoon, the mission tried to check out the situation in Abydos and the Kharga Oasis by phone. Both places had reported violent unrest but damage to Cultural Heritage could not be confirmed.

On February 15th the mission, accompanied by the office manager of the Dutch Institute, left early to Saqqara. After some initial difficulties it was possible to have a conversation with the local SCA official. He was telling us about his experiences during the time of looting in Saqqara and Abu Sir. After that the mission visited several sites at Saqqara, following a provisional list of reported damages. In Abu Sir it was, due to time constraint, only possible to visit a few places reported to be affected. The mission decided it was very important to visit Dahshur, and especially the De Morgan warehouse where looting had been reported that supposedly took place until the day before the mission arrived. Although strongly discouraged to go there and with all sorts of constraints, the mission found that the doors and windows of the warehouse had recently been walled in (the mortar still being wet). The accounts of the local guards were not encouraging. At the end of a day enriched by a constant sandstorm, the mission visited the red pyramid of Snefru at Dahshur.

On February 16, the mission still explored further possibilities to support training of Cultural Heritage Protection staff in Egypt and left back in direction of Vienna in the afternoon.

Results

Memphis

The museum was seemingly untouched. No broken windows in the office building, no signs of vandalism. The shopping stalls were equipped with the usual goods but no personnel. There might have been demonstrations in front of the museum.

Later info learns that there is supposed to be a warehouse containing objects somewhere in the environment; however the mission did not know at the time, so possible damage to this facility was neither checked nor confirmed.

Assessment of Memphis by the Director of the Austrian Archaeological Institute at Cairo, Irene Forstner-Müller, Joris Kila and Karl von Habsburg.

Even the souvenir shops at Memphis remained untouched.

Saqqara

The museum and the main storage facilities next to the main office building were untouched according to the SCA inspector, but could not be visited.

During the tour of the premises the mission went first to see the tomb of Mereruka—it looked seemingly undamaged.

Teti—undamaged

Tomb of Kagemni—the door was opened by vandals but now it was welded shut, supposedly no damage.

Unas Pyramid—was especially opened for the mission, obviously closed since a long time and was untouched.

Tomb of Isisnofret—door was welded, supposedly unharmed

Tomb of Maya—clear signs of vandalism (broken locks, broken pieces of wood), supposedly no looting. The entrance to the famous reliefs was sealed with an SCA seal so it could not be visited. It was guaranteed to be in perfect order. The mission had no real reason to doubt this, since reliefs were generally left untouched.

Tomb of Tia & Tia—cupboards for reliefs were not locked, though reliefs look untouched. Some cupboards were sealed but definitely only after the break in.

Tomb of Horemheb—seemingly untouched, same as Tia.

2 brothers—new locks, doors welded shut, definitely broken into before. The same applies to Nefer.

The guard house at the entrance to the site
is intact and the police is back on duty.

Chamber of the Unas pyramid.

Abu Sir

The mission was told by a very helpful SCA inspector about illegal diggings. Supposedly they went no deeper than 50 cm and were already filled in again. But the illegal digs were too far away to be checked within the limited time available. It was decided to visit only the Mastaba of Ptahshepses as an example. This one could not be locked, and the mission was told that there had been people there but no damage could be immediately assessed.

Dahshur

The mission went to see the De Morgans storage facility. It was recently broken into several times up to February 14th, but now the doors and windows were walled off. The roof was secure. The mission found ammunition shells around the compound. Important pieces were supposedly brought to other more secure warehouses, but there was no doubt that looting on a big scale took place.

Lessons Learned

The mission was definitely necessary and very well received as shown by the encouragement of the local staff on site, once they were convinced that the mission was about Cultural Heritage Protection and not about journalism or tourism.

A crucial element of the mission proved to be the reach-back capacity at the home base (office of Dr Thomas Schuler in Chemnitz/Germany) that was constantly furnishing the newest information and coordinating contacts.

The mission would not have been possible without a concentrated effort from the people in public positions, diplomacy and the military. A basic condition for the operation was the willingness of the participants to go and take certain risks without waiting for insurances. The disappointment that other big NGOs and GO's dealing with Cultural Heritage, had not yet managed to send experts or assistance to Egypt could be heard from all sides.

Suggestions for the Future

It is important to plan further missions in Egypt in the near future, since only a very small portion of areas where damage was reported could be surveilled.

Assessment of Abu Sir by the Office Manager of the Dutch Institute at Cairo, Tilly Mulder.

De Morgans storage facility, Karl von Habsburg and Joris Kila.

It is strongly suggested by the mission that a conference in Egypt should be planned in the near future to analyze the security situation at archaeological sites, on how to deal with emergency situations and how to create contingency plans using the Egyptian example.

Military contacts and training about protection of cultural property are indispensable, this is for instance mandatory under IHL (1954 Hague Convention and Protocols) and is still not put into practice in many countries. The damage and access problems would have been less if the international community realizes this and would live up to the treaties they sign not only in word but also in practice.

Acknowledgements

The mission would like to recognize the support they got from the Ministry of Archaeology, the Minister Dr. Zahi Hawass and the whole staff of the SCA in Egypt in these very difficult and tense times.

The mission would also like to recognize the outstanding support by the Austrian Embassy, the Cultural Attaché, the Defense Attaché and the Director of the Austrian Archaeological Institute in Cairo.

Without the personal support of the office manager of the Dutch Institute, Tilly Mulder, and her perfect and convincing command of the Arabic Language, a lot of the goals of the mission could not have been achieved.

Only the help of the many individuals the mission met in Egypt, but also those helping with information from abroad, made the success of the mission possible.

Links

The photo documentation of the mission can be found at http://www.blueshield.at/.

INDEX

www.ingramcontent.com/pod-product-compliance
Lightning Source LLC
Chambersburg PA
CBHW071230230926
51849CB00001B/66
9789004215689